Strind⦿
and Autobiography

Strindberg
and Autobiography

Writing and Reading a Life

Michael Robinson

Norvik Press
1986

Forthcoming titles:

Sigbjørn Obstfelder: *A Priest's Diary,* edited and translated by James McFarlane
Bjørg Vik: *An Aquarium of Women,* translated by Janet Garton
Hjalmar Söderberg: *Selected Short Stories,* translated by Carl Lofmark
Annegret Heitmann (ed.): *No Man's Land* - an anthology of Danish women writers
Irene Scobbie (ed.): *Studies in Modern Swedish Literature*

Our logo is based on a drawing by Egil Bakka (University of Bergen) of a Viking ornament in gold foil, paper thin, with impressed figures (size 16 x 21 mm). It was found in 1897 at Hauge, Klepp, Rogaland, and is now in the collection of the Historisk museum, University of Bergen (inv.no.5392). It depicts a love scene, possibly (according to Magnus Olsen) between the fertility god Freyr and the maiden Geror; the large penannular brooch of the man's cloak dates the work as being most likely 10th century.

© 1986 by Michael Robinson
All Rights Reserved
ISBN 1-870041-00-3
First published in 1986 by Norvik Press, University of East Anglia, Norwich, NR4 7TJ

Norvik Press has been established with financial support from the University of East Anglia, the Danish Ministry for Cultural Affairs, the Norwegian Cultural Department, the Norwegian Cultural Council, and the Swedish Institute.

Publication of this book has been aided by a grant from the Swedish Institute.

Printed in Great Britain by the University of East Anglia, Norwich

iv

TILL SIV

CONTENTS

PREFACE

This is a book about Strindberg and about autobiographical writing, about how a particular writer projects himself in language, the problems this entails, the subterfuges it engenders, about how he finds and loses himself there. It therefore attempts to place this central aspect of Strindberg's project upon a more nuanced and substantial footing than the familiar tradition of biographical criticism in Strindberg studies normally permits, and does not restrict itself only to those works singled out by Strindberg as explicitly autobiographical. Nor, I should perhaps add, does it concern itself in any detailed way with the laborious examination of the relative accuracy of the life Strindberg attributed to himself – whether, for example, the description of his early years in *The Son of a Servant* as a time of fear and hunger is in fact belied by the evident plenitude in the way of food and drink as chronicled in his father's household accounts. In any case, the myth a writer generates about his own experience is as significant a fact as any other, and a writer like Strindberg merely accentuates the way in which all of us live our lives as fictions in terms of the available narrative and plot structures, structures that incorporate those personal symbolic landscapes which (as Strindberg well knew) are in large part unconsciously fostered by the prevailing doxa or mythologies. I am aware, however, that the approach employed here remains partial. Notwithstanding his achievement in other fields, all of which, including his scientific preoccupations deserve to be taken seriously, Strindberg's major achievement remains his drama. A consummate creator as well as player of roles, the mosaic work of character which he elaborated in his theatrical projections is an essential complement to the life traced in his prose works, and deserves to be studied as such. Moreover, like Janine Chasseguet-Smirgel, in her analysis of Strindberg in *Pour une psychanalyse de l'art et de la créativité* (Paris, 1971), "Je n'ai pas manqué toutefois d'être frappée par la pauvreté relative des thèmes des oeuvres biographiques si on les compare à la richesse des élaborations dont ces mêmes thèmes sont l'objet dans l'oeuvre dramatique." Maybe the occasion to explore this elaborated wealth of drama will one day present itself.

As it is, in the protracted passage of this study from its inception into typescript and on to print, there have been numerous developments in Strindberg studies. Not least has been the inauguration of the new National Edition of Strindberg's Collected Works, the necessary replacement for John Landquist's long-serving *Samlade skrifter.* But so far only a small proportion of the anticipated seventy-seven volumes has appeared, none of them central works in Strindberg's autobiographical sequence, and I have therefore continued to use Landquist's edition. Hopefully, however, this will be one of the last books on Strindberg to do so.

Over the same period, there has also been a welcome increase of interest in Strindberg, both in the United States and in Britain. Beginning with Evert Sprinchorn's important *Strindberg as Dramatist* (New Haven, 1979) and reinforced by Harry Carlson's *Strindberg and the Poetry of Myth,* Walter Johnson's edition of the plays, new, accessible translations of *Inferno* and *By the Open Sea,* and the publication in Britain of biographies by Olof Lagercrantz and Michael Meyer, it is at last becoming possible to envisage a time when English readers will be able to make a more accurate assessment of Strindberg's achievement in all its facets, though much still remains to be done, particularly in the way of translation. And perhaps, too, this will be accompanied by a more adventurous approach to Strindberg in the theatre, both as regards the selection of plays for production and the manner of their staging. The British theatre has accommodated Ibsen with relative comfort for many years, but it remains largely uncomprehending, even hostile, to the type of stage interpretation which Strindberg's plays require.

My debts in writing this study are several, and of different kinds, all invaluable. Part of Chapter One has appeared in a slightly different form in *Scandinavica* 23:2 (1984); I am grateful to the editor for permission to reprint it here. Some formulations from Chapter Three, again somewhat altered, were deployed in a paper on "Autobiography and Biography", given at the British Scandinavian Conference at the University of Wales in 1985, and published in the Proceedings of the conference.

While working on the original version of this study, I benefited from two generous grants from the Brita Mortensen fund at the University of Cambridge, and one from Clare College. These were of great assistance to me in enabling me to undertake research in Sweden which was decisive for the direction of my work. For three months in 1979 I was also the fortunate recipient of Strindbergssällskapet's Strindberg Fellowship in Blå tornet; I am truly grateful to them for providing me with the opportunity to immerse myself in the minutiae of Strindberg's life and manuscripts, a task made easier by the helpful staff of the manuscript department of the Royal Library in Stockholm.

On a more personal level, I owe an enormous amount to Göran Printz-Påhlson for his advice, sympathy and intellectual example in working out my ideas on Strindberg and autobiography, as well as to Ulla Printz-Påhlson for her frequent and generous hospitality. I am also grateful to Elinor Shaffer for her lively interest in this project, and to James McFarlane, both at an early stage in my work and latterly for the care and patience he has bestowed in helping a computer illiterate to transform his typescript into print by way of modern technology. Needless to say, any errors that remain are indubitably my own.

Finally, my debt to Siv for her support and encouragement in an enterprise whose outcome was sometimes in doubt is incalculable.

CHAPTER ONE

Writing a Life:
An Approach to Strindberg's Project

> He has dived under, in the Autobiographical Chaos, and swims we see
> not where.
> - Carlyle: *Sartor Resartus*

In the bravura discourse on writing which forms the improbable introduction to
a correspondence in which he will inscribe himself on the heart of his first wife, Siri
von Essen, Strindberg declares: '*A writer is only a reporter of what he has lived* '
(I:190)[1]. The emphasis already placed on this sentence in the original has helped to
foster the notion that, when writing, Strindberg merely transcribed remembered
experience from the text recorded in his mind directly to the page in front of him. It is
as if the rudimentary phonograph which furnishes his late experimental novella, *The
Roofing Feast*, with an underlying structural image for its stream of consciousness
technique, provides the critic with an apt metaphor for this recording and writing
process. Just as the machine reproduces the music that is already traced on a
cylinder so, each time the novel's protagonist awakens, 'the cylinder in the
phonograph of his mind began to move again, emitting all his latest memories and
impressions, but strictly in order exactly as they had been "recorded"' (44:61). If for
Rousseau memories are ineffaceably 'gravé dans mon âme',[2] for Strindberg they are
ineradicably printed upon the mind, and sustained by what he had come to regard as
the authority of Swedenborg, his later work assumes 'that every least thing that a
man has thought, willed, spoken, done or even heard and seen is inscribed on his
eternal or spiritual memory; and that the things there are never erased.'[3] However
difficult it may be to decipher, the past always takes the form of writing, at times
uncomfortably lucid and conveniently linear, as in the instance from *The Roofing
Feast*, at others burdened with resistance and only

> A line with many coils upon it
> like the image of a script
> on blotting paper - back to front -
> forwards and backwards, up and down
> but in a mirror you can read the script (51:80).

In every case, however, this trace is the precious and indelible sign of an individual
life and presence. As the Teacher in the dramatic fragment, *The Isle of the Dead*,

points out, memory is 'our capital', the reading required of us if 'we are going to make use of our true dreams or our experiences!' It is the place where each man's story is written even as he lives it, an account which is at once a personal narrative and a moral ledger, a codex of his life and the index of his vice or virtue. Without the written text there would be no man: 'If in one moment you could lose all remembrance, you would be like a book with white pages, less than a new-born child, and have to begin all over again!'[4].

Indeed, it is all too easy to capitulate to such images and accept at face value a conception of writing as the mere and immediate transcription of the lived into the written, especially when they are reinforced by the arguments with which Strindberg fervently advanced the utilitarian aesthetic he adopted during the 1880s. Even when composing historical fiction he insisted that 'the warp is always taken from my own life'(VII:154), and since he invariably maintained that writing predicates the experience of the writer as its foundation ('to be able to portray every facet and hazard of life one must have lived it'(46:72), he states, in *A Blue Book*), he frequently contends that an author's only proper and possible subject is himself. Like Rousseau, who argued that 'Nul ne peut écrire la vie d'un homme que lui-même. Sa manière d'être intérieure, sa véritable vie n'est connue que de lui',[5] he claims the autobiographical prerogative and extends it to other genres. Apparently disdaining the lure of invention, he asserts the precedence of the experimental autobiographical narrative, *The Son of a Servant*, over the fictional *The People of Hemsö*: 'Not a novel, for the genre is false, we only really know fragments of other people's lives, and can only write one novel, the one about our own life'(VI:335). And what he particularly values is the author's presence in the text. After reading Edvard Brandes's play *Superior Force (Overmagt)*, he tells him: 'Of all the things you've written, this seems to me the most full of life, because you have given something of yourself. And what else should one give, when one knows so little about others!'(VII:33), and more than twenty years later he criticises Birger Mörner for having failed to achieve the drastic display of his 'entrails' [*inälvor*] that alternately disgusted and compelled him in his own writing: 'I've now read your book! All right! But you must write about yourself, about the important, remarkable things you have yourself experienced....But you don't want to, because opening your belly is painful (=Harakiri).'[6] In fact Strindberg repeatedly stresses the continuity between living and writing, and even their identity. In a disarmingly simple observation from the Inferno period, he informs Torsten Hedlund that he is 'returning to [his] book! Although it is not a book; it is a life!'(XI:100), while he explains to his sister, Elisabeth, that the art of the writer depends not upon invention but on the uninhibited exploitation of personal experience. To write does not mean 'making up things that have never happened; to write means relating what one has lived', and what endangers such an undertaking is not a lack of ability, since 'anyone with education can write, that is to say, put his thoughts on paper', but reticence, a reluctance to give oneself 'to the paper' and so achieve 'the greatest form of pleasure and comfort'(III:41-2) as one's reward for releasing what is within.[7]

For his insistent misgivings about the moral propriety of imaginative writing are accompanied by a personal drive towards exposure and introspection which links the early assertion that 'what we have been seeking to compile for thousands of years is the natural history of the human heart, and everyone can and must make their contribution' (I:198), with the later declaration 'imaginative writing will gradually cease to exist. The future should see the setting up of offices at which at a certain age everyone anonymously handed in a truthful biography [sic]; it could become the data for a real science of man if such a thing were needed.'[8] In any case, Strindberg was well-equipped to engage in continuous and rigorous introspection, and he often claimed to have mastered the complex art of regarding himself and his life objectively. Indeed, what distinguished him from critics of his subjectivity was, according to a letter of 1895, precisely his ability 'to objectify [him]self' (X:351), a faculty he bestowed in turn upon The Unknown in *To Damascus* (29:175) and The Stranger in the chamber play *The Burned House*, who describes how he 'now regarded [him]self as another, and observed and studied this other and his fate, which made me insensible to my own suffering' (45:106), and in later years Strindberg frequently envisaged the past he had lived through as if it were the plot of a superior dramatist in which he was both actor and spectator, or the text and its reader. An expert in what Nietzsche termed 'the art of staging and watching ourselves,'[9] he thus caused Falkenström, one of the figures in whom he contrived this objectification, to remark in the novel *Black Banners*: 'It has in fact seemed to me from an early age that my life was staged before me so that I would be able to observe all its facets. This reconciled me to my misfortunes, and taught me to perceive myself as an object' (41:196).

Several factors, to which Strindberg himself sometimes draws attention, nurtured this tendency. There was what he once called 'that damnable old faith of duty and asceticism', his early pietism, which his Norwegian colleagues, Bjørnson and Jonas Lie, both regarded as the fundamental stratum of his character. To Lie the engaged polemicist he knew in the early 1880s, who advanced the claims of a socially conscious, scientific literature at the expense of the imagination, was a concealed but fanatical Pietist, passionately attracted to martyrdom, while Bjørnson perceived that regardless of his later experience, Strindberg remained, morally at least, faithful to the Pietism of his youth.[10] And when, in *The Son of a Servant*, Strindberg came to analyse the religious perspective which in spite of everything continues to animate the text in which the judgement is made, he refers himself, if somewhat disparagingly, to 'Christianity's individualism, with its eternal burrowing into the self and its imperfections'(18:239), and indicates how 'Christianity's egotistical criticism of the self had accustomed him to occupy himself with his self, fondle it, cosset it, like another beloved person'(18:271). 'This habit of self-examination, which he derived from Christian soul-searching'(18:213) acted as a stimulus, both to the continual inspection of himself in the mirror of his words, and in a lifelong inclination to identify with a series of Romantic protagonists (Karl Moor, Manfred, Cain) who have in common a disposition 'to appear interesting in their own eyes'(19:99), and in whom he also saw himself reflected. As Nils Norman has observed, in his astute study of Strindberg's early religious ideas and experience:

That the psychological training involved in evangelical Christianity was of enormous significance for Strindberg as a writer, is obvious. When Strindberg became a Naturalist in the eighties, this also meant a return to behavioural patterns which had been implanted in him during his evangelical years. The confessional vein, which is already apparent in his early writing, but which first comes to the fore as a dominating feature in *The Son of a Servant*, has his youthful religious self-scrutiny as its self-evident precondition.[11]

In Strindberg's case, therefore, the autobiographical enterprise is clearly related to the introspective religious tradition which Georges Gusdorf calls 'pietist', a non-literary tradition initially, consisting of works written with no explicit artistic intent or thought of publication, in which various individuals recorded their spiritual life in writing. However, the scrupulous observation of his thoughts and motives, which the believer was encouraged to perform, prepared a context in which later writers (Gusdorf points to Rousseau, Herder, Goethe, and Kierkegaard) thought and wrote. Thus spiritual autobiography moved from the private domain of correspondence and diary (at the most, confidential texts open only to a select group of readers such as Strindberg wrote for his youthful mentor, Edla Heijkorn), via exemplary and cautionary personal histories, to the commercial world of published literature, a trend which, in the 1880s, and culminating with *The Son of a Servant*, Strindberg sometimes suggests he is anxious to reverse. As Gusdorf writes:

> Le rôle du piétisme, dans l'histoire de l'autobiographie, aura été de susciter une conversion de l'attention vers l'espace du dedans... Lorsque diminuera la part de l'exigence religieuse, celle de la psychologie augmentera d'autant. Et l'autobiographie littéraire moderne naîtra de la désacrilisation de l'espace du dedans. Ceux qui ne s'examinent plus devant Dieu et en fonction de Dieu verront s'ouvrir à leur curiosité, à leur inquiétude, une région autonome de l'être humain.[12]

But if the habit of constant self-scrutiny originally encouraged the combination of self-assertion and public confession that characterizes so much of Strindberg's autobiographical writing (the one resisting and the other conceding the guilt he had become accustomed to seek and find), the desire to bear witness, which leads him to the extraordinary claim that he not only tells the truth but is the truth ('But in me there is a brutal animal instinct for truth...which compels me to be truth' (IV:168)), finds additional encouragement in both Kierkegaard, whose 'subjective demand for truth liberated and encouraged the Strindbergian subjectivity',[13] and the theories of Naturalism.

The discovery of Kierkegaard, whose impact on the young Strindberg is documented in volume two of *The Son of a Servant*, acted as a further spur to self-analysis and moral self-scrutiny, provided an example of how to distribute and objectify the different sides and drives of the self among invented and pseudonymous characters, and introduced him to the idea of experimenting with standpoints and to seeing his life as a series of stages, as well as to the art of 'living immured within one's own personality to be one's own witness, one's own judge, one's own prosecutor, to be in oneself the one and only!'[14] In Kierkegaard's description in his *Essay in Experimental Psychology*, *Repetition*, of the young man who was captivated by the theatre 'and desired to be himself carried away into the midst of that fictitious reality in order to see and hear himself as an *alter ego*, to disperse himself among the innumerable possibilities which diverge from himself, and yet in such a way that every diversity is in turn a single self',[15] there is, too, an anticipation not only of Strindberg's method of characterization but also of the species of shadow play into which he enters in *To Damascus*, in order to project himself and the events of his life in the mirror image of the stage. Moreover, Kierkegaard offered Strindberg grounds for regarding his passion for writing as a calling (*kallelse*), a sacrifice (*offer*), and a duty (*pligt*), so partly allaying that 'distaste for art' (IV:144) which always haunted him as 'Ghosts from my youth, when I was a pietist' (II:362). By placing his production in the category of the ethical rather than the aesthetic, he was able to accept the 'indescribable' pleasure writing gave him, as well as 'this wonderful turning inside out of the soul...which is the precondition of art'(I:325).

By purporting to represent the real and not the beautified, Naturalism also assuaged, if only temporarily, the same misgivings. With its scientific pretensions, what he termed 'this microscopic view which wants to penetrate to the core of the matter' (II:357), afforded a theoretical framework for his native disposition, and Nietzsche's malicious description of the current literary trend as one in which 'the showy words are:...being "scientific" (the *document humain*: in other words, the novel of colportage and addition in place of composition)'[16] provides an apt summary of Strindberg's many comments on the need to abandon a literature derived from the imagination during the 1880s. Not that he was the first to argue the scientific and documentary value of autobiographical writing at the expense of fantasy and invention: in *Monsieur Nicolas*, Restif de la Bretonne had claimed 'Ce n'est pas pour m'historier que j'écris, mais pour démontrer les causes et les effets des actions humaines. Voilà ce qui nécessite une foule de détails. C'est un livre utile qu'on lit ici, et s'il est amusant, ce n'est que son second mérite.'[17] But with *The Son of a Servant*, Strindberg certainly embarks upon the single most extended attempt at the scientific literature which possessed the imagination of his French contemporaries. Flaubert's remark, 'Quand on aura, pendant quelque temps, traité l'âme humaine avec l'impartialité que l'on met dans les sciences physiques à étudier la matière, on aura fait un pas immense',[18] and Zola's demand for 'une littérature expérimentale' in which 'l'écrivain est un chirurgien qui, pour aller jusqu'au cœur, coupe dans la chair d'une main paisible et ferme, sans fièvre aucune',[19] preface Strindberg's argument that literature 'ought to emancipate itself totally from art and become science' (V:339); and the four volumes, in which he dissects himself in accordance with the prevailing view of the writer as a counterpart to the surgeon or physiologist, are in fact continuous with the scientific investigations to which he afterwards devotes himself. They represent an attempt to proceed beyond the constructions he accused

Zola of having placed on observed or invented lives (and the criticism of Zola for pretending to know 'what goes on in other people's heads' (18:456) in the Foreword signals the autobiographical nature of *The Son of a Servant* in a discussion which otherwise deflects precise generic identification), while as 'an attempt at the literature of the future' (18:455), they approach the 'livre de pure analyse' which Edmond de Goncourt believed might represent 'la dernière évolution du roman'.[20]

Conceiving his life as a scientific project, each of Strindberg's principal autobiographical ventures is therefore not only a Kierkegaardian experiment with standpoints but a text in which he is 'Laborator und Experiment-objekt auf demselben Mal' (XIII:262). *The Son of a Servant* is considered 'a development of the naturalist novel, incorporating history, psychology, social milieu, together with the writer's opinions on the matter' (V:295), 'an attempt to emancipate literature from art' in which the author 'has merely taken the corpse of the person I have known best and learned anatomy, physiology, psychology, history from the carcass' (V:344). The next stage, *A Madman's Defence*, is the outcome of 'an experimental psychological analysis' (VI:242) in which Strindberg transforms himself and his environment into a field of research, cultivates the virus of jealousy, explores the hinterland of insanity, and turns his private life with Siri von Essen into a public laboratory in which he tests his views on marriage, so accomplishing an extreme instance of that type of *dédoublement* often encountered in Naturalism where, as Maupassant observes of the writer, 'Il semble avoir deux âmes, l'une qui note, explique, commente chaque sensation de sa voisine de l'âme naturelle, commune à tous les hommes'.[21] In *Inferno*, meanwhile, he embarks upon 'the study of man' (XI:104) to which he redirected his attention after the spectacular investigation of the natural world and man's place in nature which he conducted in the early 1890s, and writes up the experimental data gathered in the letters to Torsten Hedlund and his *Occult Diary*, while *Alone*, written in 1903, incorporates a theoretical blueprint by means of which he seeks to explore and disarm his future as well as placate and preserve the past.[22]

In any case, of course, Strindberg palpably fails to achieve that impartial and impassive detachment from his material which a number of contemporary writers considered appropriate to the objectivity that was an essential component of the experimental method as understood by contemporary science.[23] Indeed, the impersonality of the experimental method, which 'aura pour résultat de faire disparaître de la science toutes les vues individuelles pour les remplacer par des théories impersonnelles et générales',[24] posed a direct threat to the self which Strindberg guarded so jealously and whose preservation and distinction is one of the underlying purposes of his autobiographical project. As Claude Bernard stressed in his *Introduction à l'étude de la médecine expérimentale*, the treatise on scientific method which exerted so potent an influence on Zola's *Le roman expérimental*: 'L'expérimentateur doit alors disparaître ou plutôt se transformer instantanément en observateur.'[25] But to disappear was an option Strindberg rigorously declined, and like the grounds upon which Naturalism eventually proved inadequate to the questions he asked of it, in part precisely because of the dilemmas inherent in a literature which affects 'la nudité d'une leçon d'anatomie',[26] these tensions in his approach to writing will shortly require elucidation, for it is often in relation to the easily accepted metaphors and images through which Strindberg describes his project that, on investigation, it becomes most discrepant and opaque. Nevertheless, it is clear that in the conception of literature to which he so often gestures, that is, a combination of the kind of autobiographical and confessional material which both Herder, in 'Von Erkennen und Empfinden der menschlichen Seele', and Goethe, in his desire for a history of the personality, wanted to see collated and published, and the *document humain* advocated by the Goncourts and Taine, the role of the imagination in writing is normally treated as secondary to the facts of the author's life:[27] 'Of course, you have the freedom to use your imagination,' he remarks, in a significantly concessionary addition to his letter on writing to Siri von Essen (I:198). It serves to augment what life offers and provides 'the protective disguise' (VII:138) when the material to hand is too intimate for immediate publication, as is strikingly the case with his almost contemporaneous account of events at Skovlyst in 1888 in the novella *Tschandala*, where he literally dresses up his revelations about his landlady, her bailiff lover, and his own entanglement with the latter's sister, in seventeenth-century costume.[28] Otherwise, however, at least until after he develops a modernist aesthetic during the Inferno period, Strindberg continues to maintain that 'the imagination, which has been regarded as creative, that is to say, able to make something out of nothing, is only the gift of organization, which arranges the memory's greater or lesser wealth of impressions and puts each of them in its place.' (17:193)

Prefaced by such statements, it is perhaps not so extraordinary to recall that, until recently, it was an accepted practice in Sweden for the actor who played The Unknown in *To Damascus* to wear a mask representing Strindberg's features. In its immediate erasure of all difference between the writer and his text, this custom affords an eloquent image of the long tradition of biographical criticism in Strindberg studies, where the writing is generally mapped neatly back on to what is known of the life it ostensibly transcribes. That what is known is often only recoverable through Strindberg's highly personal account is, however, a nicety which leaves such criticism largely unruffled. In its concern to identify the text with its author and to reconstruct from it only the image of its progenitor, it attributes any noticeable discrepancies in the transcription of known facts to the realm of authorial inadvertency, and habitually glides from the names of the characters to those of Strindberg and his contemporaries. Thus Strindberg's first biographer, Erik Hedén, illustrates his discussion of *The People of Hemsö* with a recent photograph of 'Gusten in *The People of Hemsö* as an old man', and even Torsten Eklund grows so frustrated with the discrepancies between *A Madman's Defence* and the facts of Strindberg's life that consideration of the work's veracity provokes the resigned comment: 'Moreover, the material is clearly designed with an artistic aim.'[29] In this critical tradition, life and work are understood to reflect one another without significant distortion, and a text like *The Roofing Feast* can therefore easily be reduced to the status of a transparent report from Strindberg's third marriage.[30]

Since the interval between the events of Strindberg's life and the material of his writing is certainly traversed more rapidly than with most authors, criticism is not unjustified in observing this proximity; but in its tendency to annul all difference and engage with novels and plays only as forms of more or less impeded autobiography, this approach denies many texts their potential polyvalency of meaning as literature. Indeed, it even negates the possibility of an imagined literature since, as Kierkegaard points out, 'all poetic production would *eo ipso* be rendered impossible and unendurable, if the lines must be the very words of the producer, literally understood.'[31] Unfortunately, however, where Strindberg is concerned, impurities abound and fact and fiction are frequently only imperfectly distinguished, either through the impassioned carelessness of an author personally engaged in the recorded events, as in *A Madman's Defence*, when the equivocal figure of 'fröken Z' is inadvertently unfrocked towards the end of the text as her real life original 'Miss David' (ED:247), or with intent, as when, in retrospect, he deliberately aligns his later destiny as it is recounted in *Inferno* with the fate of the central character of his first major work, the historical drama *Master Olof*.[32] Thus an alternative critical method, which regards even *A Madman's Defence* and *Inferno* as fictional entities independent of the life of their creator, also affords too partial an approach. Eric Johannesson's penetrating study, *The Novels of August Strindberg*,[33] for example, provides an antidote to the excesses of the biographical tradition which is of great service in demonstrating the artistry with which Strindberg composes his narratives, but it cannot account for the duplicity with which he moves back and forth, from one domain to another, either in the relationships a text proposes between the lives of actual persons in a real environment and its own internal narrative logic, or the uses to which it was put by its producer. Generally, disguises are transparent or bestowed on a system of minimal displacement (in the Inferno material, for instance, Poles become Russians, and Norwegian painters, Danes); footnotes and textual allusions sometimes direct the reader to other fictional or non-fictional segments of the developing corpus of texts to which Strindberg signs his name; and even in achieved works of fiction (for example, in the statement 'They lived in Norrtullsgatan, to the left of Observatory Square' (14:40), in the short story, 'The Rewards of Virtue', or the Student's remark, 'I'm said to have come into the world in the middle of bankruptcy proceedings' (45:153), in *The Ghost Sonata*, both of which evoke information about Strindberg's early life that is explicitly developed in *The Son of a Servant*), there are rents in the text through which his life flows. They are solicitations in which he draws attention to himself, apertures where he allows himself to become visible to the eyes of his contemporaries and to the critical gaze he intends should one day trace his whole career. For he frequently maintains that he is only to be apprehended in the entirety of his writing ('My writings are me!' (XV:223)), and that the truth about him is to be found not in the world, but in 'the thousands of printed pages' (19:278) wherein their author is dispersed, to be constituted subsequently from what Michel Foucault terms '[the] relationships of homogeneity, filiation, reciprocal explanation, authentification, or...common utilization'[34] which exist between the various texts.

Hence his concern that nothing he wrote be lost or overlooked, as in one of his several premature testimentary letters (on this occasion to his short-term collaborator on the ironic comedy, *Comrades*, Axel Lundegård) in which he urges him to see that 'my collected works, *everything* I have written, every word from newspapers, almanacs, at home and abroad, including my letters, are published when the time is ripe, in Flensburg, Leipzig, Copenhagen or Chicago' (VI:297). Every word must be available for the reader to be in a position 'to see as deeply into a soul as can be seen' (VI:298), for like Kierkegaard he conceived of the work as a whole, shaped and orchestrated and yielding itself only to the informed reader. It is a play of signifiers in which he has 'multiplied himself' (*polymeriserat sig* - 18:459), and where his self is distributed throughout the totality of texts from which 'the enlightened reader' (18:459) may reconstruct the author and his life amid the cluster of Johans, Axels, Falk(-enström)s, and their companion Teklas, Marias, Gustavs, and Borgs, characters in whom Kierkegaardian pseudonymity is sometimes coupled with Balzacian recurrence in novels, plays and autobiographies: 'And if his collected works are ever published,' Strindberg writes, of one of these multiplications, 'not a word should be changed, but all the contradictions resolved in the common Kierkegaardian title: Stages on Life's Way' (40:46).[35]

This is Strindberg's larger project, which establishes a context in which all his writing demands recognition as in some degree autobiographical. And, of course, most writing accommodates such a reading. Thus Nietzsche considered every great philosophy 'a confession on the part of its author and a kind of involuntary and unconscious memoir;'[36] Derrida's continuing deconstruction of Freud has uncovered the autobiography in *Beyond the Pleasure Principle* as well as in *The Interpretation of Dreams*;[37] and works of fiction offer innumerable opportunities for the pursuit (if not the capture) of the author since, as André Maurois observes, 'la création artistique n'est pas une création *ex nihilo*. C'est un regroupement des éléments de la réalité. On pourrait montrer facilement que les récits les plus étranges, ceux qui nous paraissent le plus loin de l'observation réelle, comme les *Voyages de Gulliver*, les *Contes* d'Edgar Poe, la *Divine Comédie* de Dante ou l'*Ubu Roi* de Jarry, sont faite de souvenirs.'[38] Indeed, an invitation to trace latent or overt transpositions and transformations of lived experience into writing that does not necessarily advertise its autobiographical substance is implicit in most post-Classical literature where the reader is encouraged to discern not only what Edward Said has called the 'idiolect' that signifies the 'irreducible individuality' of the author,[39] but also the more or less submerged fragments of the great confession which, since Romanticism, it has been the custom to seek and find in literature: as Strindberg retorts, to criticism of *To Damascus*: 'Why does Norddeutsche Allg. Z. go on about autobiography? Doesn't Goethe state in Aus meinem Leben that all his work was a Confession? Isn't Faust a diary?' (XIV:223). But this pursuit entails a vastly more sophisticated process than the tradition of biographical criticism normally allows for. If the author's life lurks at the base of a literary work, where it provides the deep structure of experience retailed in the text, then no more than literature as a whole is a simple reflection of the society of which it is part, does this underlying sequence of events appear in the text without refraction, distortion, addition, and inevitably subtraction. Besides retaining a sense of the text's diversity, therefore, following the autobiographical trace involves a recognition that the obvious signposts of intent in a text may prove misleading, and that the transfer of a life into the text of its written inscription inserts it into a circuit of communication where it is traversed by other forces, the demands and constraints of language and genre, and what Roland Barthes calls 'the image-repertoire, which oversees, controls, purifies, banalizes, codifies, corrects [and] imposes the focus (and the vision) of a social communication,'[40] as well as by those forces which the narrator does not know, or knows only obscurely, his unconscious and the prevailing ideology, which constantly undercut any desire he may have to fit the word neatly to the world. As Strindberg knows from his own self-study, characters are 'conglomerations of past and present cultures, scraps from books and newspapers, fragments of people, torn scraps of fine clothing that has become rags, in just the same way that the soul is patched together' (23:104), and he proceeds with what Paul de Man has termed the blindness which yields insight,[41] whether he is writing autobiography or fiction.

To comprehend Strindberg's enterprise, therefore, requires neither the simple matching of fact to fiction, nor the removal of his work to an independent realm for contemplation as a series of self-contained realities, but an eye for the unarticulated forms which mediate its production, for the non-transparencies in the text, and for those symptoms of an unseen meaning which may reside even in the most prominent and constant of his images, in for example his claim to be the lucid purveyor of truth or the bearer of a spectacular destiny. In the interplay between the lived and the written, moreover, it is the work that illuminates the life, not the reverse, and for the reader both constitute texts to be interpreted. As Fredric Jameson notes:

> It should be observed that, where the older biographical criticism understood the author's life as a context, or as a cause, as that which could explain the text, the newer kind understands that 'life' or rather its reconstruction, precisely as one further text in its turn, a text on the level with the other literary texts of the writer in question and susceptible of forming a larger corpus of study with them.[42]

But it requires, too, an awareness of the context in which writers were prepared to render up their lives to a literature in which the reader expected to discover the figure of its author in the text. For although an extreme instance, Strindberg's flagrant exposure of himself to the public gaze, in which he attempts to convey 'my story stark naked' (VIII:188), was only conceivable because it encompassed a potential inherent in the literary institution of a period for which writing was published and read as essentially self-revelatory. In a market where the novel was the dominant article of self-display, Maupassant, in remarking that 'nous ne diversifions donc nos personnages qu'en changeant l'âge, le sexe, la situation sociale et toutes les circonstances de la vie de notre *moi*',[43] might still imply that diversity and even invention remained an option, but a comment by Edmond de Goncourt in his

Journal (the publication of which was itself a symptom of the time), betrays the growing impatience with invention, at least on the part of a sophisticated reader: after criticizing Zola for the kind of 'fabulation' with which Strindberg also took issue, he observes that 'Je ne suis intéressé que par un roman où je sens dans l'imprimé, pour ainsi dire, la transcription d'êtres en chair et en os, où je lis un peu ou beaucoup des mémoires d'une vie vécue.'[44] In an earlier period, Shaftesbury had already lamented that 'The whole Writing of this Age is become indeed a sort of Memoir-Writing';[45] but Strindberg now frequently took up this development in defence of his own practice, as when, in a letter urging the publication of *Miss Julie* and *Creditors* upon a publisher who recoiled at what he took to be their character of improper private revelation, he pointed out that 'in our days everything is intimate and Confessions are the height of fashion'(VII:144), and went on to remind him of recent examples, among them Zola's *L'Oeuvre*, (with its 'pretty intimate scenes in bed with his wife'), Goncourt's *Les frères Zemganno*, Jonas Lie's *Ett Samliv*, and Victoria Benedictsson's *Pengar*, in which he detected a transparent account of the writer's marriage, down to 'her husband's hairy chest'. This claim is repeated some five years later, again with reference to *Pengar*, in order to defend the exposure of his own marriage in *A Madman's Defence*' (IX:224), and a similar argument is used to exonerate writing *à clef* in the essay 'On the General Discontent' ('Om det allmänna missnöjet'), where he includes both Dante and Dickens among the 'out and out scandal-mongers' (16:46). Apart from indicating that Strindberg's manner of reading resembled Goncourt's, however, and that his approach to a text was often vehemently partial, the evidence he marshals does suggest that contemporary writers at least sometimes invited such attention. In short, Strindberg's writing is part of a movement in which the textual encounter between writer and reader seems more immediate than hitherto. At times, in *Inferno* or Maupassant's 'La Horla', Hamsun's *Hunger* or Huysman's *En Route*, where the writer assumes the burden of the experience recounted in his text with minimal pretence, this writing resembles a *document humain*, and it is therefore not surprising that, in what Conrad describes as a 'task which mainly consists in laying one's soul more or less bare to the world' where 'everyone who puts pen to paper for the reading of strangers...can speak of nothing else' than himself,[46] this trend should coincide with the development of the kind of purposeful occultation practiced by Henry James and Mallarmé, who wished to preserve both literature and themselves from too direct and impertinent a gaze.

This approach applies particularly to the more modest of Strindberg's projects, that selection of his works which in later years he suggested should be published under the collective title 'The Son of a Servant' as a continuous account of his 'life's saga' (XIII:28). The 1909 preface to the second edition of the original *Son of a Servant* is evidently written as a foreword to the whole sequence, as it is enumerated in an unwieldy conception he sent to his German translator, Emil Schering, in 1904:

One thing, while I remember it. If I die soon, will you collect and publish, in *one volume*, under the title 'The Son of a Servant' these works:

1. The Son of a Servant
2. Time of Ferment
3. In the Red Room
4. (Fourth part of this work, manuscript at Bonniers)
5. Die Beichte eines Thoren
6. The Quarantine Officer's Second Story (from Fagervik and Skamsund)
7. Inferno
8. Legends
9. Alone.
10. The Occult Diary since 1896.
11. Correspondence, letters.

This is the only monument I desire: a black wooden cross and my story! (XV:38)

That the project represents more than a passing whim is confirmed by similar lists to his publisher, Bonnier, and the writer Gustaf af Geijerstam (XV:42, XIII:28), and among his surviving papers a further reformulation of the table of contents is written on a concept entitled 'The Son of a Servant (to be published after my death with this title in one volume).'[47]

Given the ambiguity which surrounds the nature and genre of every one of these texts (the refusal in the 1886 Foreword to identify *The Son of a Servant* as 'novel, biography, memoir... apology...confession' (18:452), for example; the narrative frame of *A Madman's Defence*, with its duplication of writers between the preface and the text; the claim of *Inferno* to be only a transcription of the Narrator's diary; the extraction of the pseudo-fictional 'The Quarantine Master's Second Story' from the autobiographical novel, *The Cloister*, which was not published until after Strindberg's death; and the way in which the first person narration, absence of names, and fictional inclusions places *Alone* in the no-man's land described by Philippe Lejeune in his recent influential attempt to establish the generic boundaries of autobiography on the basis of the writer's contract with his readers as 'Pacte = 0: non seulement le personnage n'a pas de nom, mais l'auteur ne conclut aucun pacte, - ni autobiographique, ni romanesque'),[48] it is evident that Strindberg nevertheless experiences a need to distinguish these writings from the remainder of his production in what represents a kind of autobiographical pact with those who study his work. Although he may sometimes yield to the temptation to relocate a work in the domain of fiction, it exhibits, for all the flux of categories that now exists in the relationship between autobiography, *Bildungsroman, roman intime*, confessional novel, case history, self-analysis, diary, and letter, a desire to achieve a coherent, consequent, and continuous account of his life. And it is precisely in relation to these works which most obviously seek to take possession of their author's past self and the life he has lived, that the image offered by The Unknown's Strindberg mask reveals a fine irony. For however closely writing retraces the events it records, and whatever the degree of veracity it achieves, it simultaneously covers over and masks the life it is employed to recover. Language displaces the past: the past is replaced by language and the genres into which it settles, and which in turn impose a shape not only on the past but on a reader's response to its reproduction. Thus language interposes itself as a screen between the reader or spectator and the events projected in it, and it is by no means a gratuitous play on words to see, in any subsequent account of the lived experience, both a further recovery and a fresh re-covering. For, more evidently than most discourses, the autobiographical demonstrates that writing is secondary. Even in cases of almost immediate transcription (for example, in those parts of Anais Nin's *Journals* in which she attempts the instantaneous capture of experience 'before it is altered, changed by distance or time'),[49] whatever incites the writer to write is separate usually in place and always in time from the act of recording. What is narrated or described is developed, enriched, and impoverished as it is transposed into the domain of the written; moreover, autobiography is not a one-way mirror but a composition, and the image of the self that is captured there is not a reflection but something created by the act of writing, an act which is itself an event in the life, an action which produces rather than reproduces the life.

Although part of the writer's life, therefore, and capable once written, of playing a role in the inauguration of other texts, autobiography remains a supplement. That is, it follows after the life it narrates until it reaches a point where, by a neat reversal, it becomes the life narrated. For the obsessive autobiographer such as Rousseau or Strindberg, writing is partly a means of organizing identity, of recuperating the dispersed fragments of personality, and, through the mediation of language, of creating his own image in the cohering structure of literature, and almost any event may stimulate a revision or a fresh attempt. A single page of Strindberg's favourite Lessebo writing paper survives as witness to one such aborted attempt. It merely lists a handful of dates, 1849, 1857, 1867, 1877, 1893, 1901, 1904, in a column down the page, all of which (except tantalizingly and provocatively the second) are easily associated with significant events in the succession of birth, university, marriage, and divorce, which form the most obvious chronology of his life.[50] Meanwhile, in another inventory, headed 'Excremental hells' (*Träckhelveten*), the reading of Swedenborg's *Arcana Coelestia*, where those who once delighted in sensual pleasures are described as finding their *post mortem* delight in sewers, urine and dung, has provoked a further recapitulation in search of continuity and order that is governed by the idea of an excremental hell. Before issuing in the Swiftian disgust which sometimes characterizes his later writing ('Children enter the world in excrement, live their first years in excrement'), and in an urgent addition in crayon in which he once again demands to know 'Who am I?', the list succeeds in incorporating a large reach of the past among places which he has repeatedly described in the autobiographical sequence and *To Damascus*:

The dustbin in the yard at Clara, where I played as a child by the toilets.
Loviseberg, cowshed, cesspits, tobacco plantation, putrid ponds with
leeches and dead cats.
Norrtullsgatan 12. In the flat. Grev Magnigatan.
Lästmakargatan - the dining room window was directly opposite the
toilet.
Norrmalmsgatan in an old whore house with the toilets beneath an
open sewer.
The situation when Baroness W. declared her love for me and the old
codgers W. went through the room with the out-house lantern
Skovlyst: Excremental hell and Swine hell.
Dornach: Excremental hell.
In Gravesend: the closets.
Rue de la Grande Chaumière opposite the toilet.
Orfila opposite one; above one; and a view over 150 toilets
The yard at Madame Charlotte's where we ate between the dustbins
and the toilet.
The Rose Room at Klam was directly opposite the toilet.[51]

But as even this minor example suggests, the image of the self and its past
established in language gradually replaces its source, and the natural sequence of
events in the life becomes an interpreted series, a retrospective reconstruction which
confers on the discrete particulars of existence the coherence, order, and elaboration
of a destiny. What is unwritten, meanwhile, becomes the unlived, and each recorded
moment or fact is a component of the image comprehended by the text. Thus one of
the main drives articulated in Strindberg's writing, the instinct for truth which
provokes 'a hazy desire to rip off one's clothes and go naked' (16:110), which is
often advanced in evidence of his autobiographical probity, is itself an element of the
personal myth embodied in the writing. Whether, as in the 1880s, he appears in the
guise of the iconoclastic rebel, Loke, or, after his Inferno experiences, as the
reluctant prophet, Jonah, Strindberg, the truth-sayer, who unmasks the web of
deceit and lies with 'the simple, raw language of truth' (54:227), is only one aspect of
the almost archetypal self-projection which his writing has imposed upon his
readers. And hence what matters is not to ascertain whether what Strindberg writes
is true or false in any pedantic, literal sense; what matters is only what he wrote of
himself, either wittingly or not, of what may be deduced from both the sequence of
autobiographical works and the totality of his writings since they hold not merely
other versions of himself but belong to the single endeavour to apprehend his
experience of the world. Eventually rejecting Naturalism, he would maintain that
the natural world had not developed like a Darwinian chain but formed a complex
lattice-work of relationships: 'The plants are not developed like a chain but...the
whole is a net' (27:679). His life, too, as he lived and wrote about it, came to
resemble not a continuous linear progression of events but a network of discontinuities,
repetitions, and contradictions for which he sought a more sensitive means of self-

representation than the developmental Naturalist account, with its stress on physiological and psychological cause and effect, one that was alert to the often unconscious, seemingly trivial, and apparently random fragments of being as well as to its steady, onward flow.

Moreover, if it is the continuous desire to represent himself in language which eventually convinces Strindberg of the need to go beyond Naturalism, it also accounts for his refusal to confine himself to the customary autobiographical model, that is, the single retrospective text involving a return to childhood and the retracing of the writer's origins and development, which distinguishes autobiography as a genre from related forms such as the historical memoir (in which the emphasis, as Strindberg himself observed in commenting on the exclusion of events surrounding his trial for blasphemy in 1884 (19:227), is placed on an account of external matters rather than on an examination of the personal life), the short episode or *souvenir* (which covers only a period in the subject's life), the intimate journal, auto-portrait, essay or diary (all of which are discontinuous or do not take the form of a retrospective prose narrative). According to Philippe Lejeune, it is this singleness 'qui rend particulièrement solennel et émouvant l'acte autobiographique.'[52] A man can produce only one such autobiography, Lejeune argues, for in writing of himself he will become, if he has not already done so, once and for all, who he is. Having reconstructed the unity of his life in time, the prospect of change appears at an end, if only in the closure achieved in the consummation of the autobiographical act in which he has given his one life its definitive form.[53] This is the singular task which Strindberg performs in *The Son of a Servant*, which he often regards as a book composed in the face of death, the vivisection of a corpse in which he achieves the posthumous perspective of the comprehensive autobiographer who falls back upon his origins in the face of a foreclosed future and dissects his naked body: as he wrote, to Edvard Brandes:

> If you only knew how pleased I am that my book has made an impression on you. For all my demagogism, I think I am too genteel to write for the mob. I have cut a caper before, I have no doubt been an unwitting clown, who 'put it on', who dressed up, made faces, anything to attract people's attention. But this time I regarded myself as dead, paid no heed to the inquisitive snout of the common herd, forgot myself more than it seems...and tried to be the most difficult thing of all: honest. (V:350)

In his study of Stendhal, Lejeune notes how 'sans doute l'idée de la mort (mort affective...et après 1830, mort sociale) était-elle nécessaire pour briser un instant le dynamique systèm de relais vers l'avenir, et induire un retour aux origines,'[54] and his analysis is suggestive of the context in which Strindberg sought a way out of the 'mort sociale' of the trial arising from *Getting Married* by writing his autobiography. 'I regard myself and my talent as dead and am now writing the saga of my life in a peculiar form of novel', he tells Brandes, 'I believe that in that way I will be able to analyse myself and discover what makes me tick' (V:306). Indeed, each autobiographical volume is written 'confronted by death' (18:458) or 'devant la mort' (IX:339), but this is underlined in the case of *The Son of a Servant* by the fiction of seeing his life as past, a fiction partly sustained by his use of the third person to objectify himself as 'Jo/han'[55] and regard himself, at least in theory, from the standpoint of a research scientist writing a report on an unusually interesting case.

However, in later years Strindberg adds further instalments in other narrative modes and from greatly altered perspectives. When, therefore, Lejeune asserts, of the traditional autobiographical model, that 'ce récit une fois écrit il sera difficile de la recomposer autrement. Aucune approache fraîche et directe du passé ne sera plus possible, on ne pourra plus le voir qu'à travers le récit qui en aura été fait',[56] he is in fact describing precisely the situation of intertextuality which Strindberg contrives. His past is written and rewritten, lived and relived, across a succession of texts that comment upon each other as well as upon the life they record. The method is dynamic in order to encompass change. Continuity and discontinuity, which Francis Hart sees as the essence of autobiography since, as he argues, 'effective access to a recollected self or its 'version' begins in a discontinuity of identity or being which permits past selves to be seen as distinct realities, yet only a continuity of identity or being makes the autobiographical act or purpose meaningful',[57] are dialectically related, so that the narrator is constantly confronting himself as he was, as he knows himself no longer to be, but as (once written) he cannot easily escape or disavow. 'My disharmonies', he tells Schering, 'reside in the impossibility of stitching my previous points of view together with my present ones' (XV:146), a difficulty that is compounded by the republication, either in new editions or in translation, of works embodying opinions he now abjured. But subscribing as he does to the post-Romantic ideology of unfettered, organic personal development, and contemporary as he is to the debate on evolution, it is not surprising that Strindberg should expect and value growth and change, both in society and the individual. To bind himself to a single standpoint or a fixed programme would undermine his often-vaunted 'freedom to "grow" freely' (VII:39), and in a letter of 1894 to his old friend, Littmansson, he defends the mutability for which his contemporaries frequently criticised him by arguing what is perhaps the central tenet of his undertaking:

> You bore the seeds of growth within you, but you didn't cultivate your self with brutal egoism. You couldn't create several persons out of yourself; you couldn't like Münchhausen and I, pull yourself up by your hair and lift yourself out of your scepticism; you couldn't search out yourself and use it to correct the other conventional selves which others had poked down into your soul; you couldn't rise above your self. (X:150-1)

When, therefore, Robert Sayre writes of Henry Adams (who likewise procured a posthumous perspective for himself by adopting the third person form in his autobiography) that 'the *Education* is not a response to some other experience, not a way of memorializing some other insight or achievement that has given life significance; it is a response to that moment in life at which an examination of life became essential',[58] he could be describing *The Son of a Servant*, which represents the necessary 'balancing of accounts with the past' (19:250) to which Strindberg was compelled by the encounter with Darwin, Socialism and Atheism that he describes in the final volume. But also implicit in the final pages is an awareness that Johan will not remain as he is at the point at which the book concludes. Consistent with the view that growth is continual, Strindberg continually outgrows himself. What begins as a summing up, therefore, becomes in the course of its writing, the grounds of 'a later enterprise, whatever that may turn out to be' (19:250), and when he completes the text he is on the point of taking leave of Johan: when next encountered, in *A Madman's Defence*, he has become Axel.

Moreover, once the initial autobiography catches up with the life at the moment of writing, the texts produced thereafter (*A Madman's Defence, Inferno, Alone*) foreshadow modernism. They become the substance of the life itself. The life is lived with the writing in mind, and the latter becomes not an addendum to experience but part of the event, no longer the documentation of the career in recollection but something calling attention to itself, to its career as text, to its own life as part of the autobiography of its writer, a central event more important now than the events recorded in it, or rather, constituting a version of events to which his future life must consequently conform. In the narration of *Inferno*, one observes the situation described by Robert Adams with reference to *Ulysses*, of 'the presence of the artist within the work of art, not simply as an overt and dramatic character (Stephen Dedalus), but as the *terminus ad quem*, the retrospective arranger, the manipulator of the characters, and perhaps even the secretive and willful manipulator of the manipulator',[59] and since he is living through the writing of the text, what appear to be possible transformations and deformations of the past become Strindberg's present experience. Thus this all-pervasive intertextuality affects the relationship of all his other texts to those of his autobiographical sequence and to the life they variously apprehend. When reproduced in literature the events of this life have already been worked over and winnowed, in memory. They undergo further changes, elisions, compression, displacement, and extension in the process of transformation, and depending upon the genre chosen, similar material assumes a different form in separate works.

Furthermore, the exploration of analogous material in different literary texts has placed a figured screen between the writer and his past, and the wife Strindberg depicts as his own in *A Madman's Defence*, for example, is not only regarded in the light of the theories advanced contemporaneously in the essay volume, *Vivisections*, but refracted by the images of Bertha in *Comrades* and Laura in *The Father*. As Maurice Gravier rightly points out, therefore, *A Madman's Defence* should not be considered as merely the key to the dramas of the same period; this narrative is also constituted by the texts which surround it and which (in *Miss Julie, Creditors,* and *Playing With Fire*) it colours in turn, and it is therefore equally appropriate to enquire not in what way the novel provides a biographical explication of the plays but

> ...dans quelle mesure le travail que Strindberg a fait pour dessiner les personnages de *Camarades* ou de *Père* ne l'a-t-il influencé, lorsqu'il évoquait dans la *Plaidoyer d'un fou* les rapports et les faits et gestes de la baronne, d'Axel et du Capitaine.[60]

The Father, for example, certainly implants the idea of a wife who tries to destroy her husband by driving him insane into the evolving narrative of Strindberg's own marriage, where it feeds upon misgivings he had long entertained regarding his mental stability. The drama thus transfers from the stage to his private life, as one of the letters to his friend Pehr Staaff, in which he explores the literary possibilities of this material, makes clear: 'It will be interesting to see the outcome of the drama' (VI:266), he declares, with his customary appetite for experience he can turn to literary account. And if, therefore, some five years later he complains 'I have been married for 13 years - and don't know who I've been married to' (VIII:177), it is not unreasonable to attribute his doubts to the practice of literature, with which his life is so easily confused. As he remarked, on one much-quoted occasion: 'I don't know if *The Father* is a work of the imagination, or if my life has been' (VI:298).

The question raised by Strindberg's writing is thus not how faithfully it reproduces its anterior experience or the accuracy with which it reflects the real but rather, how well does he in fact know himself when, in the otherness of the written text, the writer is also written, the subject is also an object, and the discourse of the self is not single and irreducible but dialogic and even polyphonic? The mask *he* adopts with his use of language may be precisely that, and what therefore now demands investigation are the ends to which he employs his writing and how he can adequately represent himself in a medium, language, which he in fact considers inherently mendacious.

CHAPTER TWO

Writing Out and Repetition

The psychical process which originally took place must be repeated as vividly as possible; it must be brought back to its *status nascendi* and then given verbal utterance.

- *Studies on Hysteria*

One other thing! Because both my stories concern people in quarantine, you must not think that this is my own story or stories - that is more deeply buried!

- The Quarantine Officer's Stories

I

In his study of Romantic literary theory, *The Mirror and the Lamp*, M.H. Abrams examines a tradition in which the nature of art is predicated in terms that 'turn on a metaphor which, like "overflow", signifies the internal made external', and he remarks in particular upon the way in which, with Romanticism, the Aristotelian notion of the relief which art affords the spectator becomes 'silently shifted to denote the healing expenditure of feeling in the poet himself.'[1] He quotes Byron's blunt comment, 'If I don't write to empty my mind, I go mad', and draws attention to John Keble's Oxford Lectures in which the thrust of much earlier thinking is impressively reformulated. Keble, who follows Hazlitt and anticipates Freud in observing a relationship between poetry and the fulfilment of ungratified personal desire, distinguishes primary poets as those 'who, spontaneously moved by impulse, resort to composition for relief and solace of a burdened and over-wrought mind', and discerns in poetic creation 'a safety-valve preserving men from actual madness.'[2]

With his desire 'to write a book about the lot of us in order to liberate myself' (XI:300), Strindberg's writing has been widely regarded as an unusually transparent instance of such a venture, whereby he effects an often immediate and sometimes tempestuous emotional discharge of the excitations accumulated in everyday experience. Sustained by the daily therapeutic practice of literature, it is argued,[3] he converts his life into language and so removes affects that would otherwise remain strangulated and occasion pathogenic results. Indeed, Strindberg stresses the

19

cathartic nature of writing on his own account, and readily identifies with the tradition discussed by Abrams. In *Alone*, for example, he quotes Goethe on the relief to be gained from 'transforming whatever delighted or distressed me into a poem or image...in order to bring peace and order to my inner life' (38:198). Like Keble he regards poetry as a safety-valve ('My habit of converting experiences into poetry opens the safety-valve (*säkerhetsventilen*) for an excess of impressions, and replaces the need to speak' (38:192)); and in the account of Johan's discovery of his vocation as a writer, in *Time of Ferment*, he provides a paradigmatic description of the cathartic action of creation upon the creator. Although Johan has already attempted to satisfy his need for self-expression in a number of ways, he finds them all (declamation, painting, acting) at least partly inadequate. For while it will often be painting that eventually helps him to 'show himself to himself' when 'the small, cramped letters on the page lay there dead' (19:18) and he could not write, it did not as yet enable him 'to express what he wanted to say'. Equally, while he may occasionally stumble upon a role in another man's text that corresponds with the words he would himself like to utter (in both Schiller's Karl Moor and Wijkander's Lucidor 'he had discovered his inner feelings expressed in print, and therefore he wanted to speak with their tongues' (18:313)), he discovers that as an actor he is normally called upon 'to shout out empty meaningless words' (18:332), since what a character says does not carry the burden of his own unexpressed ideas and feelings.

Disappointed in the theatre, therefore, and denied advancement there, he seeks to save face and re-establish his 'battered, wounded, torn' self by escaping into the imaginary world of *The Army Surgeon's Tales (Fältskärns berättelser)*, a popular collection of stories by the Finnish writer, Zachris Topelius. But whether by accident or subsequent design (and it certainly fits the crucial retrospective episode of *The Son of a Servant* precisely), the story he reads reminds him of his own familial situation at a moment in his life when he is at odds with his father and his stepmother, yet longing 'for reconciliation and peace'. To achieve a vicarious satisfaction, therefore, and to amend reality, he 'spins' a daydream in which his stepmother reconciles him with his father, a scenario which is accomplished 'by organizing memories from the past, removing some things and adding others' (18:340), or as Freud was to define the process, in 'Creative Writers and Day-Dreaming', 'the wish makes use of an occasion in the present to construct, on the pattern of the past, a picture of the future.'[4] Once this is accomplished (and the Narrator doubts if something so effortless and irresistible 'could be called work, for it went of its own accord, and was none of his willing or doing' (18:341)), it only remains to write it down. The relief is then immediate and comprehensive. It felt (and the image is typical of the bodily metaphors, either surgical or purgative, to which Strindberg often resorts in order to describe his compulsion to write) 'as if years of pain were over, as if an abscess had been lanced' (18:341).[5]

However, the role and function of Strindberg's conception of writing as catharsis has never been thought through in relation to his accomplished work, which raises a number of insistent questions especially as regards the margin of overlap implicit in the frequently drawn comparison between his attempt 'to see as deeply into a soul as can be seen' (VI:298) and the theory and practice of psychoanalysis, which Freud, in one of his first attempts at an adequate metaphor for the abreaction of repressed material, compared to 'the opening up of a cavity filled with pus, the scraping out of a carious region.'[6] What in fact does the often aggressive desire to speak out ('att tala ut') represent? Does it remove the effects, as Strindberg often suggests, or is the material with which he works only fastened the more securely as he returns each day to his life in writing? Is his attempt to reveal himself in words a symptom or its cure, or is the language in which he formulates his life only a means of solace, like the chemical formulae with which he manipulates the natural world in his scientific essays, where exactitude is often sacrificed to the consonance of mathematical harmony? Moreover, given Strindberg's ability as a consummate player as well as creator of roles, how far may the autobiographical writing, which prompted the psychologist Gösta Harding, to maintain that 'apart from his genius as a dramatist, the most remarkable thing about Strindberg seems to me to be his capacity for self-treatment – auto-psychotherapy',[7] be regarded as consonant with the talking cure developed by Freud from Breuer's fortuitous discoveries in the case of Anna O, and what, if anything, is to be made of the striking synchronicity wherein (as Gunnar Brandell points out) 'Strindberg during his Inferno crisis to some extent carried out a self-analysis, albeit presented in religious and moral terms, at virtually the same moment as Freud was embarking upon the self-analysis which forms the basis of *The Interpretation of Dreams*'?[8]

The problem is therefore twofold: the questionable nature and efficacy of Strindberg's attempt to meet his claim that suffering may be expunged merely by writing it down (e.g. XIV:217) raises what Guy Vogelweith calls 'le problème si délicat des rapports entre psychanalyse et littérature,'[9] and at precisely the moment when the former discourse was taking shape, a point which lends further encouragement to the tempting notion that the endeavours of Freud and Strindberg run parallel to one another. For there is, certainly, a remarkable degree of shared ground. As heirs to an impulse in European thought that Henri Ellenberger terms 'the unmasking trend...the systematic search for deception and the uncovering of underlying truth,'[10] they both detect in man not merely a deliberate intention to lie, to himself as well as to others, but a powerful inner resistance to truth, which is sustained by the fiction of a world that corresponds to our desires. Strindberg's insight into the mechanisms of repression and self-deception, for example, often suggests Freud's shrewd and intricate explorations. He knows we punish ourselves for hidden wishes, what he calls our '*önskesynd*' (46:193), as well as for the crimes and peccadilloes we actually commit, and he recognizes that man has 'an ability to keep obnoxious impressions from him, which borders upon the miraculous' (48:854), while in his later works he frequently dramatizes the dilemma to which Gerda confesses in *The Pelican*, when she responds to her brother's ruthless unmasking of family secrets by crying, 'I knew it all along, and yet I didn't know it...It didn't reach my consciousness, because it was too awful' (45:253).

More immediately, however, the kinship between Strindberg and Freud is largely a matter of the precursors and contemporaries they have in common. For both in detail and in its general tenor their work inhabits an intellectual milieu which is populated by Schopenhauer, Hartmann, Ibsen, Nietzsche, and Taine,[11] and in the 1880s Strindberg, like Freud, became conversant with contemporary psychology. By his own account he consumed 'a whole literature of insanity' (VI:78), and the writings of Ribot, Maudsley, Galton, Bernheim, and Binet figure in his letters, his libraries, and his works, as he sought to implement the current demand, articulated here by Maudsley, in *The Pathology of Mind*, for 'a scientific demonstration of the strict order and necessity of the chain of events of the person's life history by a patient unfolding of his action on circumstances and of their action on him.' 'Sane or insane,' Maudsley continued, 'a man's history is his character, and the full and exact explanation of his position in life, whether eminence or madness, would be the full and exact disclosure of his character,'[12] and by combining autobiographical and religious traditions of introspection with contemporary psychological theory, Strindberg attempted such a disclosure in *The Son of a Servant*, just as other developments in the field, for example Bernheim's work on hypnosis and suggestion in *De la suggestion et de ses applications à la thérapeutique* and Charcot's research into hysteria at La Salpetrière, are as significant for what Strindberg called his 'artistic psychological writing' (VI:335) in *Short Cuts (Genvägar)*, 'The Romantic Organist on Rånö', *Vivisections*, and *By the Open Sea*, as they are for the contribution of Charcot's student and Bernheim's German translator, Freud, to *Studies on Hysteria*. Conversely, Freud, as Brandell suggests, may well have read Strindberg's study of the hysteric, Tekla, when *Short Cuts* was published in the *Neue Freie Presse* in 1887,[13] and the influence he subsequently exerted upon literature is in any case only a reversal of the situation in the early days of psychoanalysis when Freud was caught up in the literary as well as the scientific developments of the period. As Brandell points out, in his stimulating study, *Freud - A Man of His Century*, the Paris to which he came in 1885 to study with Charcot, at a time when Strindberg had just embarked upon *The Son of a Servant*, was the centre of 'a general ideo-historical and literary context, which may be called that of psychological naturalism', and 'Freud's new system of psychological understanding and his self-analysis during the 1890s are, from one point of view, the culmination of a long-lasting collaboration between humanistic men of letters on the one hand, and doctors and researchers on the other.'[14] Indeed, the resemblance between the two domains was at times so close that in both *Studies on Hysteria* and the Case History devoted to 'Dora', Freud found it necessary to distinguish his compelling and ingenious narratives from the psycho-pathological studies in which contemporary fiction abounded,[15] an endeavour of some urgency when literature aspired to the status of 'scientific analysis' and employed 'all the tools of the new science of psychology' (MD:17). *The Son of a Servant*, Strindberg maintained, was not 'an *Ehrenrettung* or book of exculpation, it is a soul's analysis, anatomic psychology' (V:356), and he told Ola Hansson that Naturalism had brought literature to the point where invention had been superseded by psychology: 'Don't you see yourself that you are moving from synthetic literature into the psychological thesis!' (VII:248). Thus when he attributes his own technique to Axel Borg in *By the Open*

Sea, the account reads (apart from the final modest disclaimer) as a striking anticipation of the course Freud would take when he added his self-analysis to the library of Naturalist case histories and thereby transformed the genre: 'And in order to verify the correctness of his observation he used himself as a psychological preparation, cut himself up living, experimented on himself, constructed fistula and fontanelles, subjected himself to an unnatural, often repulsive spiritual diet, but then - paying careful attention to the bias exerted by the presence of the experimenter in the experiment - avoided using himself and his life to establish a norm for others' (24:65).

This analytic standpoint was in fact endemic in Naturalism, which affords many instances of a *dédoublement* similar to the investigations undertaken in *A Madman's Defence* and *Inferno*. Stressing the split into experiencing self and observing consciousness, the Naturalist writer often presents himself as a spy upon his own mind, someone who watches himself live and then composes a report on what he has seen. Thus Alfred Binet records Alphonse Daudet's response to an investigation into the nature of thinking, where Daudet describes the 'horrible analytic and critical faculty' underlying his writing and argues that it is 'like an internal watcher, impassive and unmoved, a *double*, inert and cold, which in the most violent broadsides of *Le Petit Chose* was observing all, taking notes and saying the next day: A nous deux!'[16] Directed outwards, moreover, in the Vivisector's role which Strindberg cultivated in the late 1880's, this faculty not only permitted the writer to use his inner life as 'a carcass for dissection' (V:364), but also foreshadowed the analytic situation. Thus, in his one-acter, *The Stronger*, Y's silence enables X to talk herself into understanding the past, and in *Creditors*, as Strindberg pointed out to his French translator, Georges Loiseau, 'Tekla, qui mène une existence inconsciente comme les femmes...est emmené par Gustave de réfléchir sur elle-même, devient devoilée devant soi-même, est rendu consciente' (X:76)

But of course the similarity here is superficial. Gustav,'l'assassin psychologue' (X:77) reveals what is concealed in Tekla's discourse to its speaker only because he is personally involved in the drama. His mastery of the situation depends upon deception. Spurred on by his own hidden wound and motivated by a desire for revenge, the past he reconstructs by encouraging others to talk of it, is as much a part of his experience as it is of theirs. For as his author repeatedly discovers, 'one is not alone in the possession of one's experiences' (V:356): the past, that is, is not singular but shared with those among whom one lives, and out of the web of conflicting interpretations the Vivisector therefore seeks to establish the primacy of his own account: as Strindberg informs his publisher, concerning the third volume of *The Son of a Servant*, 'I analyse an event from a psychological point of view, and I relate it in my way, after others have related it in theirs' (VI:86).

Nevertheless, his desire to 'peer down into the hidden' (24:35) and bring 'life in the hidden' (37:68) to light is an undertaking he takes seriously, and the technique of allowing 'his memories to run through the history of his personal development, as far back as he could trace it, in order as it were to seek his way up to his self and be able to read in the past stages his probable fate' (24:44), to which Strindberg often refers, is again one that seems to derive from Freud rather than precede him. Each such 'refresher course' (24:65) represents an attempt on Strindberg's part to review his past, bring it back into the present, and transpose it into language, and as in Freud's advocacy of a similar procedure, his method bears traces of another literary movement, Romanticism. Both writers inherit what Philip Rieff calls 'the Romantic insight that equated artistic creativeness with the process of unconscious truth-telling in general,'[17] and Freud's idea of the discourse in which the patient might circumvent repression and reclaim his past is, like Strindberg's conception of writing as the immediate transcription of experience, authenticated by the notion of inspiration which frequently accompanies a view of poetry as the cathartic expression of overpowering emotion. Indeed, in many respects inspiration emerges as another royal road to the self, and both Freud and Strindberg take encouragement from the same predecessors, notably Schiller, who is quoted at length in later editions of *The Interpretation of Dreams* and serves to authorize inspired discourse in *The Son of a Servant*,[18] and Ludwig Börne, whose sketch 'Die Kunst in drei Tagen ein Original-Schriftsteller zu werden' caused Freud to write the clarificatory 'A Note on the Pre-History of the Technique of Analysis' (1920), and supported Strindberg's case in the theory of writing he sent Siri von Essen: 'Reproduce what you have experienced, I wrote to her, for you have lived a life with harrowing changes; get hold of a pad of paper, a pen; be frank and you will become an author, I quoted, following Börne's recommendation.' (MD:50) For although Strindberg initially enlisted Börne to combat a conception of genius which granted the elevating visitation of inspiration to an exceptional few (this, he argued, was 'an out-of-date falsehood' (I:187) since the spread of literacy made literature accessible to anyone who wished to write, much as Freud's account of the artistry displayed in dreaming was also sometimes taken to suggest that art itself was thus open to all), he in fact suppressed his mistrust of inspiration's improper ease and believed 'that in his fever the writer is led in the right direction' (VI:103). 'The artist', he stated, 'works unconsciously, creating like nature by chance with an incredible wastefulness, but in the moment when he, *post festum*, tries to think his work over, to analyse it, he wakes from his half slumber, and falls to the ground like a sleepwalker' (27:630), and by employing images of somnambulism and hallucination, he depicted the writer as a medium awaiting a visitation ('But it doesn't come to order, nor when I please. It comes when *It* pleases'(54:472)), just as Freud sought to establish the most favourable conditions for the unconscious to reveal itself in the patient's discourse. Abandoning in turn both hypnosis and suggestion, he arrived at Free Association where, he concluded, *It* spoke most clearly.

And it was when Strindberg made a virtue out of the fact that he wrote best when he hallucinated (IV:80), and deliberately submitted himself to the drive of his fantasies (as he wrote to his friend, the botanist Bengt Lidforss: 'I often put myself into a state of unconsciousness, not with drink or the like, for that awakens a host of memories and new ideas, but by distractions, games, play, sleep, novels, and then I let my brain work freely, without bothering about the outcome or consequences, and

something then emerges which I believe in, just because it has grown inevitably'
(VIII:239-40)) that he arrived not merely at the most remarkable prefigurations of
Freud in his writing, but also at a method which resembles Freud's technique and
anticipates the shift from a linear to an associative autobiographical mode that is
implicit in Freud's theories, and in the example of *The Interpretation of Dreams*.
Firstly when painting according to the technique of *skogssnufvism*, which he
introduced in 1892 (IX:40 - the name, literally 'wood-spiritism', is derived from a
folk tale concerning a boy who mistakes a tree trunk for the wood sprite, so
displaying the kind of double vision demanded by his own works, with their dual
exoteric and esoteric meaning), and then in the seminal essay of 1894, 'Des arts
nouveaux! où Le Hasard dans la production artistique', in which he develops a
theory that is implemented in literary texts such as 'Deranged Impressions' and the
letters he wrote to Torsten Hedlund during 1896, he deliberately lays himself open
to chance ('that propitious chance, which has made so many discoveries' (27:130))
and adopts a random manner of creation, a 'free-hand drawing' (X:206) or
associational method (X:64), which he believes nature also employs, in order to
penetrate what he terms 'le rideau du conscient' (VR:66) and read the normally
invisible deeper syntax that underlies the calligraphy of the surface. As he describes
the process in 'Des arts nouveaux!':

> Dégagé de la peine de controuver les couleurs l'âme du peintre dispose
> de la pleinitude des forces à chercher des contoures, et comme la main
> manie la spatule à l'aventure, toutefois retenant le modèle de la nature
> sans vouloir la copier, l'ensemble se révèle comme ce charmant pêle-
> mêle d'inconscient et de conscient. C'est l'art naturel, où l'artiste
> travail comme la nature capricieuse et sans but déterminé. (VR:58)

Thus he evolved a type of 'naturalistic clairvoyance' (28:59) which encourages
what he later termed 'the appearance of the unconscious' (46:190). By improvisatory
techniques either adopted or invented, he essayed a type of 'art fortuite' (X:177) in
which customary mechanisms of repression were suspended and his unconscious
life was free to reveal itself. Perhaps taking his cue from Leonardo, to whom he
refers in *A Blue Book* (46:190), and responding during the 1880s to Max Nordau,
whose collection of essays, *Paradoxes*, includes the description of a child's game in
which a series of random dots are linked to form the image of a person or object,
Strindberg describes how 'a painter (can) see figures in the sawdust which is strewn
on the shop floor by arbitrarily linking one point with another, seeing figures in other
words where there are none' as early as *Flower Paintings and Animal Pieces*
(22:269). Not surprisingly, too, he showed an interest in automatic writing, in the
Rorschach blot, and in Kerner's 'kleksography' which revealed 'the operator's very
innermost unconscious thoughts, even such as he didn't wish to recognize as his
own, but nevertheless must' (46:191). Moreover, attributing substance to his
fantasies and to his dreams ('Nothing comes from nothing, and fantasies, like
dreams, possess full higher reality' (XI:236)), and fashioning an instrument of

exceptional sensitivity in what he termed his 'inner eye' (XI:268), he was able, although still confined to the discourse of romantic fiction, an occult world of doubles, ghosts, and mesmeric suggestion, to discover a fresh autobiographical dimension in the 'strange occurences' that composed themselves into the significant pattern of life with the aid of free association and skilful interpretation. It is as if he employs the method outlined in his proposal to illustrate the book of Job 'in an occult manner' (XI:288) and lays a fine paper over events to catch their imprint, extracting from the trivia of his daily life, its chance encounters, the detritus of the streets, his haphazard reading, and obsessive images, a gigantic *frottage* wherein he can trace his life's design. 'I believe that if one only refrains from hardening one's heart a great deal is revealed' (XI:157), he confided to Hedlund; esoteric meaning was to be found even in the gutter of everyday Parisian life; and as Marcel Réja remarks, in his informed preface to the first French edition of *Inferno*, on which he worked with Strindberg, by observing

> la législation du hasard...tous les petits détails, les incidents fortuits que nous ne jugeons pas dignes d'un seul moment d'attention, il les dépiste avec un soin jaloux, les confronte et les fait hurler de force à nos oreilles, qui veulent être sourdes, et les fait briller violemment à nos yeux qui veulent être aveugles.
> Il combine en système inquiétant ce que nous éliminons systématiquement du domaine de notre attention. Tandis que nous les mettons sans plus d'enquête sur le compte du hasard, il adopte ces enfants abandonnés, et cherche à leur constituer une famille, une signification, un but.[19]

Or as The Unknown explains, in *To Damascus*: 'Life, which was earlier a great nonsense, has gained a meaning, and I perceive a purpose, where before I only saw chance' (29:10).

Thus, as Göran Printz-Påhlson points out, Freud and Strindberg are also united 'by their experience that in the inner life nothing is wasted, everything comes back in one form or other.'[20] 'To throw light on things by tracing what is manifest back to what is hidden,'[21] delights them both; they share a passion for interpretation and discern in fortuitousness a key to a more deeply inscribed reality where the play of chance becomes a determined network repeatedly producing 'a coincidence which cannot be chance' (X:153). At much the same moment they become alert to the intermittencies of conscious life through which another order of being may be glimpsed, to what could be gleaned from what Freud once termed 'the rubbish heap...of our observation',[22] in the seemingly banal details and *objets trouvés* out of which Strindberg fashions his *Occult Diary, Inferno* and *To Damascus*, and which forms much of the material in *The Psychopathology of Everyday Life*, Freud's second psychoanalytical book and the one in which, by a nice stroke, he quotes Strindberg for the only time.[23] For what Strindberg unveils in the Inferno material is very much 'our double existence, obsessions, our nocturnal existence, our bad conscience, our momentary baseless fears' (XI:293) as they manifest themselves in the action of what the Surrealists would call *L'hasard objectif*. As in Breton's post-Freudian narrative, *Nadja*, or Aragon's novel, *Le Paysan de Paris*, a predominantly urban environment casts up images and objects that accord with the writer's unconscious desires and fears, and if the language in which Strindberg conveys his findings is sometimes less precise than Freud's measured tone, it is nevertheless continually reaching out to accommodate comparable insights:

> My inner being is mirrored in my dreams and so I can use them as I use my shaving mirror: to see what I am doing and avoid cutting myself. The same applies to certain 'occurrences' in waking life - but not all. For example, there are always bits of paper lying in the street yet not every bit of paper catches my attention. But if one of them does, then I pay attention to it, and if there is something written or printed on it that has some connection with what is occupying my thoughts, then I regard it as an expression of my innermost unborn thoughts. And I am right to do so. For if this bridge of thought between my inner self and this outer thing did not exist, a transfer could never take place. (38:135)[24]

It is this tension between apparent randomness and a concealed personal order which dictates the emergence of a radically new form of autobiography in *The Interpretation of Dreams*, where a life is no longer written according to the causal, chronological sequence that the rational consciousness extracts from the remembered past, but is reclaimed from the data of dream by association and analogy, regardless of temporality and no longer impeded by a concern to distinguish between what is fantasy and what is real since, as Freud later makes plain, what we remember is all we possess and our 'phantasies possess *psychical* as contrasted with *material* reality.'[25] Even in the process of remembering, the past becomes dismembered, as Freud realizes in his account of the dissection dream ('The task which was imposed on me in the dream of carrying out a dissection of *my own body* was thus my *self-analysis*')[26], and individual identity as the continuity of consciousness through time thus becomes no longer so certain or essential a principle of autobiography. Meaning is not enchained, as the nineteenth-century mode adopted in *The Son of a Servant* suggests, in successive events that are conveyed by a narrative where temporal sequence is elevated into a causal one, but embedded in the obsessions, repetitions, and intermittencies cast up in the course of narration, during which the self reconstitutes itself around patterns of memory, complexes of association, and correlations in literature and myth. For, as John Sturrock remarks, in an essay on the autobiographer whose practice has responded most thoroughly to Freud, Michel Leiris: 'the power of association, of bringing into the light mnemonic instead of temporal contiguities, has infinitely more to tell us about our permanent psychic organization than the power of chronology.'[27]

And this is a major aspect of the Inferno process. Having placed his experience under the control of contemporary psychological theory and taken introspection to its respectable limits in *The Son of a Servant*, Strindberg now submits himself to conditions in which he contrives, firstly to experience the derangement which others had only studied, and then to write his own case history.[28] In his experimental records, the Hedlund letters, *The Occult Diary,* the first drafts of *Inferno*, and *Inferno* itself, he re-explores the data of his life according to his experimental associative technique until, in *To Damascus*, where 'everything recurs' in the form of 'dead men and beggars and madmen and human destinies and childhood memories' (29:45), he projects himself on to the mirror of The Unknown and is able to monitor his experience with a subtlety that sets ajar that door to the past to which he, like Freud, so often refers,[29] through which his guilt and neurosis emerge with unprecedented complexity, not as a single extended strand but in a web of metaphor and myth, a network of interrelationships wherein the past reveals its continued potency in the present and the present re-illumines the past.

But if these manifold similarities encourage the notion that by transposing his life into language Strindberg achieves not only a temporary release of effects in words but mastery over their causes as well, it is more likely that he stops where Freud began, namely at the point in the 'Preliminary Communication' to *Studies on Hysteria* where Freud and Breuer describe how:

> The injured person's reaction to the trauma only exercises a completely 'cathartic' effect if it is an *adequate* reaction - as, for instance, revenge. But language serves as a substitute for action; by its help an effect can be 'abreacted' almost as effectively. In other cases speaking is itself the adequate reflex, when for instance it is a lamentation or giving utterance to a tormenting secret, e.g. a confession.[30]

For while he may bring the buried past back into his texts, Strindberg does not perform the labour of interpretation which Freud came to regard as the necessary extension of the talking cure if the latter is to be effective, a development in his thinking which marks the methodological shift from catharsis to psychoanalysis, whose 'aim was no longer to abreact an affect which had got on to the wrong lines but to uncover repressions and replace them by acts of judgement which might result either in the accepting or in the condemning of what had been formerly repudiated.'[31] Indeed, Strindberg is not looking for a cure; he wants to go on writing since, as he remarks, 'I found existence pure bliss so long as the writing continued, and do so still. It's only then that I live' (54:467). Moreover, it is not necessarily the deepest or the most remote layers of his personality that this unburdening process is directly engaged in tapping, but a recent, often minor, affront to his self-image (a day's residue in fact) that demands prompt relief. And while Strindberg perceives the process by which an affect can be abreacted through language as clearly as Freud and Breuer (in both *A Blue Book* and *Black Banners* he relates an anecdote in which an acquaintance had, by speaking, 'freed himself from a painful impression so completely that it was erased from his memory' (41:128)), the solace which writing affords is shortlived and normally confined to the effacement of immediate discomfort. It offers a means of redress in times of adversity and its habitual practice renders the present endurable, but as a type of secondary revision of experience, it does not substantially modify the personality. Rather, the narrative or drama in which fragments of the past arise is a recreation which repeats and adapts the autobiographical material, and the text, like the last stage of the dream work, connects the disconnected, systematizes and reshapes the mnemonic data which is already, as Freud notes in his essay on 'Screen Memories', formed 'unconsciously - almost like works of fiction',[32] and establishes relationships between the manner and the matter of the utterance whereby it conforms to expectations of an intelligible whole that are often already fulfilled by the genre in which it is cast, and which, to the extent that it is conventional, depersonalizes what is entrusted to it. To employ a formula of Philippe Lejeune which is particularly apt when applied to Strindberg: 'C'est une tentative d'alchimie poétique, plutôt que de chimie analytique.'[33]

This verbal alchemy already colours the most immediate of the ways in which Strindberg formulates an affect in words, his letter writing, where even more promptly than by writing for the press, he could perform what Torsten Eklund sees as one of the essential tasks of his project: '...to keep the public up to date with his more or less private misfortunes and sufferings.'[34] At times, indeed, he keeps selected correspondents informed on chosen aspects of his life by almost daily reports, each letter taking up the tale even as it is unfolding, and in some cases, for example in the letters to Pehr Staaff in 1887 on the disintegration of his first marriage, it is clear that he is discovering, or inventing, or recomposing this life in the very act of writing about it. It is as if he allows the words to have their say, following them where they care to take him, in what is effectively a trial run for the novel they conjure up, *A Madman's Defence*.

Given the importance he placed on letter writing as the model for writing in general, the letters are obviously of particular relevance to a project in which the boundaries between different written discourses tend to dissolve into a single life of scription. They represent perhaps the quintessential method of self-representation since they afford a true *multiplicité du moi* in the different projections each correspondent elicits, and he frequently uses an extended correspondence as a mirror in which to observe and analyse himself. But his practice resembles a soliloquy rather than the dialogue which an exchange of letters normally evokes. As he reminds one of the first in a series of reflectors with whom he enters into a sometimes entirely written relationship, 'You are used to my speaking in the first person Singularis' (I:27), and in telling both his youthful confidant, Eugène Fahlstedt, and Jonas Lie that they need not answer the letters he intends sending them (I:122, IV:180), he acknowledges that his correspondence is not intended for a full and reciprocal communication.

At its most intense this practice produces a form of externalized inner monologue, a type of public self-address in which Strindberg analyses his situation and inspects himself. In a succession of correspondences, he deftly secures a balance between intimacy and distance that permits him to concentrate on himself, and especially in relation to Torsten Hedlund he is able, in the crucial stages of the

Inferno crisis, to use the other as a screen on to which he projects his inner turmoil in order to interpret it. He arrives, in short, at a remarkable complement to the analytic situation, or rather, at the almost contemporary situation contrived by Freud in relation to Wilhelm Fliess for the conduct of his self-analysis. 'I need you as my audience,' Freud wrote to Fliess,[35] much as Strindberg required Hedlund to be the distant intimate of his intellectual isolation, and Paul Roazen's remark, 'On the one hand, Freud needed his own isolation, even if he grumbled about it; yet he also sought an uncomprehending blank screen in Fliess,'[36] could as easily be applied to Strindberg's relationship with Hedlund, who was enlisted to receive what Strindberg extracted from himself by experimental techniques involving introspection and free association, and then transferred to paper: 'Read what I write without criticism, without resistance, and don't prevent me from running on,' he instructs Hedlund, 'for I am growing as I write this, and perhaps you will too' (XI:240). And yet, quite clearly, Hedlund was forbidden to place his own constructions on the material Strindberg offered him. As always, the latter's resistance to other interpretations of his experience remains firm: he refuses the transference which Freud came to see as part of the psychoanalytical situation, and when Hedlund comes too close, he breaks off with a letter that confirms the one-sided nature of their entire correspondence: 'Your appearance in my life always seemed to me like a mission, and your person, which I don't know and have never seen, remained an abstraction to me the whole time' (XI:393).

This abrupt end, and Strindberg's subsequent return to literature in order to alleviate his conflicts in art, helps to distinguish the writer from the subject in analysis. It belongs to the nature of the pact under which an analysis is carried out that the subject lies on a couch and talks, suppressing nothing, however trivial or exceptional, that comes to mind. He is in the presence of a listener, the analyst, who receives this discourse, responds to it with questions, and prompts the subject towards an interpretation of his own words, returning them to him in order that he may amend and augment them. Moreover, this interruptable discourse is not only modified by the immediate response it elicits; it is also supported or betrayed by the other eloquent signs emitted by the subject. As Freud observed, as early as *Studies on Hysteria*, the gestures, intonations, facial expressions, and silences of the subject can be as revealing as his words.[37] Although it is tempting to compare the analyst to a blank page on which the analysand writes his story, the actual situation is thus one in which spoken discourse is clearly distinguished from the written, however direct or immediate. It is a question of unveiling the hidden and unknown discourse transmitted by the subject, a discourse conveyed and audible only in the words he nevertheless speaks with the conviction that they mean what he says, to a listener who helps him to bring it into the open, recognize himself in it, and accept it as a more faithful account than the one he is accustomed to tell. The subject has need of the other so that the opaque material of his discourse may achieve clarity and coherence. He presents it to another in order that it be given back to him, that eventually in the exchange of words, he will possess his own discourse instead of being possessed by it, that he will, as Bernard Pingaud points out, in his essay

'L'Ecriture et la cure', 'enfin parler sa propre parole au lieu d'être parlé par elle.'[38]

Conversely, the writer's language, which is normally produced at a desk and consigned in silence to the page, is addressed to an absent reader, whose response does not modify the text. Although the features of the reader whom the author would like to see elaborate its codes are often implicit in the text, there is no guarantee into whose hands, or when, it will fall, and whatever the writer imagines he has intended with his text, this intention is not only impossible to impose but actually not recoverable as such by the potential reader, who may well discover that the text embodies meanings at variance with what the writer believed himself to have written. The situation of the autobiographer in particular is irremediably narcissistic. Engaged in the creation of his own image he is, irrespective of any desire to surmount his resistance and unearth the aetiology of his character, left to his own linguistic devices, without the assistance of an interlocutor. Alert to the constraints of form and genre, and to the determinacies of other books and lives, he is occupied with composing a discourse that is shaped and closed, not untidy and open-ended, as in analysis. And where the endeavour of psychoanalysis is to penetrate the image which the subject has formed of himself, the autobiographer elaborates a specular image in a narrative given over to the establishment of order and coherence, consciously manipulated, highly crafted, and felicitously expressed. Moreover, the object of the cure sought in analysis is deliverance, which means that having said all that matters the subject may be silent and move on, whereas the writer continually returns to his writing and multiplies the texts. Hopefully, the patient finally becomes himself; the writer, however, achieves the status of a subject only vicariously by projecting his personal myth in a work that is then detached from him in order to embark upon its own career. As Pingaud observes: 'La personnalité conquise de l'écrivain, c'est l'oeuvre elle-même.' [39] But once conquered this personality is immediately lost again, as a product now external to the self which produced it. Once written, the text and its author part company, so compounding the sense of lack and misprision with which his commital to a written existence may in any case impart to the writer. To recapture himself he must begin again and then again, only to lose himself in each set of words he leaves behind. For if the cure is singular, the work is plural and may therefore be, as Pingaud suggests, 'le modèle de toute fixation', since even when he seeks to deliver himself from obsessive themes and images, the writer only succeeds in fixing them outside himself, in the now foreign monument of the text, where it is the words and not their substantial producer that are 'l'objet même du discours'.[40]

II

Certainly, Strindberg's attempt to write out the past assumes, for its author as well as for the reader or spectator, every sign of a fixation. From the Inferno period onwards, the phrase 'Allt går igen' (Everything repeats itself) constantly recurs to point the structure of plays where repetition is a major organizing principle for transforming an otherwise unbridled reality into significant pattern, and pure continuity into interpreted, meaningful sequence. Sometimes proffered as the wisdom of experience ('Anyone aged forty, knows everything: life functions so simply; everything is repeated, everything comes again'),[41] repetition reveals how the unexpected consistency of events prompts what Freud describes as the uncanny 'idea of something fateful and unescapable where otherwise we should have spoken of chance.'[42] 'Then no matter how life shaped itself, I always found continuity or repetition,' the Stranger observes, from amidst the ashes of his childhood home, in *The Burned House*: 'there are scenes in my life which have occurred many times' (45:98). And the ageing Strindberg, whose obsession with chains of significance and networks of correspondences sometimes leads him to find a consolation in a mode of thinking that Freud would consider regressive in its propensity to animism and the narcissistic overestimation of subjective mental processes, generally goes out of his way to re-encounter the past. This is one facet of a repetition compulsion that permeates the Inferno material, where it continually suggests a fate arranged, although not always consciously, by the author himself, and which also directs his steps in the account in the *Occult Diary* of a walk through Stockholm on 22 September 1906 along streets that remind him of his past, and which concludes: 'Then went home to Karlavägen; and I thought: this is really like an "Agony" or the very moment of death, when the whole of life passes before one, and I decided to write about this morning walk, during which, in an hour and a half, I had been given a review of my life until now.'

For rather than fade into forgetfulness, the past becomes increasingly tenacious the more Strindberg writes and the older he grows. Thus, ever more aware of himself as the sum of his years, the Strindbergian protagonist in the guise of The Unknown, The Stranger, The Hunter, or the Narrator of *Inferno*, relives and re-examines, repeats and replots the constituents of a life which is continually doubling back upon itself and is always inclined to return to its origins: as the Lawyer tells Indra's Daughter in *A Dream Play*, 'Life consists of doing things again....you must retrace your steps, return by the same path, and suffer all the horrors of the process, the repetitions, the repetitions, the repetitions' (36:290). Indeed, repetition is the principle upon which a number of important late works (*To Damascus, Crimes and Crimes, A Dream Play*) are organized, and in so far as the principle underlying his writing is also the governing principle of a life in which Strindberg creates situations, engineers coincidences, and contrives to 'bring about events which never or very rarely happen in fact,'[43] his later autobiographical texts are uncanny arrangements of what in Freud's terms is already 'uncanny' experience. Thus *Inferno* emerges as the accurate account of a life previously lived through the purposeful creation of 'Das Unheimliche'.

Many allusions indicate the intellectual provenance of Strindberg's idea of repetition. Apart from the popular conception that at the moment of death the dying man's life passes before him in review,[44] he frequently alludes to Kierkegaard's concept of *Gentagelsen* (Repetition), to Swedenborg's idea of a *post mortem* 'livsrevy' (review of life), and to his own often articulated notion of life as an infernal scene of torture for crimes committed in a previous existence, a notion which he readily combines with the image of an inexorably grinding mill in order to endow the insistent retention of the past with a meaningful moral context, as when The Unknown describes how he 'saw my whole life unreel as in a kind of panorama from my childhood, through my youth, right up to... and when it came to the end of the reel, it began all over again; and the whole time I heard a mill turning... and I can hear it still...Yes, now it's here too!' (29:100). According to one of his glosses on Swedenborg's correspondences, the mill, an obvious metaphor for remorse and conscience, represents 'scrutiny' (47:530), and its implicit purificatory aspect is clearly expressed by the Teacher, in *The Isle of the Dead*, who describes how 'all you have lived, small as well as large, both good and evil, is ground in the mill of memory, ground and ground until the gray husks and chaff are sifted out and blown away by the wind. Then only the fine meal remains, which is baked into the snow-white bread of life for eternity.'[45]

But in all of Strindberg's obsessive bids to discover a sensible pattern in his life there is, whether here in the study of its insistent repetitions or previously in his many early attempts to interpret his destiny in what he sees as the ravaging effect of Nemesis upon those he encounters, a passionate desire for coherence that precedes all theory. As Brandell points out in his reading of *To Damascus*, the continual re-run of the past, either as a reminder of events from which he cannot free himself ('I have moments when the memory of everything horrible I have experienced collects as in an accumulator' (X:219), he tells his friend, Littmansson), or as the duplication of actual situations, is standard neurotic practice, and Strindberg is characterized both by an acute sensitivity to coincidence, parallel, and repetition in everyday life, and an inclination to repeat entire situations, to discover himself in familiar circumstances where the same roles are distributed to new protagonists. 'When I encountered *that* person, I remembered *that* one from the past' (45:98), the Stranger explains, in *The Burned House*, and Brandell rightly remarks upon the way in which Strindberg conflates his first two marriages in the text of the play, where the lineaments of his earlier relationship are uncovered in his rapidly foundering second attachment.[46] In retrospect Strindberg might try to turn the persistence of his memories and the sense that experience is a 'circulus vitiosus' into the claim that he had foreseen his fate at twenty 'when I wrote my play *Master Olof*, which has become the tragedy of my own life' (28:191);[47] in practice, however, the tendency of the same material to reappear across many years reveals not merely the tenacity but the impermeability to writing of certain pathogenic recollections. With their overlapping lists of titles, motifs, and references to episodes from a past already given frequent expression, the surviving papers in the Royal Library in Stockholm demonstrate how the same topics recur as if each fragment were somehow seeking its place in relation to all the others, whereby the whole constellation of headings would eventually add up to a life. Thus, for example, the episodes of the wine bottle and of his late arrival at Klara school, which are both treated extensively in *The Son of a Servant*, reappear once again among the jottings for later works, and he finds it necessary to retranscribe the Biblical narrative of Hagar and Ishmael which, as a determining aspect of his self-image dating back at least to the mid 1880s and already explicit in the title of his first volume of autobiography, was a story which he must by then have known by heart.[48]

Most pertinent, however, is the evidence in these papers that the episode which haunts his writing more than any other, what he on one occasion calls 'The Irremediable' (*Det Ohjelpliga*) and on another merely 'Affaire W - - - - -l',[49] remains the least written off of all his preoccupations. At any moment material from his relationship with Siri von Essen and her first husband, Carl Gustaf Wrangel, is likely to nudge its way into a text, and for all the artistic mastery of two such central achievements of his 'artistic psychological writing' as *Creditors* and *A Madman's Defence* in which he explores this material, he does not gain a corresponding psychological mastery over the situation they encompass. Invariably associated with feelings of guilt, shame and self-reproach, which provoke him to repeated and vehement denials of what he considers the prevailing view of him as a seducer, a role Strindberg repeatedly evokes in order to repudiate it with elaborate casuistry,[50] it is, moreover, clear that the special potency of the Wrangel material resides in its ability to activate the archetypal Oedipal scenario, with its *a priori* role for the remainder of his life. The return to Norrtullsgatan 12 that is depicted in *A Madman's Defence*, when Wrangel, with Siri von Essen at his side, opened the door of what had been Strindberg's childhood home from 1864-67, and again in 1871-72 (and for once he could be excused the characteristic exclamation, 'What a freak of fate' (MD:28) in his re-telling of the encounter), reconstitutes the framework of a family around the rootless young man of letters, whose 'raw dissipations' are dispelled by an atmosphere of 'family peace' and 'homely comfort' (MD:28). 'The austere memories which were associated with the house where she lived'(MD:34) awaken; 'the lost child' becomes 'a member of the family' (55:22,65); and past and present fuse in his memory as he discerns a rival in the (to him) strikingly masculine baron, and an object of desire in the 'virgin mother I had dreamt of' (MD:44). 'Gradually mother's pale face fused with the baroness's exquisite features' (MD:78), Strindberg writes, as what appears a caprice of destiny gives way to its real determination in nature and the narrator at last possesses the woman of his dreams, only to ask: 'Is it an abnormal instinct? Am I a product of nature's whims? Are my feelings perhaps perverse, since it is my own mother I possess? An unconscious incest of the heart?' (MD:135)

Once incurred, moreover, the guilt or debt (*skuld*) demands repayment, and the currency at Strindberg's disposal is writing. The possession of Siri and the destruction of his new family ('I could never separate you in my thoughts,' he wrote in dismay to Wrangel, 'I always saw you together in my dreams' (I:304))[51] feeds the treadmill of his mind, where it quickly takes its place on the plane of myth, first as one among the innumerable repetitions of the Fall that Strindberg, like Rousseau, inserts into his own history, and then as the inescapable harbinger and burden of his entire destiny. 'It was thus written "Norrtullsgatan"', he notes; and then, more fully: 'Affaire Wrangel was foreseen, foreshadowed, therefore necessary. Firstly I am forced and tempted to the first divorce; then I am punished because I obeyed the

34

command. The unreasonable (*oefterrättlige*)'.[52] And while the impression he likes to give, both in the early letters and in the Inferno material, of being pursued by a malignant fate or possessed by some daemonic power, owes as much to the legacy of Byronism as to a personal fate neurosis, the duplication and triplication of this experience in successive marriages, each marked by a characteristic exogamous object choice, demonstrates a compulsion to repeat experience whose underlying drive he in fact noticed himself. For when, at the dress rehearsal of *To Damascus* in 1900, a relative observed that the Norwegian actress, Harriet Bosse, who played The Lady, and who was shortly to become Strindberg's third wife, 'was just like Aunt Philp (my sister Anna)', he rapidly perceived a whole train of likenesses for The Unknown's partner, each one more revealing than its predecessor:

> ß (Bosse) is like (1) my second wife (who she has played in Damascus); (2) my sister Anna; (3) my mother (4) Mlle Lecain, the beautiful English woman who wanted to capture me in Paris; and who was like them all: often made a warm motherly impression, so that at Mme Charlotte's I often wished myself under her warm beautiful woollen coat as in a mother's womb.[53]

Thus if *A Madman's Defence* affords the clearest articulation of the preoccupation with incest that often surfaces in Strindberg's account of himself, the identification between his sister Anna, his mother, and sometimes one or all of his wives to date, as here, in *The Occult Diary*, indicates material that is never worked through. Already present in *The Son of a Servant*, in the contrast he draws between his 'sisters, of whom the eldest resembled his mother' and 'sexual love' (19:127), it appears in *The Cloister*, where he describes how 'everything erotic' in his feelings for Miss X 'had been repressed' because she resembled 'his own eldest sister' (C:34), and again in a late note where he recalls both how he had been taken for Siri von Essen's brother, and that 'Gunnar Heiberg found my sister like my second wife'.[54] Evidently he cannot 'cross out and go on' (34:108) any more than the Captain in *The Dance of Death*, whose advice this is,[55] and it becomes clear that, as he writes, 'Everything is dug up, everything repeats itself!' (30:215).

This archeological metaphor, so similar in scope to those in which Freud depicts the subterranean nature of traumatic memory traces, is often employed by Strindberg to indicate the relationship of the present to the past. For example, in *Creditors*, Gustav identifies 'the secret wound' from which Adolf suffers with a 'corpse in the cargo you're hiding from yourself' (23:203), and before he ruthlessly brings what is buried to light, he indicates the more normal process, which is to 'work, grow old, and pile masses of new impressions over the hatchway, so the corpse remains still' (22:204), an idea to which he returns in both *The Dance of Death* (34:40) and *Fagervik and Skamsund* (37:9). But Strindberg's own predicament is more complex, for the writing by which he lives is both a means of laying the past to rest and the route whereby it re-enters the present. In spite of a hopeful suggestion in the material related to one of his late self images, the hero and poet Starkodd, that activation of the repressed is only a temporary effect of language ('the latent memory rises up only when he sings, but he forgets afterwards'),[56] Strindberg generally acknowledges that there 'is no drink which extinguishes memory without stifling life' (45:276). Memory is exempt from the decay that afflicts the body (44:74), and as in *To Damascus*, where The Unknown exclaims 'Burn! Quench! Burn! Quench! But what won't burn is unfortunately memory - of the past!' (29:212), the burden of the past resists destruction even by what Strindberg calls 'the terrible business of writing, which threatens to burn me alive' (IV:239). Indeed, as he tells Siri, it is precisely 'When one becomes warm from a memory [that] the words come by themselves, one doesn't know from where' (I:197), and like memory or 'the infernal coal fire' of sexuality, which is 'lit to burn right to the grave' (28:362), the writing to which he is committed (and which he so frequently associates with fire)[57] is similarly unquenchable because ultimately it is not required to uncover or excavate the past but to cover it over and bury it in words.

The process is described in the *novella*, 'The Romantic Organist on Rånö', an apparently slight tale which sketches, in its account of the apprenticeship and aspirations of the young church organist, Alrik Lundstedt, and his later service in the poor parish of Rånö, the portrait of an artist whose practice, if not his achievement, resembles Strindberg's. For in allowing his 'all re-creative mind' (21:236) to transform whatever he sees or experiences into something else, Lundstedt's behaviour conforms substantially to the definition of the poet as 'a man who possesses imagination, that is an ability to combine phenomena, see connections, arrange and sort out' (22:269), in *Flower Paintings and Animal Pieces*; and as Karl-Åke Kärnell demonstrates, in the final chapter of his stimulating study of Strindberg's imagery, *Strindbergs bildspråk*, when Lundstedt 'relates things to one another in similes and metaphors through free association on the basis of some likeness between the things',[58] he uses a method that Strindberg employs in the majority of his scientific writings as well as in his fiction.

Characterized by a word which Strindberg frequently adopts as a synonym for art, Lundstedt is endowed with the 'gift of playing' (*att leka* -21:254). That is to say, the playful pursuit of likenesses, in which he habitually indulges, not only allows him to people his solitude and enrich his impoverished daily existence; it also provides him with a means of interpreting and so disarming the world. With the aid of metaphor and simile, he is able 'to knead the whole of creation according to his fancy' (21:243), so as to master its multifariousness, subordinate it to his desire, and reduce the power of the unknown and the unfamiliar to disturb him. Normally inhibited and (like Strindberg) constrained in his speech, metaphor affords him an 'outlet for his feelings' (21:215) and compensatory 'shivers of respect for his own greatness and power' (21:236), while an ability to discover analogies between diverse phenomena or between past and present, normally permits him 'to play the disturbing impression away' (21:240). In the opening paragraph, for example, he eases the anxiety of his departure for Stockholm by transforming the moon into 'a large, friendly face, with a broad, good-natured smile' (21:194), which he then applies to the aspect of his employer, of whom he is afraid, and the calm induced by this transposition is also evident in a later episode, in his encounter with the organ in Jacob's Church, 'which bore no resemblance to anything else in nature or in art and therefore disturbed him, oppressed him, and made him feel he was under this work of man's hand' (21:218). Disturbed by the anomalous and fearful of a chaos he cannot control, Lundstedt therefore resorts to metaphor and simile as he seeks 'to trace its forms back to other things and thereby to draw near to it, bring it down to him and be calm' (21:218).

What underlies and prompts Lundstedt's artistry, however, is not merely a delight in playing but the desire to forget, a compulsion to conceal the past. 'Playing, a way of concealing' (21:250), the Narrator defines at one point, with the subterfuges of everyday life in mind, and in the analytical seventh chapter, where the summary of Lundstedt's past shifts the Hoffmannesque, Romantic narrative in the direction of a modern case study, it is stressed that the ability 'to play' only began after the disappearance of his mother, as a means of allaying the guilt, which her obscure and violent death had provoked in the young child, beneath a mound of memories.

Strindberg's insight here is twofold. Firstly, he provides a striking account of the aetiology of a mental trauma, and of the way in which Lundstedt gradually represses his feelings of guilt beneath

> a thick covering of earth and stones, a whole cairn of other memories, to prevent it from rising up again. And when the trivial events of his drab little life could not provide material fast enough, he played events into being, masses of impressions, and piled up fabrications, hallucinations, imagined sounds in order to construct a thick layer that would cover the dark spot. And as soon as an impression had become a memory, it assumed reality, and was placed like a new stone on the cairn over the one there buried, which was unable to rise up. And so what was buried became as unreal or as real as if it had never occurred, dissolved, evaporated, and disappeared for long periods at a time. (21:245-6)

In demonstrating Strindberg's understanding of the subtleties of repression, this passage combines, as Göran Printz-Påhlson has pointed out, the folk image of the way in which the restless dead are supposed to be prevented from returning to haunt the living by the placing of a stone on the disturbed one's grave each time it is passed, with an analysis that clearly prefigures the use of archeological metaphor by Freud.[59] But having described how Lundstedt conceals the past beneath inventions contrived in play, he draws the narrative closer to his own experience in relating how 'a kind of urge (had arisen) in Alrik to mix the real and the unreal, a desire to deceive himself had been implanted, a need of avoiding any confrontation with reality had grown up in him' (21:246), thus evoking the testimentary letter to Lundegård in which he makes the often-quoted remark 'I don't know if The Father is a work of the imagination, or if my life has been', and adds the less frequently observed rider, 'If light is shed on this darkness, I will collapse in pieces' (VI:298). By losing himself in roles, Lundstedt prevents the discovery of his secret and blocks the past off from himself, and yet, just as Strindberg finds relief in the practice of literature, he, too, finds a way of relieving himself of his feelings by relating his story in a manner no one else could understand: 'He had discovered an expressive outlet for his own feelings and perceptions in music, through which he could tell his story, without anyone else understanding what he said or becoming suspicious that he had a secret.' (21:246)

But secondly, and even more prescient than the way in which Strindberg depicts how Lundstedt secures forgetfulness of an all too faithful memory, is his account of the dramatic collapse of these defences wherein the past surges back and overwhelms the present. It is evident that the advances made to Lundstedt by the housekeeper on Rånö, Miss Beate, are open to a sexual interpretation, at least in Lundstedt's troubled mind, and that, in forging a link between past and present by the repetition of what passed on some earlier occasion, her encouraging gesture to the tongue-tied young man somehow makes it impossible for the obscure events surrounding his mother's death to remain repressed: 'He had been woken up and could not go back to sleep.... What had struck Alrik most forcibly was that the stranger's eyes could have the same expression, that her arm could make the same gesture, when she laid her hand upon his knee, and this similarity stretched like a thread between the past and the present and everything between ceased to exist' (21:247). And whether or not Strindberg intended the connection to be made, the malfunctioning of Lundstedt's strategies of repression, in which 'face to face with a powerful reality he could not contrive to play the disturbing impression away' (21:240), illuminates several of the more light-hearted episodes earlier on in the story. For whatever the nature of Lundstedt's involvement in his mother's death (and it is difficult not to concur with Harry Carlson's suggestion that the idea, if not the fact, of incest plays a role, since this would also fit Strindberg's other explanation of Lundstedt's behaviour, namely the atavistic amorality which the isolation of life in the skerries fosters (21:190)), it is evident that even in the first part of the narrative, Lundstedt's 'play' has been of particular importance for his relationships with women. Seated at his post in Jacob's Church, he had elaborated an entirely imaginary relationship with a beautiful girl in the congregation, whom he calls Angelika, and when, later on, his defences are penetrated by Miss Beate and reality overwhelms him, his forlorn wish remains 'to rather have Angelika for ever than the house-keeper on the manor for life' (21:243). Real women, as the narrative indicates on several occasions, always render him speechless, which is why, in the solitude of his organ loft, he elaborates his Angelika fantasy in the first place. As Carlson observes, 'real women provoke irruptions from his unconscious where memories of the past collide with deep urges from the present, and where guilt and anxiety reside,'[60] and when the onanistic retreat which had once preserved him from the blandishments of the whores of Tyska Prästgatan is dispelled by Miss Beate's importunate gesture (and the gulf between past and present dissolves when he perceives her similarity as a woman who 'wanted him' (21:243) with the women of the town), the memory of his mother is metamorphosised, as woman so often is in Strindberg, into a whore.

What eventually permits Lundstedt to rediscover 'the gift of playing' and so 'be calm afterwards' (21:251) is the knowledge that others, too, 'possessed their secret corners, where they hid bodies, covered them with words, hid them under flowers, wreathes, ribbons, showy texts' (21:250). By recognizing that subterfuge is general, and that words often provide 'the protective disguise' (VII:138) on which it depends, 'The Romantic Organist on Rånö' anticipates a theme that dominates much of Strindberg's production after *Inferno*, when his life-long experience in the manipulation of language confirms that men live not in the real world but in their imaginative projections. That Strindberg himself uses language 'to bury' the past and so escape a sense of guilt is something he virtually admits when, in a letter to Harriet Bosse during the writing of what would become *A Dream Play*, he recalls: 'I am writing 'The Growing Castle', great, beautiful as a dream...I wander here like the Organist on Rånö and *transform* ruins' (XIV:131). Elsewhere he goes further. In *Legends*, for example, he writes openly of the use he makes of dream: 'Do you know what makes life bearable for me? That I sometimes imagine it is only half-real, a horrible dream, which has been inflicted on us as a punishment' (28:316); and in a *A Blue Book* he argues that 'in order to be able to live one must be like a sleepwalker and one must also be a poet, dupe oneself and others' (46:142). For many of the characters of the later works, the past is covered by a veil they are reluctant to part; to them the ability 'to play' or 'poetise' (*dikta*) is essential, as an exchange in *The Dance of Death* indicates:

> Kurt: I've noticed how you've fabricated (*diktat*) your life, and fabricated what surrounds you, too.
> Captain: How else could I have lived? How could I have stood it?....Then there comes a moment when the ability to fabricate, as you call it, stops. And then reality stands forth in all its nakedness!...It's terrifying. (34:108-9)

It is a view which the Captain (like the Father, a writer in uniform) shares with his author: as Strindberg wrote to his old confident, Littmansson: 'And besides, when reality fails you, then invent an existence for yourself, as I have invented a person when I became tired of myself' (XIV:217).

More immediately, however, it is possible as Kärnell suggests, to relate Lundstedt's practice to Strindberg's general method in the years preceding the Inferno crisis. If, in explaining how 'I live in my work, looking before me, sometimes looking behind me, in my memories, which I can treat like a child's building blocks, making all kinds of things out of them, the same memory serving in all kinds of ways for *one* imaginative structure' (38:173), he eventually clarifies the playful use to which he puts voluntary memory (and as he adds, 'since the number of arrangements is limitless, I derive a sense of infinity from my games'), a comment of Goethe's, also quoted in *Alone*, suggests that writing in general provides him with the means 'both to rectify my conception of the outer world and to bring order and calm to my inner life' (38:199). Where writing affords 'a sense of infinity', it lends events 'an impression of premeditated design' (38:192), and in reading his life or accounting for any single event in it, Strindberg is continually engaged in 'seeking likenesses everywhere'. For Strindberg everything must signify, and intent on extracting a meaning from each fragment of experience, he is driven by the 'imaginative and emotional need for unity, a need to apprehend an otherwise dispersed number of circumstances and to put them in some sort of order,'[61] which Edward Said sees as inherent in narrative, to seek the universal design that encompasses his life, to accomplish, in the discovery of what he terms 'analogies = correspondences = harmonies' (27:357), the tranquil formula of peace for which he strives. For disorder pained him and the unexplained offended. They instilled 'a disharmony which makes me ill' (28:145), a sensation in which mental turmoil manifests itself in physical discomfort. Confronted by the composition of nitrogen, for example, which he describes as 'formless' (27:164), he writes to Lidforss of 'a certain discomfort at the thought of the current view of the composition of air and water; I feel a lopsidedness (*snedhet*) in the whole of my being when I think of the contemporary theory of air, an oppression which I never experience when I regard a natural object' (VIII:239). Similarly, he tells the Norwegian novelist, Alexander Kielland, that 'when I see something go haywire or a stupidity or injustice take hold, I am askew (*sned*) in my body until I can sort out the question' (VI:110): it offends the sense of beauty referred to in *A Dream Play*, where the spectator is invited to draw a comparison between unaligned candlesticks and the moral and intellectual disorder of a house 'gone off the rails' (*på sned* - 36:257), and of which he writes, in a late note on 'The Imperfections of Life': 'If one is born with a sense of beauty which begins with order, and if one is brought up to complete orderliness, the whole of existence thus becomes an affliction...If I lose a coat button, and get an ill-matched button sewn awry (*på sned*) so that my coat is twisted, I become ill, I can't help it!'[62]

But whether he writes of his own life, the natural world, the history of Sweden, world history, or the moral order he attempts to discern behind them all, Strindberg's desire is 'to perceive the coherence of the disordered' (24:51). What he seeks is a 'Homogeneous cosmos' (46:231), as he entitles one section of *A Blue Book*, and behind the superficial scientific rigour of the still Naturalist discourse of *By the Open Sea*, there is, in Axel Borg's 'scientific equations which could from what appeared to be only a few premises (or which seemed few, because the links had been forgotten) draw new conclusions, where as in a chemical compound two older ideas merged with one another and formed a new conception' (24:50), already a theory of metaphor metaphorically conveyed, that supplants the chain of evolutionary theory in which he had previously tried to locate himself. Proceeding by associative leaps and metaphorical couplings rather than by patient deduction and the methodical accumulation of data, he delves into his memory to organize the world ('only through his enormous accumulation of memories could he relate all the things he viewed to one another' (24:42)) and discovers, like Lundstedt, how 'to make nature intimate with himself' (24:126). 'It makes me calm [*lugn*] to know' (24:126), Borg admits, and in its stress on peace or calm his remark suggests the many occasions on which Strindberg's own speculations prompt him to exclaim 'How calming [*lugnande*] it is to be able to explain everything!' (27:599) or admit that 'with this premise there is order and calm in nature!' (27:174), speculations, moreover, which sometimes lead him to abandon the words in which he formulates his life for other formulas of peace. The not over-scrupulous manipulation of chemical formulae, of atomic weights, and of the comparative measurements of phenomena, both man-made and in nature, are, like his recourse to the Kabbala, number magic, and theories of periodicity in history and the individual life,[63] speculations in 'Celestial Arithmetic' (46:274), in 'the formulae according to which the plans for the work of creation are drawn up for our planet' (27:538), and all these attempts to decipher the code of 'the master builder who has created the world with number and proportion' (46:403) and read his signature in such 'messages to earth' (27:234) as meteors, stones, the wings of butterflies, the petals of flowers, the flight of birds, and the formation of clouds, are ultimately intended to instil calm in the author of the script in which all these communications appear, Strindberg. 'The thought that we are everywhere at home and a part of the cosmos provides a feeling of homeliness and security' (46:231), he asserts in *A Blue Book* (a comment arrived at by a method glossed by Freud in *New Introductory Lectures on Psychoanalysis* when he observes: 'analogies, it is true, decide nothing, but they can make one feel more at home'),[64] and the complementary discovery to the knowledge that 'everything repeats itself', namely that 'everything is in everything, everywhere' (allt är i allt, överallt - 27:262), abolishes chance and reveals 'the endless continuity in the apparently great disorder' (27:560). Thus the hidden order and beauty of 'la cryptographie céleste' (27:246) intimates to Strindberg that his life, too, must possess a meaning if only he reads (and writes) it aright.

But even in a world conceived in terms of repetition, where 'everything is in everything' and 'everything repeats itself', writing offers a means of achieving a periodical renewal that it is easy to regard as a self-analytical cure. There is, first, the confessional impulse evident in many letters (for example, those to Bjørnson in 1884 (IV:144) and von Steijern in 1892 (IX:29)) in which Strindberg seeks out an addressee to whom he feels an obligation to 'ransack his heart' (IX:29), a process that is also sketched in 'The Romantic Organist', where the Narrator describes how Lundstedt 'bore his guilt and wished to be free of it. He wanted to go straight to the pastor and tell him how everything had happened, be spoken to firmly, take his punishment and then be calm [*lugn* -21:251].[65] This process is largely a matter of the attempt, evident throughout Strindberg's production, to alleviate the sense of guilt which is a fundamental constituent of his experience. 'I long for a torture which will re-establish my sense of balance in my relationship to society, so that I don't have to go on feeling in debt', The Unknown declares (29:124), while the Narrator observes, of Johan, in *The Son of a Servant*: 'He wanted to have a real punishment; it would restore the balance; it would relieve his remorse' (19:88). The desire to achieve tranquility in this respect is conveyed in terms of debit and credit, of a need to balance the books, settle accounts, and draw up a balance sheet (*bokslut*) in which 'he set off debt (or guilt - *skuld*) against debt' (44:78). For as Ruskin noticed, in *Unto This Last*, the goddess of guilt and revenge, Tisiphone, was 'a person versed in the highest branches of arithmetic and punctual in her habits',[66] and Strindberg is able to evolve these ideas so neatly because the semantics of payment and debt and those of guilt are the same in Swedish as in several other European languages. They permit a link between morality and economy that allows the structural identity of guilt and debt, contract and duty, price and retaliation, in 'this muddled account of in and out, debit and credit, which is called life' (40:78). Moreover, both debt and guilt are retentive of the past like autobiography, and the idea of moral creditors, of accounts to be settled before life may proceed, is an insistent one in a project where justice and revenge are interchangeable terms.[67] Initially presented as components of a Naturalist justice in which what is written is employed to restore the balance violated by the experience of a life with no recourse to the divine (hence his boast 'I take care of my Nemesis Divina myself' (VII:298)), each book represents an instance of debt collecting, the consequence of an irrepressible need to speak out and 'restore the balance' (22:157): 'Il fallait que je te dise cela!', he tells Frida Uhl, as he will Harriet Bosse, 'parce que chez moi la revanche est un sentiment inné, irrésistible qui joue le rôle de justice, un instinct de rétablir l'équilibre' (X:299), and after each public inspection of accounts his impulse is often to remark: 'A debt is paid and we were quits' (22:157).[68]

Thus the rhythm of Strindberg's production frequently follows the sequence described in *Black Banners*, where the Naturalist writer, Zachris, conceives a book which explicitly recalls the writing and publication of the account of Strindberg's first marriage, *A Madman's Defence*:

> There was now only one way to free himself from the poison: to write her out of himself; to put it all down on paper and then burn the manuscript, after it had been read by those closest to him, or if he was in need, to publish it in Germany. This thought revived him. To be able for once to say openly everything that had for years oppressed and pained him, at the same time unravelling the whole of this account which had simply run on without any reckoning being made; to be able to defend himself, and -why not? be revenged!
> It would be to begin a new life, wiping out all the old. (41:213-4)

This movement from a desire for self-expression, by way of a compulsion to unravel the past to drawing up a statement of accounts, defending himself, and finally, having obtained his revenge, to beginning a new life, is common to Strindberg's autobiographical writings, which are written 'in order to untangle my thoughts and free myself' (XI:268). For renewal and the new are evidently at the heart of a process which is, particularly in *Inferno*, at once intellectual, moral, and artistic in its intended metamorphosis. Just as his attempts during the 1890s in his scientific writings to elide the distinction between the inorganic and the organic demonstrate his overriding preoccupation with immortality and the imperishability of matter, of 'life's existence everywhere' (27:228) where 'everything flows into everything else' (27:687) and 'nothing can cease to exist' (27:245), so the images of transformation and metamorphosis, which characterize this writing, indicate a concern with the idea of rebirth or immortalization which centres upon himself. Thus, from observing the transformation of a larva into a moth ('The larva is dead within the chrysalis, yet it lives and rises up...a higher form in beauty and freedom' (27:245)), Strindberg develops his conception of 'nekrobios' (XI:114), or life in death, which encourages him to hope that like Saul he too 'will be transformed into another person' (XI:157). 'Am I sloughing off my skin?', he asks, in the essay 'Deranged Sensations', 'am I in the process of becoming a modern man?...I am as nervous as a crab which has cast off its shell, as irritable as the silkworm in the process of transformation' (27:606), and in *Inferno*, where the modish discourse of the *detraqué* gives way to the no less up-to-date discourse of religious conversion, he relates the history of his 'education to a new life' (XI:283) as the outcome of a process he has actively promoted rather than passively undergone, a 'vita nuova' (XI:83) wherein he seeks simultaneous confirmation of his personal immortality, his moral salvation, and a form of art. Similarly, 'dead in both a physical, moral, and economic sense' (V:277), in *The Son of a Servant* he performs what he regards as an autopsy on his own corpse in order 'to begin again, undeluded, purged' (VI:69); 'écrit devant la mort' (IX:339), *A Madman's Defence* is also presented as an alternative to death (MD:9); and in *Alone* he describes how

> ...by cutting off my links with other people I seemed at first to lose my strength, but at the same time my ego began, as it were, to crystallize, to concentrate around a kernel, where everything I had ever experienced collected, was digested and then used as nourishment for my soul....This, at last, is to be alone: to spin oneself into the silk of one's own soul, to become a pupa and wait for the metamorphosis, which will not fail to come. Meanwhile one lives upon one's experiences, and by telepathically living the lives of others. Death and resurrection; a new training for something unknown and new. (38:128, 145)

Moreover, each succeeding autobiographical volume does not merely retrace the past. Rather, the process is a dynamic one, in which self-discovery, 'coming to terms with oneself and the past' (38:147), is continually renewed and constantly deferred. Each time he achieves 'the synthesis of all the hitherto unresolved antitheses of my life' (38:147), the result is not a final summation but a temporary halt, only to find that 'by studying the whole of my life I have arrived at discoveries which I did not expect' (VI:116). In contemplating the old self he has recreated in language, he finds that when the narrative catches up with the present it re-opens the foreclosed future onto a new life which will in turn compel additional texts. Having written his own obituary, 'the corpse stands up and publishes his memoirs' (V:320), and it is by recovering his steps that Strindberg proceeds along the road to Damascus.

Repetition thus evokes the dialectic once formulated by Kierkegaard and pondered in that form by Strindberg, whereby 'what is repeated has been, otherwise it could not be repeated, but precisely the fact that it has been gives to repetition the category of novelty...when one says that life is a repetition one affirms that existence which has been now becomes.'[69] For in the narrative discourse produced in autobiography, the repetition of the life once lived is imbued with difference: it is fashioned anew. And where Freud certainly identified a kind of destructive repetition which stresses 'the perpetual recurrence of the same thing',[70] with the death wish, a form of repetition that may well suggest Strindberg's continual reproduction of the same interpersonal situation, there is also a type of repetition that cannot be defined simply in terms of reiteration or mechanical replica, and which serves the pleasure principle rather than the drive to destruction. It is constructive and pleasurable because it transforms a passive predicament into an active situation, and in Freud's work the *locus classicus* for this type of repetition is the celebrated description of the child's game, in *Beyond the Pleasure Principle*, in which a cotton reel attached to a piece of string is thrown away and then recovered to the accompaniment of the vocables 'fort' and 'da'. Here, Freud deduces, the passive situation of being overpowered by the absence of the mother is transformed by the child into an active mastery of the disagreeable experience by inflicting a simulacrum of the event upon itself. In this game, which is 'repeated untiringly', and in all play in which 'the child passes over from the passivity of the experience to the activity of the game,'[71] there is in miniature that constructive repetition which Freud had previously recognized in his essay 'Remembering, Repeating, and Working Through', where in describing the transference in which the patient repeats the repressed material as a form of contemporary experience rather than as the reconstruction of the past, he remarks:

> We may say that the patient does not remember anything of what he has forgotten and repressed, but acts it out. He reproduces it not as a memory but as an action; he repeats it, without of course knowing that he is repeating it....As long as the patient is in the treatment he cannot escape from the compulsion to repeat; and in the end we understand that this is his way of remembering.[72]

In this discussion, repetition emerges not as a reproduction of a previous event, of something already present in the subject's mind, but as the production of a piece of real experience, and as Freud points out, in relation to such psychical processes as phantasies, emotional impulses and thought connection, the irony of this type of repetition is that what is repeated is something that is not recalled: 'In these processes it particularly often happens that something is 'remembered' which could never have been 'forgotten' because it was never at any time noticed - was never conscious.'[73]

And it is on the ground of an analogous absence that Strindberg's autobiographical narratives constitute themselves. For although narrative (and especially autobiography) implies that it is the repetition of an antecedent presence, that it retraces ground already covered and repeats events that have already occurred, it is in fact the case that it 'repeats' by creating since, as Emile Benveniste has pointed out, 'Le langage *re-produit* la réalité. Cela est à entendre de la manière la plus littérale: la réalité est produite à nouveau par le truchement du langage.'[74] Thus the volumes of

Strindberg's autobiography (and still less his novels and plays) are not the mere repetition of prior events, repositories in which the past is embalmed or interred, but the means by which he turns it to account and fashions himself anew in a text wherein the past he retraces also returns of itself to create an artistic web of analogies in which his life is no longer a succession of discrete events but a meaningful work of art whereby (like Alrik Lundstedt) he mediates his relationship with the world about him.

CHAPTER THREE

Writing, not Speaking:
Strindberg, Language, and the Self

What is said is always too much or too little: the demand that one
should denude oneself with every word one says is a piece of naiveté.
- Nietzsche: *The Will to Power*

An Author, who writes in his own Person, has the advantage of being
who or *what* he pleases.
- Shaftesbury: *Advice to an Author*

I

'If your heart is heavy and you cannot speak, then write!', Strindberg encourages
his sister, Elisabeth: 'Confide in the paper!' (III: 41-2). To reject the possibility of
speech and entrust himself to writing, to what he regards as the privacy and
inviolability of the printed page, is so peculiar and yet essential an aspect of the
presuppositions underlying Strindberg's practice that it has often been remarked, as
has the teasing contradiction it implies between the author's inordinate shyness and
the brutal self-assertion with which he permits his intimate life to circulate in print.
Two images confront one another: that of a man whose childhood modesty caused
him to conceal himself in a wardrobe when he undressed (a revelation to be made by
his brother, Axel, which Strindberg disarms by anticipation in *To Damacus III*:
'We laugh now, when we hear he only wanted to change his underclothes in the dark
wardrobe' (29:302)),[1] and the uninhibited writer whose methods so easily leave him
open to the charge of washing his dirty linen in public, as in *A Madman's Defence*:
'Now she's reached the briefs: she chooses a pair from which the tape has been
ripped, and without betraying a trace of what she is thinking, puts them on one side.
But I recognized them, since it was me who, frantic with desire , ripped them apart in
the first assault' (MD: 130-1). On the one hand, there is the writer who veils himself
in words; on the other, the man who delighted 'in being able to tear off his clothes and
go naked' (16:110).

Sustained by numerous anecdotal accounts which confirm Strindberg's partiality
for indirect communication, even with those who were his daily acquaintance or the
familiars of his house,[2] the orthodox view thus emerges of someone in whom a fear of
physical confrontation and an acute reticence in the face of friends and enemies alike
rebound in a violent desire to 'attract attention in the world whatever the price'

(I:168) through the writing wherein he exhibits himself. And yet, while evidence certainly exists to encourage Torsten Eklund in his supposition that 'there is hardly a writer who has stripped himself naked in his books as he has done,'[3] there lurks the germ of contrariety in the juxtaposition of this nakedness and the complimentary image of a man who removes himself to a distance where he cannot be observed or molested, writes, and then returns, adorned in language, to exact revenge on those in whose presence he felt unprepossessed.

This view is, of course, often anticipated by Strindberg's own self-scrutiny, which readily discloses the compensatory drives that literature is engaged to satisfy. Indeed, in the letter on writing to Siri von Essen, he explains his preference for the written over the spoken on precisely these lines. Firstly, he is inhibited in company and therefore it is 'this shyness which drives [him] to write' (I:186). Secondly, writing repairs the imperfections and slights of life and is often initiated and sustained by a desire for retribution: 'You are enraged by everything which is evil, base, and shabby', he tells Siri, whom he endows with his own sensations, 'but you cannot say so! Then write! And those to whom you weren't previously able to say all this, and who would have hated you for the truth, will applaud you!' (I:191). But it is also possible to find Strindberg acknowledging the likelihood that self-exposure might not be the candid procedure it at first appears. When Axel (in *Playing with Fire*, but the ubiquity of the name in the period 1887 to 1893 suggests a certain pseudonymity, or at least continuity of utterance) is called to account for always boasting about his wickedness, he replies, speculatively, 'Perhaps it's to conceal it?' (25:419), and a similar point is made in an exchange in *Creditors*:

> Adolf: Do you know, I'm beginning to find your frankness painful.
> Tekla: And yet it was the highest virtue you knew - you taught it me.
> Adolf: Yes, but now it seems to me you're hiding behind this openness!
> (23:238-9)

Moreover, if to write for the press is a matter of appearing with the curtain raised on a bare stage (16:143), literature involves the donning of 'the impenetrable masks' (I:193) which conceal the writer. 'There will now be two plays one after the other. That is really my genre, since one doesn't need to be seen oneself' (V:355), he tells Bonnier, while at work on *The Son of a Servant*, where he wonders if being a poet is not really a matter of trying 'to get away from himself and invent another; is it the craving to dress up, is it modesty, the fear of self-surrender, of laying bare one's shame?' (18:352).[4]

But beyond recognizing a tendency 'to make up a story which conceals the true outlines of the matter' (MD:234), Strindberg also entertains a more comprehensive distrust of language, and of spoken language in particular. This distrust is the perplexing context of his autobiographical project; indeed, it casts doubt on his attempt to represent himself in language, and is voiced so frequently, and with so remarkable a continuity of argument and imagery, that it is curious it should have provoked so little serious comment.[5] And while it does not in itself explain

Strindberg's fascination with autobiographical writing, it nevertheless serves to establish the ground upon which the continual inscription of life into the secondariness of written discourse takes place more adequately than mere shyness or a self-assertion that is fortified behind the armour of the word.

Notwithstanding the ease with which he customarily suggests that anyone can 'relate what they have lived' (III:41), Strindberg repeatedly maintains that human discourse is scarcely ever veracious but usually employed to mislead, conceal, and misinform. Whereas language in daily use is normally regarded as transparent and innocent, a clear mirror of the world or of its user's thoughts (as Emile Benveniste remarks: 'Pour le sujet parlant, il y a entre la langage et la réalité adéquation complète: le signe recouvre et commande la réalité: mieux, il *est* cette réalité'),[6] Strindberg regularly indicates a radical discontinuity between man and the world, and thought and action, which language does not mediate fully or faithfully. Indeed, language emerges as the very sign of difference, the mark of an unbridgeable fissure which it obscures but cannot conceal, and which is the token of the language user's alienation from a primary order of being in which language has no place. The apparent 'fullness' of words as bearers of meaning is therefore seen by Strindberg to mask an absence, either that of the reality which language displaces or screens, which was an important platform in his criticism in the 1880s, or of truth, whose purity is perverted by the contaminated medium of conventional language, or even of the writer's own presence, which is evoked against the background of absence by means of a surrogate that does not truly represent him.

If this last possibility is clearly fundamental to the autobiographical enterprise, Strindberg originally formulates his misgivings about language in order to characterize its social function. That 'we are not what we seem' (27:67) is a constant complaint, from *The Red Room* to *A Blue Book*, and language provides both the instrument and the evidence of this general duplicity. Men use language 'solely with the object of deceiving one another' (48:1061), extending it like a screen, 'a web of hypocrisy and lies' (17:68), to conceal their real opinions and motives. People say what they do not think or hide what they ought to say behind 'the masking and dressing up of their upbringing' (16:109), and Strindberg often paraphrases the *aperçu* attributed to Talleyrand, 'La parole a été donné à l'homme pour deguiser sa pensée', in order to point the discrepancy between the notion that language is a faithful and adequate transmitter of fact and feeling, and its essential nature as the agent of invention, falsification, and untruth. In the story, 'The Reward of Virtue', the young Theodor takes refuge in 'a phrase, borrowed from a teacher, who had seen it quoted as Talleyrand's: "No, the purpose of language is to conceal people's thoughts"' (14:50),[7] while the heroine of 'Short Cuts', after reflecting at length on the properties which make language so equivocal a possession, concludes: 'One strikes people dead with words, deceives and intimidates them with words, and a great man had written what books and newspapers so often quote, that language had been invented in order to conceal thoughts' (54:50).

Strindberg's conception of the origins of language is not, of course, unique. Karl Popper, for example, has recently argued that 'lying is a comparatively late and fairly specifically human invention; indeed...it has made the human language what it is: an invention which can be used for misreporting almost as well as for reporting',[8] and during the 1880s, at least, when Strindberg regarded the acquisition of language as a rite of passage from a state of innocence to the social world of what he termed 'The Public Lie' (*Den offentliga lögnen*), it is not difficult to discern a community of interest with both Rousseau and Nietzsche. Even in Strindberg's earliest writings, language denotes and facilitates a fall from pristine reality into the corruption of a world where illusion is fostered by words; with his departure from a natural state, the individual 'tastes the tree of knowledge' (54:199) and sinks into 'the half-darkness of fictions' (20:51), where he loses himself to art, the cognate of artifice, and Rousseau, too, imagines an unfissured pre-verbal innocence that is echoed in the language 'que les enfants parlent avant de savoir parler,'[9] but which is irrevocably lost in social discourse, where it is as if 'un mal inéluctable pervertit la société et fait du langage cultivé l'agent infectant d'une duperie universelle... Mensonge, fiction, illusion forment le milieu même où évoluent les sociétés policées. Brillante comme l'or, la parole, devenue elle aussi monnaie d'échange, rend l'homme étranger à lui-même.'[10] And just as Nietzsche remarked that 'the different languages, set side by side, show that what matters with words is never the truth, never an adequate expression; else there would not be so many languages,'[11] so Strindberg's linguistic scepticism evolves from a cultural critique that is indebted to Rousseau, into the radical questioning implicit in another recurring formula, namely 'that the different languages arose among the savage peoples in order to conceal the secrets of the tribe from the others; languages are thus ciphers, and the person who finds the key will understand all the world's languages' (45:190). Moreover, the image evoked here is 'the ancient legend of the Tower of Babel' to which Strindberg often refers, observing: 'People wished to storm heaven and seek the riddle of life, but God touched their tongues and called forth a general confusion, so that one man did not understand what the other said' (19:206).[12] And hence, as Lars Gustafsson suggests, in his study of aberrant nineteenth-century philosophies of language,[13] Strindberg also frequently appears to anticipate Fritz Mauthner or (especially in the Chamber Plays) the dramatists of the absurd in their misgivings about the capacity of language to represent the world or to convey one individual's perceptions to another. 'To exchange ideas is only a stock phrase, for no one exchanges his idea with another,' he maintains, in *A Blue Book*: 'My best friend understands approximately 30 procent of what I say, and I can see that he misinterprets every word I have said' (46:46-7). Conversations are 'a Babylonian confusion which end in wrangling and the impossibility of understanding one another' (38:127), and the idea of correspondences, which Strindberg derives in part from Swedenborg and adapts to the pressures of his own thought, is related to an ancient crisis in which 'The One God divided everything in two and into antitheses' (47:551).

Thus the obsessive research into the nature and origins of language which Strindberg undertook in his last years becomes comprehensible in terms of a quest for an undivided language, the ur-language or Adamic vernacular that preceded Babel, in which there is a congruence between what is said and the language used to say it, a correspondence between word and referent, sign and signified. And like the Pietists, Swedenborg, and the *Kabbala* (which The Unknown regards as 'the wisest of all the books of wisdom' (29:169) when he reads from an account of the Tower of Babel in the *Zohar*), Strindberg sought the translucent immediacy of this lost primal speech in Hebrew, where he believed he could discern its features: 'One does not need more Hebrew than to be able to distinguish the article (ha) and the plural endings (im and ut) from the root, in order to hear echoes in a biblical concordance of a language which has probably been the same everywhere' (47:562). Furthermore, he suggests that visual correspondences indicate that writing also stems from a primary script. In a note 'On the Ur-Language and the Confusion of Babel', he reports his accidental discovery that Mongolian, normally written from right to left and from the top to the bottom of the page, 'resembled Arabic, particularly the old form which is used on Kufic coins' (47:531), when it is placed on its side. Moreover he likewise considers that 'the figures on the shell of a tortoise would have served the ancient Chinese as a model for the oldest written characters' (47:513), thus provoking the encouraging footnote: 'Anyone who wants to undertake comparative philology can buy the shell in Birger Jarl Arcade for 1 krona 50' (47:514).

The relevance of these apparently trivial speculations for Strindberg's concern to represent himself in language may be appreciated if the conception of language as something that conceals and misleads, instead of serving to enlighten and communicate, is recognized at the heart of one of his primary categories, 'the law of accommodation', which he formulates in *The Son of a Servant*. Previously, in the polemics of *The New Kingdom* and *Like and Unlike*, he had argued that 'by living together, one is forced to place restraints on oneself that only long to be broken; conventions, politeness, etiquette, all that is necessary, but it is a terrible necessity, because it is falsehood' (16:90). He had been concerned with the public lie and enquired, like Max Nordau, whose popular exposure of late nineteenth-century hypocrisy and humbug, *The Conventional Lies of Our Civilisation*, he briefly considered 'the Holy Writ' (IV:9), how

> ...if we are born in lies and grow up surrounded by lies; if we are obliged
> to lie every time we open our mouths in public, or come in personal
> contact with any of the political and social institutions of the day, if we
> are in the habit of always speaking and acting differently from the way
> we feel and think, of enduring the perpetual contradiction between our
> inward convictions and the outward phases of life as a matter of course,
> of considering hypocrisy as worldly wisdom and duty and sincerity as
> extravagance...it is possible to retain a sincere and upright character?[14]

Now, in turning inwards to examine himself, he comes to see how all social intercourse prevents one from being (to take the phrase literally) oneself, since 'when one talks to someone one adapts oneself slightly in their favour, when one talks to another, one makes a concession to them, and if one did not do this but said exactly what one thought, the conversation would end with everyone spitting in one another's face and walking off, never to meet again' (19:177-8). Insertion into the circuit of linguistic exchange is to lose one's self. Within the symbolic order of language, in the act of speaking, one becomes another, or as many others as one converses with. Through his self-study, therefore, Strindberg discovers not character but characterlessness, and when he regards the contradictory images of his past self at the end of the first volume of *The Son of a Servant*, he discerns not a single, unique presence, but a multitude of personae assumed according to circumstance and company:

> That was the law of accommodation, which Johan did not know about. People were like that: there was an instinct to adapt oneself, which rested partly on calculation and partly on unconscious or reflex actions. A lamb to one's friends, a lion to one's enemies.
> But when was one being true to oneself, when was one false? Where was the self - which supposedly constituted one's character? It was neither here nor there, but in both places at once. The self is not any one thing; it is a conglomeration of reflexes, a complex of instincts and desires which are alternately suppressed and unleashed! (18:218)

That linguistic competence involves the ability to use language to sustain the duplicity social life requires, is an idea Strindberg never relinquishes. In a late fragment, headed 'The Logic of Conversation', which expands upon a section in *A Blue Book* entitled simply 'Logic' (48:1061), he argues that 'for the most part opinions are rooted in the flesh' and describes how any overheard conversation will shock a listener by the way in which the speakers accommodate themselves to each other's point of view.[15] Such scenes occur or are evoked in numerous texts (*Alone, The Ghost Sonata, A Blue Book*) where a tension between speaking out and remaining silent is a central motif, and increasingly, as the title of a late Vivisection suggests, character is confirmed in Strindberg's mind as a series of roles demanded by successive situations: 'N'est-ce pas que l'on s'adapte à chaque instant aux hommes et aux choses, que la réalité si variable et oscillante nous fasse varier, et que nous jouons la comédie de la vie sans la savoir?' (VR:126). Indeed, the deviousness inherent in the social use of language is depicted as so prevalent, unconscious, and essential a part of the 'accommodating complaisance, without which intercourse becomes impossible',[16] that Strindberg's reaction appears excessive. There seems no reason why he should not accept his insights with the scepticism expressed in a letter to the poet, Verner von Heidenstam: 'My writing: a seeking after the truth! Idiotic in itself perhaps, for the truth is only conventional!' (VII:92). And yet the reverse is true. Although the mendaciousness of the medium in which it is formulated seems to undermine the discourse of the self at which he aims from the outset, it is impossible to mistake the way in which, like Rousseau and his claim that 'Ma fonction est de dire la vérité',[17] Strindberg nevertheless repeatedly presents himself as the custodian of the truth which words are supposed to belie; as he informs Harriet Bosse: 'When you talk or write to me, remember it is to a man who cannot, who dare not say a word which is not true!'[18]

The Son of a Servant is clearly a key text in establishing this reputation for candour and probity, and Strindberg's project obviously invites comparison with Rousseau's. It is not, of course, difficult to discern an affinity between the belief 'that by crowding together and mingling their existences with one another's, civilized people...no longer live for themselves but only have their being in what others think of them' (16:74), which develops into 'the law of accommodation', and Rousseau's theory, advanced in the *Discours sur l'origine de l'inégalité* (but no less anticipatory of the view of the self which the *Confessions* present), that 'le Sauvage vit en lui-même; l'homme sociable, toujours hors de lui ne sait vivre que dans l'opinion des autres, et c'est pour ainsi dire, de leur seul jugement qu'il tire le sentiment de sa propre existence.'[19] As Sven-Gustav Edqvist has shown, in his study of Strindberg's anarchism,[20] much of his early thinking is pre-figured in Rousseau's account of man's transition from the state of nature to civilization, where 'Etre et paroître devinrent deux choses tout à fait différentes.'[21]

However, the fundamental affinity between Rousseau and Strindberg lies firstly in the way in which the formulations of such texts as 'On the General Discontent' are as intimately related, in substance and imagery, to the most personal aspects of the experience related in the autobiographical volumes, as Jean Starobinski has demonstrated is the case with the *Discourses* and *Confessions*: 'A tort ou à raison, Rousseau n'a pas consenti à séparer sa pensée et son destin personnel';[22] and secondly, that the role of language in the presentation and distortion of the social self promotes a desire to commit themselves to language in a discourse appropriate to themselves. In fact Rousseau's presence shadows any discussion of Strindberg's decision to *write* the narrative of his life, and it is remarkable that while his influence on Strindberg's social and political thought has often been surveyed in detail, there have been few more than cursory discussions of their intellectual and emotional consanguinity, and this despite the role which the *Confessions* undoubtedly have as part of the constitutive literary intertextuality of Strindberg's life, and of *The Son of a Servant* in particular.[23]

In the utopian fable, 'The Isle of the Blessed', the text in which Strindberg comes closest to repeating the received message of Rousseau's account of the rise of civilization, language is again shown as the means of transforming what is into what is not: 'The children discovered that answering yes when one ought to answer no brought one advantages, such as rewards, or freedom from punishment, and therefore the lie began to flourish' (11:94-5). Similar words are used to introduce this discovery, now presented as a general law, into *The Son of a Servant*: 'One of the earliest discoveries of the awakening intelligence is that a well-placed yes or no can reap an advantage' (18:16). But what lends it authority on this occasion is its corroboration by a primal scene of truth and appearance which, like the Lambercier episode in Book One of the *Confessions*, is placed at a strategic point in the narrative of Strindberg's life, initiating much that is to follow and reverberating throughout the entire body of his work to issue in the thought and imagery of the Chamber Plays and the unfinished fragment, *Armageddon*.

In fact the scene recounts a paradigmatic event which, whether true or false, is at the core of this autobiographical narrative. And yet, even granted the chagrin of a childhood injustice and the immediacy of direct speech, which is used here in the book for the first time, its resonance seems, on first reading, disproportionate to the occasion. In a short dramatic episode of only three pages (but from which it is difficult to exclude all knowledge of the slightly longer passage in which Rousseau, at a similar point in his autobiography, is mistakenly accused of breaking Mlle Lambercier's comb), Strindberg describes how Johan is unjustly punished first for denying that he had drunk from a bottle of wine which he had not even touched, and again for denying he had lied in making his original profession of innocence. What rankles most, however, is not the punishment itself, but the way in which the child has been compelled 'to confess to something he had never done' (18:18), an outrage which rekindles the narrator's ire and prompts him to describe the family as that 'splendid moral institution...where innocent children are tortured into their first lies' (18:18).

And yet this scene, which is reinforced some fifty pages on (18:68) by the comparable episode of the iron screw nuts, where Johan is once again beaten into confessing he has stolen something he has in fact only come upon by chance in the street, is constitutive both of the work in its entirety, and of the life which sustains it. Sometimes evoked directly, but more often, as in *The Red Room*, 'A Child's Saga', or *The Burned House*, leaving its trace upon the surface of another text in the form of an analogous incident that has taken place under the intense pressure of its repressed emotion,[24] this primal scene of unmerited punishment forms part of the network of mnemonic material in an opening chapter which is, like the first book of the *Confessions*, where the Lambercier episode is similarly complemented by the later scene of the stolen ribbon, which concludes Book Two,[25] at once 'le premier acte du drame, et le drame tout entier.'[26] As René Bourgeois has observed, in an essay, 'Signification du premier souvenir', in which he makes much of the punitive scene which opens the autobiographical narrative of another of Strindberg's French precursors, Jules Vallés, 'La plupart des premiers souvenirs sont dangereusement significatifs et révélateurs non d'une réceptivité passive mais d'une volonté de reconstruction systématique,'[27] and the account of Strindberg's earliest years in *The Son of a Servant* is already a kind of retrospective prolepsis. It not only performs its ostensible purpose, which is the recuperation of the past; it also delineates the features of a destiny that will be continually repeated, firstly in the developmental, genetic model of the 1880s, in which the man grows from the seeds of his physiological, psychological, and environmental inheritance, into the person he was always destined to be (or, as the first volume concludes, to remain: 'And thus he stepped out into life! To evolve and develop, and yet to remain forever the person he was' (18:219)) and then, when Strindberg renounces his Naturalism and no longer wishes to regard himself as continuous with nature, as emblematic of the fate allotted him in this, the terrestrial, phase of his drama.

Both these views are implicit in the episode. Seen from the perspective he employed in the mid-1880s, the scene projects an image of childhood innocence savagely abused in an environment that, ironically, predicates truth as the paramount virtue:

'In Johan's home truth was worshipped' (18:68). It represents the moment of passage recorded in 'The Isle of the Blessed' and is restated many years later by Gerda, in *The Pelican*, when she observes: 'People call one wicked if one tells the truth...so I learned to say what I didn't mean, and then I was ready for life' (45:246). All the authority of the psychological and sociological discourses employed in the book combine to pin-point the critical moment when the child is expelled into a society that accepts the evidence of appearances before the testimony of truth. Quite simply, when he speaks the truth Johan is heard to lie. His accusers disregard the words he uses to represent himself and so fail to judge him as he knows himself to be, while his innocence as yet denies him access to that fluency of speech which would enable him to appear as others see him.

The traumatic nature of the episode is also evident from the way in which it recurs throughout Strindberg's writing, from the errand boy in *The Red Room*, 'who was far too young and innocent to be able to get himself out of a fix with a lie' (5:320), and who is beaten because he tells the truth, to the Son in *The Pelican*, who reminds his mother of how, when he told her 'what I saw in the abode of sin, you said it was a lie, and you struck me as a liar' (45:265). But even within the confines of the emphatically Naturalist discourse of *The Son of a Servant*, there are intimations of another reading of the text submitted by life, which will eventually come to preoccupy Strindberg with increasing urgency. When the episode ends, Johan has been cast in a role that does not suit him; seen a fissure open up between himself and others, and between appearance and reality; encountered the ambiguity of right and wrong; and become an object of suspicion on the periphery of society, the eventual outcast, Ishmael:

> He felt like a criminal. Punished for lying, which was so abominated in
> the house, and for theft, a word never even spoken there. Deprived of
> his civil rights, regarded with suspicion, and despised by his brothers
> because he had been caught. All of this, together with the consequences,
> which were very real to him, were nevertheless based upon something
> that did not exist at all, his crime. (18:19)

Not unnaturally, too, the dilemma nurtured in the wake of this scene provokes in Strindberg a continual questioning as to whether or not he is guilty, and if not who is, and if so in what way since the punishment seems, initially at least, to precede the crime. And hence, as Martin Lamm has pointed out,[28] *The Son of a Servant* already contains the notion that 'life was a penal institution for crimes committed before one had been born' (18:39), in which the many later, post-Inferno scenarios of guilt, suffering, and punishment, and the many figures of history and myth with whom Strindberg finds correlatives for the shape and significance of his destiny, are clearly prefigured. The idea haunts many texts, sometimes discretely and impersonally, as in the description of Theodor, in 'The Reward of Virtue', who 'was sometimes gloomy and ruminative, and felt life was not as it should be. It seemed to him that some unparalleled crime must have been committed in the past, and that it was now being concealed under a mass of deceptions' (14:58). More frequently, however, its implications are personal, as when The Unknown senses how 'Fate is elaborating her plot, once again I hear the gavel fall and the chairs pushed back from the table - the sentence is pronounced, but it must have been decided before I was born, for already in my childhood I began to serve my punishment' (29:53), and it remains central to one of Strindberg's last attempts at elucidating the pattern of his destiny in *Armageddon*, where the nature and function of language are once again a major consideration.

As Walter Berendsohn has suggested,[29] *Armageddon* may well form a kind of prologue in heaven to the collected volume of Strindberg's autobiographical sequence as he conceived it towards the end of his life. It can certainly be read as such. Not only does it contain a prophetic account of a destiny which in its particulars seems remarkably like a retrospective summary of the life Strindberg saw himself as just completing, thus suggesting that its course had been artistically arranged, or plotted, from the outset (hence the statement: 'His future fate...is already written' (54:156)); it also breaks off shortly after the birth of the protagonist, Skugge, at roughly the point at which *The Son of a Servant* commences with the chapter 'Afraid and Hungry'. Moreover, in describing Skugge as someone who 'did not want to be in the way and who was not allowed to talk' (54:162), it even repeats the familiar description of Johan as 'frightened of being in the way' and unable to 'go anywhere without being in the way, without saying a word that did not disturb' (18:8, 14).

The fragment relates how Skugge (cf. Sw.*skugga*=shadow), initially called Fröjdkyss (lit. 'Kiss of Joy), becomes a shadow of his former self once he 'learned to say what he did not think' (54:152), and how he is therefore expelled from a harmonious realm of 'truth, justice...purity and innocence' (54:148-9) back down into a world called Dimona (cf. Sw. *dimma* = mist), where everything is 'ugly or false', 'distorted and counterfeit' (54:155). There he makes 'the child's first great discovery in the art of life: how to avoid trouble by dissimulation' (54:162), and the narrative ends abruptly with a scene in which Skugge 'sat in his corner and heard how the others said what they did not mean and how they spoke differently to different people and on different occasions. This, he realized, was what was called lying' (54:163).

Armageddon thus depicts the sentence passed before birth on a character whose kinship with Strindberg's earlier self-images is unmistakable, and then describes his subsequent banishment to a place which is recognizable as the 'penal institution' of *The Son of a Servant*, but which is now portrayed in the imagery of *Black Banners*, the Chamber Plays, and *A Blue Book*, as 'a prison and a madhouse with many names' (54:156).[30] It is a place of illusions, 'the world of delusion' (46:34 - *villornas värld*), where men resemble sleepwalkers, and nothing is what it seems but 'perverse, imperfect, and crazy' (46:129), a world where 'we really live not in reality but in our ideas of reality' (46:169), and 'even the man who tries to tell the truth with an upright mind, gets entangled in inherited lies and is trapped' (54:156). Moreover, what specifically distinguishes this world from the pre-natal paradise from which

Skugge is expelled, a realm where everything is 'what it pretends to be' (44:75), is language, with its capacity to deceive. And here Strindberg's own earlier intimations of a higher existence are realised in a terminology that now owes much to Swedenborg.[31] Like the Chamber Plays, *Armageddon* relies heavily upon the doctrine and topography associated with the Swedenborgian notion of Lower Earth, to which men pass at death, and where they gradually lose the ability to mask their thoughts and feelings. In time, therefore, outer appearance becomes a mirror of the individual's inner reality, and the prize of moralist and autobiographer alike, his true self, is revealed.

Yet more pertinent to *Armageddon*, however, is the sanction Strindberg discovers elsewhere in Swedenborg for his own misgivings about language. For in the sections of *De Telluribus* devoted to the inhabitants of Jupiter and Mars,[32] Swedenborg describes a type of wordless communication which Strindberg adopts and bestows upon Skugge's companions, Pärlskön and Havsdroppe: 'They spoke but little with words, but with glances and smiles' since 'they could see one another's thoughts with their eyes, and they could also show what they were thinking; their eyelids did not move, either to conceal something or in pretence' (54:151). Effected mainly by means of facial expression and adequate because of the correspondence between what Swedenborg termed interior and exterior speech, this wordless communication can dispense with the mediation of the spoken word since the inhabitants of Jupiter are unable to 'show a face at variance with the mind...because they never speak otherwise than they think.'[33] Indeed, Swedenborg's account of the development of language suggests that 'the very first speech on every earth was speech by the face' and that it is only because men learned to lie that verbal speech became a necessity. In what reads as a paraphrase not only of *Armageddon* but of Strindberg's conception of language in general, Swedenborg argues:

> that verbal speech could not have been used by the Most Ancient people, since the words of a language are not imparted immediately, but have to be invented and applied to objects; which it requires a course of time to effect. So long as sincerity and rectitude prevailed among men, such speech continued; but as soon as the mind began to think one thing and speak another, which was the case when man began to love himself and not the neighbour, verbal speech began to increase, the face being either silent or deceitful.[34]

Not surprisingly, such ideas appeal to Strindberg, who finds them reinforced at the end of the century by Maeterlinck's collection of essays, *Le Trésor des humbles* where, in contrast to speech, which cuts man off from reality, silence is described as the language of the soul and the means of true communication. To Maeterlinck, who on at least one occasion amended Talleyrand's *aperçu* by observing that speech is all too often not the art of concealing thought, but of stifling it, so that there is nothing to conceal, silence is eloquent, revealing, and non-concealing, and permits what is within a person to rise to the surface where it becomes visible to the interlocutory glance, and Strindberg, who began to translate *Le Trèsor des humbles* as a gift for Harriet Bosse, likewise often regarded silence as the discourse of virtue in his later works. 'I prefer silence', the loquacious Hummel claims, 'then one hears thoughts, and sees the past, silence cannot conceal anything... which words can' (45:190), while Strindberg himself observes: 'One ought never to speak, only signal what is most vital to meet the needs of life. And when one comes together, one should hear music' (48:917).

These convictions seem to place not only speaking but even the writing of literature in doubt, and Strindberg does in fact remark that 'the godly do not portray their marriages, and they write neither plays nor novels' (47:735). But his profoundly ambiguous relationship to language, spoken and written, does not admit so neat a conclusion. The possibility that language does not convey a perfect representation of the truth may in any case be experienced as an affront to propriety. A classic instance of this occurs in Swift's account of the Houyhnhnms, where Gulliver, 'having occasion to talk of lying and false representation', encounters a problem in conveying what he means to his master:

> ...it was with much difficulty that he comprehended what I meant; although he had otherwise a most acute judgement. For he argued thus: that the use of speech was to make us understand one another, and to receive information of facts; now if one said *the thing which was not*, these ends were defeated; because I cannot properly be said to understand him; and I am so far from receiving information, that he leaves me worse than in ignorance; for I am led to believe a thing black when it is white, and short when it is long. And these were all the notions he had concerning the faculty of *lying*, so perfectly well understood, and so universally practised among human creatures.[35]

With Strindberg, too, the possibility that language may be used to say 'the thing which was not' seems to violate not only virtue and truth but also the categories of order and disorder, and justice and injustice, so frequently associated with them. Moreover, since disorder suggests the idea of dirt, the debased work in which verbal language is an unfortunate necessity is readily linked with the notions of purity and filth which are never far removed from Strindberg's attention, as indeed, they are not from Swift's. 'He began to disturb the regulations,' Pärlskön says, of Skugge, 'he learned to say what he did not think, but his falseness could not be concealed, for whoever tells the truth has both his eyes in equilibrium like the balance on a set of scales' (54:152). Hence he is excluded from the company of his fellows 'for his breath stinks sourly and he sweats as if from the effort of concealing his thoughts' (54:153). Thus he is eventually condemned 'to lie in foul smelling filth' (54:160).

In the significative system elaborated in *Armageddon*, therefore, verbal language is specific to the fallen world of dirt (*smuts*), falsehood (*osanning*), lies (*lögn*), and excrement (*träck*), whereas the purity of wordless communication is peculiar to a situation of truth (*sanning*), purity (*renhet*), innocence (*oskuld*), and justice (*rättvisa*) as it is portrayed in the opening scene of the fragment, where a number of Strindberg's most constant and deeply-rooted desires are adumbrated. Thus, like the Stockholm archipelago or Switzerland which, according to Strindberg, have their 'great glorious nature, and therefore need no surrogate' (16:166), the purity of this landscape requires no art, nor any other kind of mediation. 'He who has nature needs no art' (47:656), he maintains, some twenty years later, and any violation of what he understood to be the order of nature always appeared to Strindberg to be, like Axel Borg's optical transformation of the archipelago in *By the Open Sea*, 'something monstrous' (24:153). This landscape also reflects his abiding preference for plants over animal life. 'It is mainly in the world of plants that I have found perfect beauty' (47:606), he asserts, at about this time, and the rarified atmosphere of the world from which Skugge falls, which is inhabited only by non-carnivorous animals and birds who discharge their waste products into the air through their lungs 'in a cleanly manner' (54:148), denotes a recoil from the brutish facts of eating, excreting, and reproducing that is similarly articulated in *The Ghost Sonata* and *The Pelican*. For almost invariably, the notion of *smuts*, of dirt and disorder, is associated in Strindberg's imagination with 'excrement, nourishment, cooks and rotting vegetables' (37:207), and with sexuality, as when Johan, coming directly from a scene with his mistress to join his sisters in the country, wonders 'what the word filth (*smuts*) means?' (19:127), and traces the disturbing image of sexual love it evokes back, by way of his sister, Anna, to his mother. Moreover, while Strindberg regularly attempts to discriminate between marriage as *ren* (clean, pure) and the temptations of the bachelor as *smuts*, the distinction frequently collapses ('to me bachelor life is filthy. Family life is finest - and yet, it's even filthier, when one roots around in it!' (XI:100)) and his later works indicate that for him, as for Max, in *Gothic Rooms*: 'There are times when I believe...that our human souls have had to creep into animal bodies. We behave like animals, we kiss with the same mouth which takes in food, and we make love with an excremental organ' (40:195).

Since language, both verbal and non-verbal, is essential to this two-edged current of desire and disgust, and since it is the medium in which Strindberg has elected to conduct his life, the tensions and taboos generated here are of crucial importance to his undertaking. As the Tempter comments, in *To Damascus*, it is precisely the most purely intentioned of wordless acts which occasions the situation from which language recoils. 'I have never understood,' he remarks, 'how a kiss, which is an unborn word, a soundless speech, a silent language of two souls, can by a sacred act be transformed into ... a surgical operation, which always ends in weeping and the gnashing of teeth' (29:340). Conversely, as Strindberg argues, in *A Blue Book*, in a section which summarizes a situation depicted many years earlier in 'Short Cuts', when the apparent conversation of the young lovers, Tekla and Robert, in fact conceals a passionate wordless discussion, language also becomes the screen behind which the discourse of desire unfolds in silence: 'The spoken word has frequently become a fig leaf which conceals shame. When you ask: "Do you love me, will you be my wife?" do you know what you are touching on then? You are really asking her, if you first may kiss her, then...and then...and then' (48:875).

Thus, in making his famous enquiry, 'Will you have a little child with me, Miss Bosse?'[36], Strindberg may be discerned shortcutting the preliminary stages of a sequence that is normally concealed behind the verbal fig leaf. Indeed, the latter is actually evoked in *Creditors*, where Gustav describes how Tekla and Adolf 'creep behind the fig leaf, play brothers and sisters, and, as their feelings become increasingly carnal, invent a relationship for themselves that is more and more spiritual' (23:207), a notion that is also present in 'Short Cuts' where Tekla asks Robert if 'their souls are brothers and sisters' and he confirms 'the invisible bond' between them. When she claims 'it seems to me, as if every word you spoke was my own thought' (54:43), they seem to be enjoying the silent communion that Strindberg later extols. However, their dialogue is not ethereal but a cloak to conceal their unspoken desire. Robert clothes the discussion in 'a veil of the wonderful... so that they moved quite unconstrainedly beneath the light veil. They spoke freely, as if behind masks' (54:43-4), moving gradually towards 'the burning words' (54:45) which pluck their veil aside to reveal, in the common memory of a youthful kiss, the nakedness of their present desire.

Thus the very silence which in theory constitutes Strindberg's ideal proves in practice to be immoral. For it is party to the veil of lies and hypocrisy which sustains social life, those 'silent agreements, public secrets which keep society together' (16:91). In *The Son of a Servant* he relates how Johan 'had learnt to speak the truth...took a brutal pleasure in saying straight out what everyone was thinking in the middle of a conversation where people were dallying with the truth' (18:217), a reaction which persists with Strindberg to the end. In *The Pelican*, the Son recognizes 'a duty to speak out' (45:246), for as the Student insists, in *The Ghost Sonata*, 'by remaining silent for too long, stagnant water accumulates and things rot' (45:208), and as Strindberg informs Harriet Bosse, since silence implies complicity in a collective deception with both private and public ramifications (on this occasion, as on so many others, he is referring to marriage), he is always compelled to distinguish himself, to make himself heard. 'A volcano of repressed opinions takes shape and it has to explode', he tells her (XIV:121), for otherwise (as The Dead Man remarks, in *The Isle of the Dead*) he will explode himself: 'Oh, that I can't keep quiet any longer, but I have stayed silent for thirty years, until in the end I got so full of falsehood I was on the point of bursting'.[37] Confronted by a society that 'wanted to hush him up' (54:71), he consequently evolves the apocalyptic notion that were the true word spoken in 'the simple, raw language of truth' (54:227), then 'society would fall apart' (17:68). This is already anticipated in his early play, *The Freethinker*, with its defiant conclusion: 'Sooner may heaven and earth collapse, than a word of the truth be denied!' (1:57), but it assumes a particular meaning in the scenes of undressing (*avklädning*) or unmasking (*demaskering*) in which the later works abound, where the word spoken in truth kills. 'Words are forms of energy of unparalleled strength' (46:193), Strindberg asserts, and the Student's deadly outburst to the Daughter at the end of *The Ghost Sonata* is conceived as a speech act in which 'He murders her with words'.[38] A similar process is depicted in *Creditors*, where Gustav talks Adolf to death, and it may be related to another recurrent belief, which again serves to link the autobiographer with the recorder of sins in the Book of Life, that when a man achieves precise self-knowledge, that is, when he sees himself (or as Strindberg may express it, his ghost or *fylgia* (23:268)) as he is, he dies: 'But when one has seen oneself, one dies!' (45:139). Or as the Hunter muses at a graveside in *The Great Highway*:

'Here rests' - yes, I knew you
but you never came to know yourself...
and you; all your life you were disguised,
your long heavy life;
and when I stripped you naked, you died! (51:77)

Strindberg thus regards the language he uses as both deadly and pure, and confronted by another, his immediate desire is often, like The Unknown's response to the Doctor in *To Damascus*, 'to speak a pure language and blow him up' (29:42). But this involves the use of 'coarse words...such words which most truly, that is to say most rawly reproduce thought' (17:68), something his sensitivity to the role of language as a carrier of impurity and sexuality will cause to haunt not only the reception of *Getting Married* (which is in any case an outspoken linguistic act from which he eventually tries to exculpate himself), but any text which seeks 'to lift the curtain' (17:67) and speak the truth. Lifting the curtain, moreover, is similar to removing the fig leaf, and like Strindberg's ambivalence about exposing himself in literature, the medium in which he performs this public undressing is also equivocal. It both entices and disgusts him as 'a raw and repulsive occupation' (V:121), and the intermittent attraction of a scientific discourse, preeminently of chemical formulae, may well satisfy a wish for a language that is immune to the contemporary accusation that his writing was 'the product of a fantasy, which finds pleasure in wallowing in filth.'[39]

However, the danger of pollution is reduced because Strindberg so pointedly avoids immediate verbal intercourse. The raw, murderous language he espouses is not spoken but written in solitude on the virginal purity of the white and silent page to which he confides what he is unable to say. These are the terms on which he constantly insists when he describes writing; they elaborate the scene in which the page is inscribed with the life of its scriptor. Although one writes what one does not say, he informs Siri, 'the secret is nevertheless kept...the whole art consists in inventing the impenetrable masks and - in keeping silent. Silence is holy. What one has once related before it has been put down on paper is lost' (I:193), a prescription which is echoed in the passage in *A Blue Book* in which he exonerates himself from the indiscretions of the press which he periodically accuses of betraying the privacy of his written discourse:

I confided it to the silent, printed word on the white page. It was a confidential communication; and the person who betrayed it was a traitor.

> Our books are made to be read in silence, to be whispered in one's ear,
> but the newspaper always speaks aloud, it shouts the secrets out, and
> therefore bears the guilt. (48:941-2)

Both Martin Lamm and Torsten Eklund have, of course, focused their attention on these and similar passages,[40] and it would be tempting to share their perplexity over the apparent disingenuousness in what seems an attempt on Strindberg's part to disclaim responsibility for his own indiscretions by transferring the guilt incurred in making them onto other writers, whose medium is nevertheless also the printed word. And equally, the distinction between writing and speech which he consistently sets up, also ask to be considered in the terms evolved by linguistics to explain the difference between the two modes of language use. Accordingly, Strindberg could be said to reject what Saussure calls 'the natural bond, the only true bond, the bond of sound',[41] in favour of the surrogate permanence and stability offered by the graphic form of words. Strindberg prefers the solitary, secondary, invented mode of writing, which arrests, fixes, abstracts from, and supplements experience, a mode of communication which eschewes the immediacy and disorder of dialogue, and which is characterized by a double absence, or occultation, wherein the reader is absent from the writing of the book and the writer from its reading, to what is regarded, if only because of the anteriority of speech to writing in the individual's life and in history, as the primary, natural, even divine mode of communication, in which the voice, borne by the breath, and guaranteed by facial expression, gesture, tone, and inflection, signifies the presence of the speaker and of his companions to himself and to others, in an interlocutory situation that binds voice and ear in the here and now. For speech proceeds from an evident context, both in terms of the perceptual surroundings and the cultural and historical background the speakers have in common. It is, moreover, interruptable, an exchange, and in its intersubjectivity, it promises an essential and immediate proximity of voice and being.[42] It also appears to have the virtue Strindberg denies it, in being immediately verifiable or, at least, open to question, since the speaker is promptly accountable for what he says (they are *his* words, unless he says otherwise) whereas writing, what Vygotsky terms 'speech without an interlocutor, addressed to an absent or an imaginary person or to no one in particular',[43] is spatially and temporally removed from its occasion, and is often placed under the aegis of death (presided over as it is in Plato's *Phaedrus*, by Thoth, the Egyptian God of writing and inscriber of accounts before the Last Judgement), a monument to pastness not only in the posthumous perspective of the autobiographer but also, according to Paul Ricoeur, in the response to all writing: 'to read a book is to consider its author as already dead and the book as posthumous. Indeed, it is when the author is dead that the relation to his book becomes complete and, in a way, intact.'[44]

In practice, however, the situation is more complex than a straightforward dichotomy admits. Strindberg is in any case suspicious of the notion of a full and present speech, and of a presence immediately recoverable from a spoken discourse that is transparent and innocent. All too often people do not commit themselves to their utterances, and in place of the noisy, soliciting, impermanence of the spoken word, in which the speaker dissipates himself, he therefore resorts to literature in order to reappropriate the presence which eludes him in speech. If the latter is where he is dispersed and misrepresented, writing is where he coheres, and in contrast to a spoken discourse in which the changing motives of the various participants determine the intermittent flow of the utterance, the written is where the discourse seems to pass under the uninterrupted control of its producer, or at least, to provide him with the semblance of control: 'Since I still cannot say coherently as much as is written on this sheet of paper', he writes, to his early benefactor, Rudolf Wall, 'I have taken the liberty of writing' (I:228).

But if in doing so he withdraws from what Ricoeur calls 'the bodily support of oral discourse',[45] this does not mean that the writing he produces is disembodied or that it becomes 'more spiritual in the sense that it is liberated from the narrowness of the face-to-face situation.'[46] Strindberg is in fact not so considerate or self-effacing as to abandon his texts to the anonymity that many textual critics regard as the domain of the written. Although he ordinarily refuses the facile à clef identifications that his contemporaries often made between themselves and the characters of his books, and eventually argued the virtue of 'the protective veil of pseudonymity' employed by 'the writer of folk songs, who effaced his own self and lived only as the echo of a song' (47:647), he felt the duty of the Kierkegaardian witness of truth (*sannhedsvittne*) to be responsible for his words, answerable for them, and discernable in them. What the reader should hear, in short, if not perceive, is 'a heart beating in every line' (II:42).

The ways in which Strindberg accomplishes this are various. A text may, as Sverker Hallén has demonstrated, be at once stridently contemporary in its literariness and a private message, directed to a single addressee. Thus the French edition of 'Deranged Impressions', *Sensations detraquées*, incorporates a passage which reads on one level as an exercise in a fashionable *fin-de-siècle* literary code of associative symbolism, and on another, as a cipher of allusions in which he warns his dubious Parisian benefactor, Willy Gretor, against interfering in his private life.[47] A situation may also arise, especially in relation to Siri von Essen or Harriet Bosse, where Strindberg uses his writing to conceive an interlocutress who was simultaneously the subject, reader, and even the actress of the roles attributed to her. As he tells his colleague, Geijerstam, Siri will repeat the role in which he has cast her: 'My wife will only play the role which is written for her, and which suits her' (VII:166). For what he often seeks to accomplish by writing is a distribution of roles in which he does not merely try to re-present himself and render his self visible; he also contrives the immediate absence of the other *and* his or her presence, both in the substance of the discourse and as its eventual reader or actor. As a passage in *Alone* demonstrates, for Strindberg writing is speech, a kind of dialogue, but one more ample and representative than circumstances ordinarily permit:

> I perceive my own thoughts as spoken words; I seem to be in telepathic contact with all my absent acquaintances, friends and enemies; I carry

on long orderly conversations with them, or resume old conversations held in convivial company, in cafes; I oppose their opinions, defend my point of view, and I am much more eloquent than when I am in the presence of listeners. (38:177)

As is the case with Rousseau, for whom writing provides the necessary substitute for the improvisations, embarrassment, and imperfections in which speech involves him, this passage illustrates that the written word affords the once aphasic Strindberg a compensatory form of eloquence in which the features of the unsuccessful encounter are recomposed in retrospect. Lacking the ability to improvise a rapid response, gauche and inept, and all too sensitive to those factors, spoken and unspoken, which impinge upon him in the interlocutory situation, Rousseau is repeatedly discomfited when he commits himself to speech and thus concludes: 'Le parti que j'ai pris d'écrire et de me cacher est précisément celui que me convenoit.'[48] Likewise it is in writing that Strindberg becomes master of himself and of his life. Only he does not intend to hide himself: there, as so many commentators follow him in remarking ('This shyness drives me to writing'(I:186)), he is not shy.

But shyness (*blygsel*) does not in itself provide an adequate explanation for this mechanism, any more than the satisfaction of Strindberg's 'urge to utter everything his thought produced' (18:64) is simply a matter of his mental health. The elaborate undertaking, which situated language at the intersection of concealing and revealing, truth and lie, purity and filth, is far more deeply ambivalent. In *Gothic Rooms*, Dr Borg supplies another catalyst of the written word in 'modesty' (*blygsamheten*): 'Modesty forbids us to speak of it, therefore it is a good thing it is written, the printed word is silent and wounds no one' (40:25), and two related passages, one comparatively early, the other late, indicate the complexity of the tension that exists between the various constituents involved. In the section 'His Best Feeling' in *A Blue Book*, the written word is described as more than just the conventional attire of thought. At its purest, it becomes both a cloak of modesty *and* a vehicle of truth:

When a man writes a letter to a really good friend, or rather, to the woman he loves, he dresses up in holiday attire; it is beautiful of course, and in the silent letter, on the white page, he gives his best feelings. One's tongue and the spoken word are so polluted by daily use that they could not speak out loud the beautiful things which the pen says silently.

This is not a matter of posing or posturing, there is no question of deceit when the soul one encounters in a correspondence is better than the one displayed in everyday life. A lover is not untrue in his letter. He does not pretend to be any better than he is, he becomes better, and at that moment he *is* better. In those moments he is true. They are the greatest life affords. (47:731)

Here Strindberg once again suggests that not only Babel but the very existence of language predicates man's fallen state - the imagery, for example, abuts such statements as the observation in *The Great Highway* on Aphrodite, born naked 'without even a vine leaf with which to cover herself, for clothes are only a consequence of the Fall of Man' (51:18). And yet, in its written form (and typically, Strindberg thinks in terms of a letter, the direct address to an absent addressee), language nevertheless represents the way in which social hypocrisy is circumvented and purity and truth achieved.

Similarly, a passage in *The Son of a Servant*, in which he discusses the discrepancies between Schiller's considered foreword to *Die Räuber*, and the furiously composed text itself, discloses the principle which permits him to accept the truth of written discourse:

> Was Schiller being truthful when he wrote the play, and false, when he wrote the preface? Just as truthful on both occasions, for man is a divided being and appears now as natural man and now as social man. At his desk, in solitude when the silent letters were written down on the page, Schiller seems, like other, generally young writers, to have been under the influence, while at work, of the blind play of his natural instincts, without consideration for people's judgement, without a thought for the public or for laws and constitution. (18:277)

Although Strindberg could sometimes reject inspiration precisely because it seemed to indicate the author's absence from the words he wrote ('How then could one dare to depend upon a writer's words, when he has written them down in a condition of partial insanity... His mind has gone its own way, and when it has arrived at the end, the writer is not there with it' (16:54)), he normally accepts 'that the writer in his fever is led in the right direction' (VII:103) and subscribes to the notion of inspiration as a privileged discourse, one that is authentic and full. It cuts through social circumlocutions and facilitates a return to the truthful, prelapsarian discourse of natural man. In such moments language incarnates the self. It is not something distinct from the writer who uses it, and no longer an instrument open to abuse. It reveals the writer because language and self coincide.

II

Perhaps the most incisive comment on all these references to whiteness, purity, shyness, silence, and solitude, was passed, however, in another context, by Charles Darwin. When Darwin came, in *The Expression of the Emotions in Man and Animals*, to review 'The Nature of the Mental States which induce Blushing', he observed: 'These consist of shyness, shame, and modesty; the essential element in all being self-attention... It is not the simple act of reflecting on our own appearance, but the thinking what others think of us, which excites a blush.'[49] Moreover, as Christopher Ricks points out, in *Keats and Embarrassment*, 'the word "self-attention" had become the supreme subject and animus for the artist.'[50] And the self-attention which Strindberg bestows on himself is, as with Rousseau, of precisely the binary kind that Darwin identifies. For if, in their writing, they place themselves out of reach of an immediate interlocutor, who might interrupt, curtail, or misinterpret their spoken discourse, they live their lives before spectators, both fancifully, in their day-to-day affairs, and in time through the words they present to the reader's gaze.

On a level determined by commercial requirements, both writers obviously publicize, as well as publish, themselves. They wish to be seen and therefore exhibit their exceptionality. 'J'aimerois mieux être oublié de tout le genre humain que regardé comme un homme ordinaire',[51] Rousseau remarks, in words that Strindberg might easily have substituted for the second epigraph to *The Red Room*: 'Rien n'est si désagréable que d'être pendu obscurément'. Or as a recent autobiographer, Ivar Lo-Johansson, observes: 'Anonymous notoriety is an impossibility.'[52]

Furthermore, this dimension of Strindberg's activity is related to what might be termed presence via provocation, in which the reaction his words incite provides evidence that he has made his mark. Again, this is a very basic level indeed. As George Steiner comments, in his essay 'The Language Animal': 'We *are* so far as we can declare ourselves to be, and have full assurance of our asserted existence only when other identities register and reciprocate our life signals,'[53] and whether by polemic, in the shock aroused by the removal of verbal inhibitions, or in the resolve to strip himself naked, writing confers a feeling of ontological security on Strindberg. Nowhere, except perhaps in Rousseau, is a preoccupation with what others see in him so apparent as in Strindberg, and it is so central a factor because the opinion others have of him prevents him from being himself. It is to their intervention that he attributes what he diagnoses as his 'will-less character': '"What will people say?"' was then a constant refrain. And thus his self was eaten away, so he could never be himself, always depended upon the wavering opinions of other people, and never believed in himself, except on the few occasions when he felt his energetic soul work independently of his will' (18:15). Moreover, these privileged moments occur when, removed from the sight of his fellow men, Strindberg experiences the plenitude that writing affords: 'When I come home, however, and sit down at my desk, that's when I live', he declares, in *Alone* (38:155), while in the chapter of *The Son of a Servant* entitled 'He Becomes a Writer', he records how 'Now at last he had found his mission, his role in life, and his disjointed being began to find its form' (18:343). It is on paper, in writing, that his self takes shape.

Unfortunately, however, as Steiner goes on to remark, the communication of presence by language is both a negative and a positive accomplishment:

> It is in the reciprocal nature of the statement of identity, in the need for echo, be it savagely contrary, to confirm one's own being, that lies the root of the Hegelian paradox: the need of one living entity for the presence of another, and the fear and hate engendered by that need.[54]

Only by provoking a response will Strindberg know his words have been received, and what his militant strategies of attack and defence clearly demonstrate is the contingent nature of his undertaking. He requires another opinion, even as he resents and rejects it. But by making a virtue of the 'law of accommodation' and utilizing the multiplicity of the self which encounters with others help him to discern, Strindberg follows Rousseau in presenting his personality as a series of shifting facades, a sequence of roles in which he satisfies a desire to be interesting at any price and also avoids both the fear of being circumscribed within the character with which he is endowed by others, and the feeling of incompleteness or rejection evoked in the suggestion that he is 'overlooked' (*förbigången*), a practice which suggests what R. D. Laing has termed 'meta-identities'. Reading Laing in the light of Darwin's far briefer observation, is to gain a substantial insight into the type of self-identity elaborated in Strindberg's (or Rousseau's) autobiographical writing:

> *In concreto*, rather than *in abstracto*, self-identity ('I' looking at 'me') is constituted not only by our looking at ourselves, but also by our looking at others looking at us and our reconstitution and alteration of these views of others about us. At this more complex, more concrete level, self-identity is a synthesis of my looking at me with my view of others' view of me. These views by others of me need not be passively accepted, but they cannot be ignored in my development of a sense of who I am. For even if a view of another by me is rejected it still becomes incorporated in its rejected form as part of my self-identity. My self-identity becomes my view of me which I recognize as the negation of the other person's view of me. Thus 'I' becomes a 'me' who is being misperceived by another person. This can become a vital aspect of my view of myself. (E.g., 'I am a person whom no one really understands.')[55]

It is the 'misperception' in what others think of them which so often preoccupies both writers. Instead of the unstable but free relationship to others which most people tolerate, Rousseau and Strindberg experience another's gaze as primarily hostile. Rousseau, as Jean Starobinski points out, regards himself as 'la victime d'un regard anonyme, d'un spectateur sans identité...le témoin hostile, qui n'est personne en particulier, devient virtuellement *tout le monde*...un Œil omniscient.' [56] Similarly, Strindberg, informed that the golden eye in a window of Klara Church which dominated the landscape of his early years, is 'God's eye' (18:27), always feels himself under observation and later maintains that 'The eye of the ruler of the world (*Världsstyraren*) is not blind' (47:704). Thus, whether the observer he detects is Ibsen, in the act of appropriating his life as the material source for *The Wild Duck* or *Hedda Gabler*,[57] or 'The Invisible One' who keeps him 'under total supervision' (XII:286), his private life is always a public spectacle.

Confronted by others, therefore, Rousseau and Strindberg seem about to lose themselves: the image which they have of their identity is undermined and fretted away by the summary conception that others form of them. 'L'essence de mon être est-elle dans leurs regards?' Rousseau asks,[58] while Strindberg reveals a recurring nightmare in which 'Someone who has lived alone goes out into the world and sees and hears. Then he discovers how everyone has created their own image of him. He sees in their expressions, hears in their words, how they have transformed him. When one of them speaks out loud and says what they think of him he finds it horrible. It is not him but another, although fashioned out of all his wickedness and that of the speaker.'[59]

This is the real source of the anguish experienced by both Rousseau and Strindberg when the words in which they speak prove inadequate as a means of self-representation. 'Qu'il seroit doux de vivre parmi nous, si la contenance extérieure étoit toujours l'image des dispositions du cœur',[60] Rousseau exclaims, in the *Discours sur les sciences et les arts*. As in Swedenborg, perfect communication would dispense with words, and when enlisted to reveal the true Jean-Jacques to his interlocutors, who traduce his image and transform his unique value into the kind of superficial, limiting category that Strindberg identifies with an 'automaton' or 'musical box', speech is wholly inadequate. 'Moi présent on n'auroit jamais su ce que je valois', Rousseau explains, and thus provides the context for his retreat to literature in order to 'rendre mon âme transparente aux yeux du lecteur'.[61] And the loss of confidence in the capacity of language to reflect the world and convey the perceptions of one individual to another, is in fact evident in its dramatic presentation to the reader (in whose eyes they are seeking to restore themselves) by means of the two paradigmatic scenes of lie and deception with which they commence their autobiographies. Just as Jean-Jacques discovered the impotence of the spoken word as a means of self-representation from his inability to lie when 'les apparences me condannoient',[62] so Johan learns that telling the truth in a house where (as at Bossey) 'lies were punished without mercy' (18:16), is no guarantee that he will be accepted for what he knows himself to be. Whether from shyness, shame, or modesty, the discovery of the theft causes him to blush, and he then compounds the supposed crime by rebutting the accusation, thus discovering that the language to which he entrusts himself does not redeem him from these false assumptions. In short, both Strindberg and Rousseau find themselves miscast, and they go on to present the moment as irreparable. 'From that day on Johan lived in perpetual disquiet' (18:18), Strindberg declares; 'Dès ce moment je cessai de jouir d'un bonheur pur, et je sens aujourdui même que le souvenir des charmes de mon enfance s'arrête là', claims Rousseau.[63] It marks an end of innocence, a close to early childhood, and the expulsion into the snares of language which repeats, on a personal level, something of the disaster of Babel - the loss of which both authors will spend a lifetime exculpating in writing.[64]

'But Johan blushes' (18:17). Even the feature which propels his fall seems to substantiate Darwin and demonstrate that the nature of Strindberg's self-attention is directed as much to what others think of him, as to himself. And from the conclusion to the first volume of *The Son of a Servant* and the Foreword to *Miss Julie*, via *Vivisections*, to the deliberations of *A Blue Book*, he insists that a person's character exists largely as a construct in other people's minds, and that in fact 'firmness of character is characterlessness.'[65] This argument, fostered as it is by the analysis of his own emotional lability, encourages him to resist the one-dimensionality of the roles in which his contemporaries would confine him (and into which, he argues, in the essays 'Is Character a Role?', (27:617f), and 'Pose and Gesture' (47:679), so many of them congeal), and to reverse the conventional notion of character, whether in life or literature, with its stress on the qualities of firmness and consistency, and the positive moral connotations they imply. This is the view of the ironically named Blacksmith in *The Great Highway*, who has forged 'a real character' for himself and proudly boasts his resistance to change (51:46), and *The Son of a Servant*, written, as Strindberg informed Bonnier, to 'explore the whole concept of character - on which of course the whole of literature rests' (V:343), may be read as a defence of the inconsistent and changeable Johan against the prevailing ideal of the 1880s and its point of departure in Ibsen's *Brand*:

> Don't be one thing today, one thing yesterday,
> And something quite different a year from now.
> Be what you have to be
> Wholly and completely, not
> A little bit here and a little bit there.[66]

As Strindberg would argue, 'Simple minds always speak of contradiction and inconsistencies, but everything that lives is made up of elements that are not homogeneous, yet have to be opposites in order to hold together, like those forces which draw unlike to unlike' (47:792). Thus he praises Ophelia as 'an unconscious attempt to present the outline of a character with all the nuances that the vulgar call inconsistencies' (50:77), and stressed his own achievement in creating, in Miss Julie, a character so overdetermined by physiological, psychological, and circumstantial influences that she emerges as strangely free of the normally inhibiting Naturalist characterization, with its stifling fatalism. His conception of the characterless character, as embodied in Miss Julie, Erik XIV, or himself, is therefore an expression of the conviction, which acquaintance with the theories of Ribot and Bernheim only confirmed, that character is not one and indivisible but many and various, and that, however sensitive its portrayal, it would always elude complete representation. As he indicated, in a typical contemporary image:

> Note how many frames must be taken in sequence by the cinema
> photographer to reproduce a single movement, and even then the image
> is blurred. There is a missing transition in every vibration. When a
> thousand shots would be needed for one arm movement, how many
> myriads would not be required to depict a human soul? The writer's
> delineations of human beings are for that reason only summaries,
> outlines, all of them imperfect and all half false. (50:77)

These difficulties notwithstanding, his own writing is largely concerned with retrieving a just image of himself from the bowdlerized versions put about by others. Superficially, he feels that people (and not only Ibsen) are continually reading and

writing his life. And just as his enthusiasm for photography did not extend to the taking of unauthorised images of himself, so he did not wish to fasten in any one else's text. Particularly in the early 1890s, his letters are filled with suppositions of plots, both in life and literature, in which he figures. Guilty himself of speculating in the destinies of his acquaintances, he infers that they are likewise engaged, thus betraying his sense of being constantly the object of other people's attention, as well as of his own. But as Torsten Eklund has pointed out, his fears were not without foundation, for he appeared in Ola Hansson's *Fru Ester Bruce* (1893), Adolf Paul's story 'Med flaska och det ärliga ögat' (1895), parts of which were revived in Paul's memoirs of Strindberg in 1915, and Przybyszewski's *Homo Sapiens* (1895), as well as in Munch's paintings and lithographs.[67] Undoubtedly, such attention contributed to the sense of persecution which dominates the early stages of the Inferno crisis, and on the way to the creation, in *Inferno,* of a formal narrative structure that would integrate the disparate parts of this experience, his letters already offer many preliminary drafts in the art of reclaiming his destiny from other hands; as he told Paul, in 1894: 'I have learned how to correct chance' (X:67). But the process is exemplified best by an earlier text, *A Madman's Defence*, which according to its pseudonymous narrator Axel, was written to pre-empt the most terrible of all conceivable destinies, namely that his wife, Maria, would remarry or 'live sumptuously [with her Danish lesbian lover] on the income of my "collected works" and trace the story of my life as seen through the eyes of a hermaphrodite' (MD:245). He has to write the true narrative of his marriage in order to defend himself against the possibility of a false, literally perverse, account.

This specific anxiety is related to a general feeling that 'people demand he perform the role they have chosen for him, and in which he then easily remains stuck fast' (48:834). It is as if by 'rubbing up against other people...he had lost the best part of himself through the law of accommodation...[and] developed into a characterless, smooth, sociable person' (24:164). Thus, like Borg in *By the Open Sea*, of whom this is said, he experiences a recurring need 'to go in search of himself in isolation' (24:102). For as the partner of yet another Maria observes, 'We are afraid of losing our identity through the assimilating power of love, and therefore we sometimes have to break out in order to feel that I am not you' (37:136), and Strindberg's own response to intercourse of any kind is described by Assir, in *The Isle of the Dead*, when, stung by the suggestion that he 'doesn't exist at all', he retorts: 'Oh yes I do, because I react to others; and if I stopped doing that, the others would engulf me with their egos, with their opinions, their fancies. They would kill me with their wills, I would cease to exist, and the whole struggle of my life has been to preserve my self.'[68]

This sense of the precariousness of individual identity, with which Strindberg invests so many of his characters, is strikingly similar to the condition that R.D. Laing defines as 'engulfment', whereby the subject's basic security is so low that practically any relationship, however tenuous, threatens to overwhelm him. Even their response is often as Laing charts it:

The main manoeuvre used to preserve identity under pressure from the dread of engulfment is isolation. Thus, instead of the polarities of separateness and relatedness based on individual autonomy, there is the antithesis between complete loss of being by absorption into the other person (engulfment), and complete aloneness (isolation).[69]

This illuminates Borg's repossession of himself, 'isolated like a cosmic splinter', in *By the Open Sea* (24:29), and accords with the image that Strindberg circulates of himself in his last years: 'In the end he cannot go out, because people's glances alight on him, penetrate his skin, and poke into his heart' (48:834). And this rediscovery or concentration of himself 'within his own skin' (37:144) is effected in his case by writing, which is an expression of 'the instinct of differentiation, not to be another but to be oneself' (VII:247). In fact the formulation 'His position was false, and he wanted it to be immaculate (*ren*)' in *The Son of a Servant* (18:117), is typical of the impulse to withdraw into the silence and purity of the printed word. For in extreme situations, personal intercourse threatens to overwhelm Strindberg and his characters with the impurity, dirt, and disorder associated in *Armageddon* with Dimona. According to Max, in *Gothic Rooms*, it is especially 'in a double-bed that one loses one's self, one's self respect, one's human dignity. It is there one sells one's soul and learns the art of concealment' (40:296), and Strindberg is haunted by the possibility that he can even be polluted in his absence by a woman's ability to draw him into intercourse with other men. As he writes in *The Occult Diary* (6 September 1901) of Harriet Bosse: 'Unknown men pollute me by the glances with which they pollute her...If she is free and has an affair with another man, she hands over my soul and transfers my love to a man, and thus causes me to live in a forbidden relationship with a man's soul or body or both!' Or as Max pithily observes: 'They seek *her*, and find *him*, for he is within blocking the way' (40:210).

In fact this spectre is often raised in the 1900s. Ten days later, he records how Harriet 'goes about befouling my soul which during my Inferno period I washed fairly clean. It is as if, through her, I entered into forbidden relationships with men and other women' (this last phrase being added above the line), and similar fears are expressed in *A Blue Book* (46:179), *Queen Christina* (39:251), and the third part of *To Damascus*, where the Tempter explains, 'I was so constituted that I couldn't go out with her in company because I felt she was soiled by other men's glances...the whole of my existence began to be perverted into a spiritual concubinage with strange men - which was against my nature which has always craved *woman*!' (29:327), as well as in *He and She*, and in the fascination with which he variously related the circulation among a group of friends, of what numerous letters and a late Vivisection describe as everyone's 'Aspasia', a figure derived from the emancipated Norwegian, Dagny Juel, whom Strindberg first encountered in the company of Edvard Munch, and later lost to the Polish writer, Stanislaw Przybyszewski. Indeed, the matter is never far from his attention, for to elide the distinction between men would, like the erasure of all difference between man and woman, be a violation of the 'natural' order his writing is engaged to distinguish and maintain: 'if differences do not keep them apart, then the whole world would be perverse' (40:267). Thus he tells an unknown correspondent that 'for the man a love affair is in fact only a delight in so far as it is between two souls, and every interference from outside seems like filth' (VII:29), warns his friend Bengt Lidforss that 'screwing a man's wife is perverse! It's a mixing of seed!' (IX:357), and explains the jealousy felt by Johan for his successor in the favours of his housekeeper on Kymmendö as a necessary act of mental purification:

> He had deposited pieces of his soul in this girl's; he had treated her as an equal, interested himself in her destiny...Furthermore, he had mixed his blood with hers, given impulses, tuned the fine strings of his nerves in harmony with hers, so that they already belonged to one another, and now along came someone else and poked his nose in where he had tried to create order, cut off his electrical contact, retuned the strings, spoiled his work and brought disharmony to his soul, which he had been careless enough to graft on to a woman's... (19:91)

In this context, therefore, where to 'wash oneself clean' (*tvätta sig ren*) and 'exonerate oneself' (*rentvå sig*) are related terms on which Strindberg often lays stress, his committal to the purity of the silent paper effects both a cleansing and a redemption from the loss of self incurred through contact with others. It is employed to preserve both his person and the categories with which he confronts the world from violation, and it is thus not entirely fanciful to see, in the solitary act of writing, an onanistic retreat that rescues him from the coition of spoken discourse, enables him to master the other in private, and seems to offer an opportunity of keeping himself intact. Indeed, at times he appears to infer such a link himself. In writing to Ola' Hansson in 1889, he rejects Maudsley's diagnosis of masturbation as a symptom of degeneration, and relates it to a symptom of 'the strong ego which does not want to sacrifice its talent for dubious children who would become his competitors' (VII:247), and in his portrait of the artist, Alrik Lundstedt, speechlessness in the face of women leads him to retreat to the private delights of his organ loft.[70]

Sometimes casually, in the coarse vein of Flaubert or the Goncourts, at others drawing the kind of parallel between sexual and verbal ejaculation that Balzac espoused, writing is in any case frequently related to sexuality by Strindberg. 'I acknowledge that a woman's embrace resembles the joys of birth when a new thought is hatched [or] a beautiful image wells up', he concedes, to Littmansson, 'but the unsatisfied sexual instinct and half-hunger transforms itself into mental power. (I have written my strongest pieces - Miss Julie and Creditors - in 30 days during enforced celibacy.)' (X:130). As Asta Ekenvall has pointed out: 'For him sexual and mental production were closely related.'[71] *Miss Julie* he calls '1st Class Seed' (X:214) with which he has 'fertilized' others, and he regards his writing in general as a godlike procedure wherein he has 'begot with myself like Zeus a whole Olympus, fools and imposters, saints and children' (X:130). Moreover, the implication is almost always the same; if in *Black Banners*, Dr Borg argues that the sexual act should be effortless, like inspiration, Strindberg repeatedly identifies writing as an alternative form of intercourse, one in which he demonstrates his prodigious potency and the fertility of his invention which peoples a world. Sometimes the two appear to preclude each other ('My former wife could do what she wanted,' he tells Littmansson (X:131), 'but I also *wrote* what I wanted, and therefore my spirit was never dominated, only my sexual impulses'), but this is not necessarily so, unless the writer is a woman, in which case Strindberg generally regards her as physiologically infertile ('with us the marriages of women who write usually distinguish themselves by their sterility' (VR:101)), since she encroaches upon a male domain and so sows (or reaps) only disorder. 'One ought not to demand of the artist, who gives, that he should become a woman - that he should receive',[72] Nietzsche remarks, in a summary of contemporary ideology, and, as Ekenvall continues, 'for Strindberg active sexuality and mental curiosity become synonymous, become potency, a proof of masculinity, while in the same way sexual and mental passivity become specific female characteristics.'[73] Thus Strindberg appropriates the scriptor's role in life and in literature, and boasts of 'everything I have shaken out of my britches! although Sweden was stony ground! Novels and poetry, plays both good and bad, histories of Sweden and China, and four kids, a fifth on the way, and *two* wives' (IX:372).

The claim is well founded. And yet Karl-Åke Kärnell is surely correct to argue that 'on the intellectual and literary level, he assigns himself the dream role of the potent man, the vigorous procreator, which periodically at least he feared he could not manage in marital intercourse.'[74] It is this which gives the edge to his insistence that Sweden's hostility towards him depends upon its hatred of 'fertility', that Viktor Rydberg's jealousy as a writer is 'the unfruitful woman's terrible envy and hatred of the fruitful' (IX:372), and that publishers either demand he 'writes chastely (castratedly)' or insist on cuts, which is to 'remove my testicles' (IV:240). For he wrote to convince his fatherland that he was potent, and he wanted every word to be published so that 'sterile and sexless Sweden will see what a fecund spirit they hated because he was fecund and they were sterile' (VI:297).

Strindberg's consolation is therefore that he 'puts other people's brains into molecular movement with my pen' (IX:374), that he 'recognizes (his) children' in another writer's book, or sends a theatre audience home 'pregnant with my mind's seed' (X:130), and he readily conceives himself the father and author to other texts besides his own: 'Strange that I should always be the Father who provides the spermatoza, fertilizes' (XI:146). But in the cluster of images concerning suggestion, seeds of thought (*tankefrö*) and molecular movement in the sphere of the mind, which dominates his writing in this register, the tension between engulfment and self-preservation remains a factor, even when the discourse to which Strindberg commits himself is written and not spoken. For if *Hedda Gabler* delights him because it seems to bear the features of *The Father* and *Creditors* (thus he writes exultantly to Birger Mörner and claims paternity: 'Observe how my seeds have fallen into Ibsen's own brain pan - and sprouted! now he bears my semen and is my uterus!' (VIII:205)), the process could easily be reversed. On one occasion, his 'mental life has received in its uterus a tremendous ejaculation of seed from Friedrich Nietzsche, so that I feel full like a bitch in my belly' (VIII:112), and he is continually on guard against being cast in the woman's role wherein he would become another man's creation and so contravene what he regarded as 'natural' law. For woman is created by man (as The Lady in *To Damascus* is given a name by The Unknown): the man 'fills her with his content and can find a good helpmate in this, his second self, which he has trained to be like himself' (17:164), and the image of 'the bitch' with which Strindberg compares himself under impregnation from Nietzsche is otherwise evoked in situations of degenerate sexuality, in *Miss Julie*, where Diana forsakes her breeding and her chastity and anticipates her mistress by coupling with 'the gatekeeper's pug' (23:120), or in the material from an unknown correspondent that contributed something to the conception of *Creditors*, and of which he remarks: 'Anna's character is interesting, a modern degenerate, who pays no heed to her stock but like a bitch, copulates with several' (VII:29). Hence Strindberg is circumspect in his relationships: 'Why don't I write to him myself?' he remarks to Edvard Brandes, of Georg: 'Because I am afraid. Afraid of him as of all fertile spirits, afraid as I was of Zola, Björnson, Ibsen, of being made pregnant with their seed and giving birth to another's progeny' (VI:134).

In the 'Battle of the Brains', which these passages delineate, each hears, in company, or in the presence of books, 'human voices bearing words, which wanted to eat their way through his ears into his brain, shed their seeds, and then like weeds choke his own sowing and transform the field he had cultivated with so much effort into a natural meadow resembling all the others' (24:77). Encouraged by the experiments of Charcot and Bernheim, and by an earlier tradition deriving from Mesmer and transmitted, in a form well known to Strindberg, by Hartmann, who claimed that 'the fundamental phenomena of mesmerism, or animal magnetism, are at length looked upon as scientifically accredited,'[75] Strindberg embraced the idea that people easily imprint themselves on one another. In *A Madman's Defence*, Axel sees the features of the Danish woman embossed on Maria's face (MD:246); in *By the Open Sea*, Borg interprets his Maria as a 'chaos of past stages, these bits of roles which she had successively played in life, masses of shifting reflexes from men, whom she had tried to win and adapted herself to' (24:114); and in later prose works, Strindberg assumes the Romantic-Realist tradition of Balzac, Hoffmann, and Dickens, in which a character's inner feelings are imprinted upon his surroundings. Inanimate matter is endowed with life. It displays a person's innermost thoughts, and bears legible traces of the past which under the informed, interpretative eye of the Narrator in *The Roofing Feast* or the compiler of *A Blue Book*, it also lays bare as a text in which to read the hidden self. As the latter observes: 'When a married man comes home from a ball with his wife, he ought to look at her handkerchief, which she has fingered the whole evening. Then he would doubtless see with whom she would most like to have danced'(46:188).

Where the relationship is one between man and woman, Strindberg's ideas are often in keeping with those of other nineteenth-century writers. Michelet, for example, in *L'Amour*, held that 'La femme fécondée une fois, imprégnée, portera partout son mari en elle. Voilà ce qui est démontré. Combien dure la première imprégnation? Dix ans? vingt ans? toute la vie? Ce qui est sur, c'est que la veuve a souvent du second mari des enfants semblables au premier.'[76] And prompted by Prosper Lucas's *Traité philosophique de l'hérédité naturelle*, both Zola and Daudet regarded woman as tied to her first lover by indissoluble physiological bonds. He imprinted on her an ineradicable trace which might be passed on even to the features of her children by other men: 'Elle ne l'aima jamais avec passion; elle reçut plutòt son empreinte', Zola writes, in *Madeleine Férat*, and again, 'Lorsque Madeleine s'était oubliée dans les bras de Jacques, sa chair vierge avait pris l'empreient ineffacable du jeune homme.'[77]

When Strindberg sees in woman an empty vessel, a clean slate, or a vacant place awaiting the creative intervention of man ('All the beauty we see in her', Dr Borg remarks, in *Gothic Rooms* (40:299), 'is only our own projections upon her white and empty screen'), his discourse is therefore not unduly singular. But it becomes more individual when, in the urgency of his desire to abrogate the scriptor's role, he continually reveals himself alert to the way in which character is engraved, traced, or inscribed by one subject on another. What fascinates him, moreover, is not the traditional concept of a secure, indelible inwardness, but the possibility of many and various editions, scripts which can be erased and traces superimposed, one upon the other. People, in short, represent white pages, which the stronger covers with his style. 'He really confirms the idea I share with the philosopher of a *tabula rasa*,' the Narrator says, of his companion, in the story 'The Battle of the Brains', 'and now, after he is newly washed, I feel a great desire to write in my handwriting on his tablet' (22:140-1). Gustav, in *Creditors*, reminds Tekla of their first meeting when 'you were a little, lovable child; a small slate on which your parents and your governess had scribbled a few lines which I had to scratch out. And then I wrote new texts, to my own liking, until you thought you were ready written' (23:256-7), and the image recurs, years later, in *To Damascus III*, when the Tempter speaks of the wife from whom he has been parted as no longer the virgin surface he had once known but 'another: she, my unblemished white sheet of paper was scribbled all over with scrawls; her beautiful, clear features were tuned in harmony with the satyr-like visages of strange men' (29:327). In this instance the experience with which Strindberg is concerned reflects conflicts in his marriage to Harriet Bosse, which are also charted in *The Occult Diary* and imaginatively explored in *The Roofing Feast* (44:49), but what he writes only confirms an earlier occasion when, in 1876, he wrote to Siri von Essen of his fear that Wrangel 'will scrape out every word I wrote in your soul' (1:350).

Character is thus presented as a fluid coalescence of numerous texts, the product of many discourses, and Strindberg indicates that people become copies or transcripts of one another. They not only bear the ineradicable imprint of their society and age (Naturalism's milieu and moment), and the genetic trace of their birth; they are also marked with the imprint of each other's personalities, and his modernity is nowhere more apparent than in his perception of the complex intertextuality of identity. The self, he tirelessly affirms, is compiled from many discourses, 'a composite resumé of parents, educators, friends, books' (18:436). But this has several implications for his autobiographical project. Firstly, common to the whole complex of imagery centred on *tankefrö* and the inscription of traces, there is a desire on Strindberg's part to be his own source, the author of himself, and progenitor of his own life. And this project is in turn interfaced with the abiding anxiety regarding his own possible lack of identity, an anxiety which can only be dispelled by writing but which, paradoxically, the very act of writing reinforces and prolongs.

The situation is intricate. In the first place, it is the white page which captivates Strindberg's imagination. For without writing he is threatened by emptiness (*tomheten*) or vacuity (*tomrummet*), an emptiness which he repeatedly evokes, and into which he fears he might disappear. Superficially, the notion is commonplace, as when, in *The Isle of the Dead*, he revives (probably inspired by Locke's image of the pre-mnemonic mind as a white paper, void of all characters, in Book Two of *An Essay Concerning Human Understanding*) the trope of memory as a book: 'If for a moment you could lose your memory, you will become like a book with white pages, less than a newborn child, and would have to begin again!'[78] This recalls the scene at the graveside of Struve's child, in *The Red Room*, where

> Falk remained bent in thought over the grave and stared down into the depths; at first he saw only a square of darkness, but gradually a light speck emerged, which grew and took on a definite form. It was round and shining, white like a mirror. It was the uninscribed tablet on the young child's coffin, which shone through the darkness and reflected only the unbroken light of heaven. (5:255-6)

What haunts him is the spectre of an unwritten character. He is afraid of leaving no real trace, of writing so faintly that, as he in fact implies in the account of a vanish acquaintance in *A Blue Book* (46:86-7), he would disappear, and it is therefore he finds it so natural, in the vivisection, 'Soul Murder', to compare the suppression of a manuscript to murder, since 'a blank space (*tomrum*) thereby arises in a writer's soul' (22:194). The missing text represents a lacuna through which the writer vanishes, and Strindberg's *angoisse* before the empty page is thus not the common dread of being unable to write, but trepidation in the face of a surface that does not signify - or rather, signifies only too clearly an absence. The white page is in fact a void which the agoraphobic Strindberg must populate, and his writing obeys an impulse to people it with words, an impulse that is betrayed in the unlikely context of the historical tale, 'At the Bier Side in Tistedalen', where he contrasts the fertility of the writer with the impotent warrior king, Charles XII, who lived 'in a perpetual aversion to providing his country with a successor to the throne'. As the doctor exclaims, over the dead king's corpse:

> Imagine, this hand, which wielded the rapier so proudly, could not coax a light quill pen across a sheet of smooth paper...then the mechanism

refused to obey, then it wavered and shook, as if he had got agoraphobia (*torgsjuka*) in the middle of the white field. Indeed, he said himself he got dizzy when he had to cross the sheet of paper. But it wasn't only that; his thoughts, which ought to have marched forward in straight columns, tripped one another up, trampled on one another's toes, and once when I read a letter to his sister, which he asked me to correct, the words lay there in long strips, tangled up as if one saw the whole muddle of his mind unwound... (12:383)

In this episode of Strindberg's long-running conflict with a figure whose role, throughout his career, approximates to that of a Yeatsian opposite, the pen is matched against the sword, and word against deed. But in the image of the king's 'torgsjuka', the text discloses a hidden identity between the two antagonists. For in both *The Son of a Servant* (18:316) and 'Deranged Sensations' (27:601), as well as by implication in the story, 'Short Cuts', Strindberg describes his own agoraphobia. Here, however, he attributes the condition to his opponent, so asserting once more the supremacy of the new aristocracy of the pen and nerves over the appearance of manliness decked out in the uniform of tradition. As such the passage resumes hostilities in a conflict that has been fought on this ground in, for example, *The New Kingdom* and *A Madman's Defence*.[79] More immediately, however, it maintains that character is clearly written as characters by those courageous enough to traverse 'the white field' of paper which, to be sure, is readily turned by Strindberg's pen into a field of battle.

Rather than establish a character which is single and indivisible, however, writing fosters multiplicity. If in general 'the danger of a long life is that the many roles begin to get muddled up, like an actor's wigs and costumes when he moves' (47:681), then the writer's life, with its multitude of assumed or invented roles which provide 'reincarnations already here [on earth]' (46:113), is especially vulnerable to the dispersal of identity. The danger is illustrated by Alrik Lundstedt's delight in metaphor, which transforms him into a Gyntian metamorphoser, a man in constant danger of fatally displacing himself, while the figure of Askanius, in the late novel, *The Scapegoat*, who 'shed his skin, and changed his character and face every ten minutes' (44:183), portrays the artist as a protean but anonymous creature who, in spite of a compulsion to confess himself (44:119), remains ultimately unknown and unknowable.[80]

Strindberg is in fact continually aware of the Keatsian paradox in which it is lack of identity that characterizes the poet. But unlike Keats, who could appreciate that 'the poetic Character...has no self', and accept that 'Not one word I ever utter can be taken for granted as an opinion growing out of my identical nature',[81] Strindberg found this possibility the cause of endless misgivings. Although he was sometimes able to transform the fact 'that the poet's life was a shadow life, that he had no self, but only lived in other selves' into yet another instance of his own fertility ('But is it so certain that the poet lacks a self because he does not have only one? Perhaps he is richer, and possesses more than the others' (18:436)), he was more inclined to regard his situation as a kind of sleepwalking in which he could easily mislay himself: 'It seems to me as if I am walking in my sleep; as if poetry and life had got mixed up...Through so much writing my life has become a shadow life; it seems to me I no longer walk on earth but am suspended weightlessly in an atmosphere not of air but of darkness' (VI:298). Condemned by the practice of writing to address himself to an absent (or an imaginary) interlocutor, the indirectness of the mediation to which he entrusts himself causes Strindberg to slip into a world of hallucination where he is disembodied and overwhelmed by a dreamlike sense of unreality. Thus, in those moments when, as it were, he comes to himself, he doubts his identity. In one of the many notes for the short fable, 'Jubal Without a Self' (38:93-101), whose significance it is easy to overlook, unless its provisional title, 'Johan Without a Self', is recalled, he observes how 'Those who change their names, lose themselves', and in another, he once again speculates on the consequences of a life-time of role playing: 'The man who denies his identity and is thereby punished by losing himself.'[82] Moreover, in so far as Zachris, in *Black Banners*, embodies Strindberg's own deeply-rooted feelings of guilt about the parasitic nature of his writing, it is precisely in a lack of identity that the writer's role playing, or facility at identification, is located. Zachris, 'a selfless jelly, an unorganised matter that lived like a truffle on the roots of others' (41:211), 'had an enormous emptiness (*tomrum*) to fill and his impressionability was unbounded. He ate people, ate up their accomplishments, fed upon their private means, and possessed the ability to enter other lives...so that he confused his person with other people' (41:48).

To confuse oneself with another, however, is the destiny from which autobiographical discourse is employed to secure the subject. It is to become another's shadow, whereas the autobiographer wishes to relate his own story, in his own language. Indeed, confronted by the common patrimony of the language into which they are forced to translate themselves when they present themselves to another, autobiographers frequently speculate on the possibility of a means of utterance that is uniquely their own. Thus Rousseau recognizes the need for 'un langage aussi nouveau que mon projet',[83] and his role as the model autobiographer is perhaps nowhere more apparent than in this desire to secede from common discourse and inaugurate his own. What he has to communicate is so singular that even to instate himself within the common vulgate by means of a radical, particular choice of vocabulary and syntax (the style with which he leaves his signature upon the corpus of language), appears too shallow a gesture. He does not want an ideolect, but his own unrepeatable language.

But this vision of discovering what another copious autobiographer, Ivar Lo-Johansson, calls 'the only right words',[84] the conclusive words which body forth 'that full utterance which through all our stammerings is of course our only and abiding intention',[85] founders upon one of the fundamental principles of post-Saussurian thought, namely that 'La propriété privée, dans le domaine du langage, ça n'existe pas.'[86] The language in which the autobiographer seeks to convey himself not only precedes him; it is also held in common with other individuals, a shared circuit of exchange in which the newcomer finds the available words already inhabited. As Mikhail Bakhtin describes it

> When each member of a collective of speakers takes possession of a word, it is not a neutral word of language, free from the aspirations and valuations of others, uninhabited by foreign voices.... The word arrives in his context from another context which is saturated with other people's interpretations. His own thought finds the word already inhabited.... When one's own personal 'final' word does not exist then every creative plan, every thought, feeling and experience must be refracted through the medium of another person's word, style and manner, with which it is impossible to directly merge without reservation, distance and refraction.[87]

But if the language at the autobiographer's disposal is embedded in the conventions of his time, is beset by the contingent emphasis of the moment, and permeated by the social and intellectual inferences of the age, it is also by composing himself in words and behaving as if the lacunary nature of consciousness were an uninterrupted, reclaimable flow, that he is compelled to wonder at his own reality. For in the continual search for self-definition, he seems regularly to disappear into the text of which he is nominally the master, where he becomes not transparent but a property of the language in which he inscribes himself. As the intimate, lived experience passes into language, it is mediated by the interrelationship between the signifiers, which come in time to stand for the experience itself. As language displaces the past and person it is employed to represent (and the notion of presence is ironically evoked by the faculty of language as representation, the fabrication of a copy that replaces the original), it establishes a metaphorical narrative that secretes and accretes meanings which surpass and undermine the intention of the author and elaborate a narrative framework that subsumes the particles of autobiographical fact implanted in it. Private experience enters the domain of language and then the formal contract of literary genre, where it is enhanced with conceptual figures and stylistic devices, and becomes an item in the institution of literature, in Strindberg's case, a material deposit of late nineteenth-century social, intellectual, and literary history, which contributes in turn to the production of other discourses, both autobiographical and critical. It is the signifier which moves into the foreground; the empirical facts of the life are transformed into artifacts; sequence is endowed with meaning and condensed into design, and the truth or falsehood of the material, so challenging a question for earlier discussions of the genre, becomes very much a secondary matter once Freud establishes that what is spoken or written and not what might have happened, is what matters. The act of stripping oneself naked in public therefore remains what it has always been, a metaphor, and the autobiographer remains, for all his effort, behind the discourse he leaves after him. The author, indeed, becomes a figure of the text.

If, therefore, the defining words continue to elude him (if he remains, as Beckett suggests, 'unnamable'), then this search for an appropriate language transforms the autobiographer into a kind of language machine, compelled to produce ever more words on his own behalf as each verbal account, having proved itself incomplete, leaves him still 'The Unknown' or 'Not I'. The autobiographer's dilemma is indeed an intricate one. If his purpose is to return to his origins and establish identity by uncovering the continuity of his personality over the passage of a significant period of time, then he is committed to narrative. For it is by means of narrative that the individual establishes a relationship with the world, which helps him to recover coherence in the face of evanesence, subdue contingency by revealing a hidden causality or pattern, and create the image of self-identity through time that enables him to act. Life can only be recuperated as a plot and a spectacle, as a story which the individual claims for his own, and in which he establishes himself as the other whom he observes making his way through the confusion and accidents of the past towards the present. This is the process which has been so finely described by Freud in his analysis of 'Screen Memories', where he elaborates the essential distinction between the acting and the recollecting self:

> In the majority of significant and in other respects unimpeachable childhood scenes the subject sees himself in the recollection as a child, with the knowledge that this child is himself; he sees this child, however, as an observer from outside the scene would see him...Now it is evident that such a picture cannot be an exact repetition of the impression that was originally received. For the subject was then in the middle of the situation and was attending not to himself but to the external world.[88]

But in spite of the inevitable rupture between the recollected and the recollecting subject, it is by the imaginative process of story-telling, in the enchainment of the text, that the autobiographer shapes his life. In fact Rousseau dates the unbroken consciousness of himself from his earliest reading, and in Mme la Tribu's lending library he discovered other exemplary plots by means of which he could create a kind of specular image of himself through identification and reverie, and Ivar Lo-Johansson, too, records the transition from a time when memories were not yet enchained, and the past had not become a narrative composition, to a more consciously structured existence when he 'began as though playing with building blocks to fabricate with the aid of my memory connections between events which I had not even bothered about before...I consciously 'invented' people and occurences, and I made a kind of poetry or sketches out of them.'[89]

The autobiographer is therefore confined to a life in language, according to criteria which are often sustained by the conventions of the alternative, dominant genre, the novel, where language also fabricates a person, and narrative condenses a life into a destiny. And as Lacan writes, of the analogous discourse of the patient in analysis, by recounting a past event 'he has made it pass into the *verbe*, or more precisely, into the *epos* by which he brings back into present time the origins of his own person. And he does this in a language which allows his discourse to be understood by his contemporaries, and which furthermore presupposes their present discourse.'[90] Thus, while the language in which the autobiographer composes his narrative allows him a point of purchase which permits him to locate himself, either by assuming a personal pronoun which is open to everyone (and which, as Francis Hart has pointed out, is chosen to perform the structural role in the narrative for which it is variously designed),[91] or as a proper name, which 'guarantees the unity of our multiplicity |and| federates our complexity of the moment and our changes in time,'[92] each entry into what Lacan has termed the symbolic order, where the subject attempts to situate himself, represents an inevitable surrender to the vast, supra-personal archives of the word *and* a rupture of the self-narrator along the lines described by Freud in 'Screen Memories', but now inscribed in his use of language.

Even the image which the writer conceives of himself, therefore, becomes to some extent a misprision, differing only in scale to the misconceptions conceived of Rousseau and Strindberg in the paradigmatic scene of their respective autobiographies. For the 'I' who writes is both the subject of the discourse and the personal, historical object of his own verb, at once present and absent in the 'I was', where he is another. He is always represented by a stand in (his appearances, as the Unnamable remarks, in Beckett's novel, 'must have been put in by other parties')[93] and as Bakhtin observes:

> Even if he is the author of an autobiography, or of the most truthful of confessions, the writer nevertheless remains, as their creator, outside the world depicted in them. If I tell of (or write about) an event which has just happened to me, I, as the *teller* (or writer) of this event, am already outside that time-space in which this event has occurred. It is impossible to identify absolutely myself, my 'I', with that 'I' of which I am telling as it is to lift myself up by the hair.[94]

Since the self is only constituted in language (and thus, when written, requires the attention of a reader to re-animate it, as Lacan's many suggestions that the signifier is that which represents the subject for another signifier insistently imply),[95] it is a verbal construction essentially different from the events it recovers, as St Augustine was already aware: 'with regard to the past, when this is reported correctly what is brought out from the memory is not the events themselves (these are already past) but words conceived from the images of those events.'[96] Autobiography is therefore not something that exists in the past, awaiting narration. It is the story told, structured, and organized with all the devices of literature, and what it does not accomplish is the denuding of the self held out by the illusory promise of a unique, full language. It remains a reflection, the site of a temporal and logical organisation by which the writer produces, from the dialectic of his narcissistic identifications with the external views of himself in which he fears capture, an opaque image which, for the moment, he imagines to be true.

These are factors in writing the autobiographical discourse of the self which become increasingly prominent the further Strindberg proceeds with his project. Although initially he avoids the first person and its enticing promise of identity, the better to analyse himself in the spatial and temporal distance afforded both by the third person and by the mantle of a name (his forename, Johan, and the significant act of nomination in which he christens himself 'The Son of a Servant', and thereby assumes a destiny on the plane of myth), he is not unaware of the way in which he becomes a creature of the text, that he is in fact engaged in an inexhaustible cycle of attempts to capture the self. Indeed, he could find in one of his mentors, Ribot, a precise statement of the contradictory nature of his undertaking: 'le vrai *moi* est celui qui sent, pense, agit, sans se donner en spectacle à lui-même; car, il est par nature, par définition, un sujet; et pour devenir un objet, il lui faut subir une réduction, une adaptation à l'optique mentale qui le transforme et le mutile.'[97] The individual's conception of himself was, Strindberg knew, an abstraction, a specular image which gave back the contour of whatever technique is used to capture it ('Where does the self begin, and where does it end?' he asks, in *Jardin des plantes*, 'Is the eye adapted to the sun? Or does the eye create the phenomenon called the sun?' (27:354)). Notwithstanding the implied consent to prevailing nineteenth-century notions of character growth and development, which the basic linearity of the narrative method in the first volumes of 'the history of a soul's development' (*en själs utvecklingshistoria*) would seem to sustain, it therefore becomes clear that Johan is not encompassed by any of the images presented of him, and that the promise implicit in this narrative mode, that eventually the subject will be seen to have become himself, that with the turn of the page he will suddenly come into sight, will not be honoured. 'The self is not any one thing; it is a conglomeration of reflexes, a complex of instincts and desires which are alternately suppressed and unleashed' (18:218), he concludes, at the end of the first volume, and when he finishes the fourth, he is no closer to a final statement. He had embarked upon the autobiography because he found, when looking at himself, only 'a motley jumble which lacks substance, which changes its form according to the observer's point of view and which has perhaps no more reality than the rainbow, which is there to be seen, but which doesn't exist' (19:277). Now, having brought the enterprise to the moment of writing a conclusion, he can only gesture towards the words themselves as the problematic and by no means final version of himself:

> Where does the truth for which he was seeking lie? It lies here and there in the thousand printed pages; look them up, collect them, and see if they can be summarized, see if they are valid for longer than a year, five years, consider if they have a chance of being so, when that requires their receiving general acceptance. And do not forget that the truth cannot be found, since it is always in the process of continual development. (19:278)

'Development' (*utveckling*) thus becomes the negation of the being he set out to find. The 'true' self, he discovers, is no fixed image but a set of tensions, mutations, dialectical oppositions, which take up the discursive formations or determinacies that impinge upon the individual and make of him a complex montage of ideas, feelings, attitudes, gestures, misconceptions, and which cannot be conveyed as a single, evolving trace, however copious and circumstantial, but as the product of many traces which cover and recover one another, as in the engraved complexity of the design upon the vase from Benares, whose surface of interlacing lines and intricate patterning provides him during the experimental re-exploration of the past in which he engaged during the Inferno period, with a more sinuous and elaborate model for the record of the self he resolutely continued to pursue.

CHAPTER FOUR

Plot and Counter Plot or:
Reading and Composing the Text of the Self

Life is that which comes already constituted in literary language.
- Roland Barthes

My life has always tended to take the shape of novels...
- Strindberg to Hedlund

I

In her analysis of the way in which the modern critical notion of intertextuality has supplanted the concept of intersubjectivity, Julia Kristeva observes that 'tout texte se construit comme mosaique de citations, tout texte est absorption et transformation d'un autre texte.'[1] Each new work invites interpretation through its relation to other texts, which provide codes and conventions with which it can be read by a subjectivity which is, in Roland Barthes' provocative description, 'déjà lui-même une pluralité d'autres textes, de codes infinis, ou plus exactement: perdus (dont l'origine se perd).'[2] Moreover, even the most personal utterance reaches the receiver as a cultural as well as an expressive inheritance. Not only the language at an author's disposal, but the forms to which he succeeds and the contemporary discourses through which he interprets and renders his lived relation to the world, the discourses that is, which constitute the system of intelligibility in his text, are suprapersonal. The text produced can therefore be apprehended in its interplay with other texts, both literary and non-literary, rather than by its reduction to a private and personal utterance that recedes into an author's subjectivity, a subjectivity that is in any case largely composed of a montage of ideas, attitudes, and emotions which the writer has in common with his society, his class, and his profession.

In relation to the writing of autobiography, where the writer's life is itself a text to be read, interpreted, and re-written, these ideas assume a particular resonance, for it is in the transcription of the discursive formations and determinacies that have 'written' the life of the autobiographical subject into the text of the autobiographer that this general intertextuality becomes most palpable. The narrated life encompasses both a text to be read by the writer in the profusion of data accumulating in his wake, and the production of a more specific reading of other texts, first by the writer who decodes the patterns whereby the past becomes readable according to the available modes of insight and representation, and then by the reader, who brings his own experience of other texts to bear on recreating the relative stability of the writer's self-projection as it is assembled and takes shape in the figures of the text.

Indeed, Strindberg frequently drew attention to the way in which the self is composed of a plurality of texts, of how identity is produced by a multiplicity of competing and complementary discourses. In *The Red Room* characters are already described as an amalgam of 'ragged scraps' (*traslappar* - 5:236), an image that is developed in a self-analytical letter to Bjørnson in 1884, where Strindberg inventories his own 'ancient rats' nest of a soul, where scraps of old Christianity, shreds of art-worshipping paganism, shavings of pessimism, splinters of general world contempt lie jumbled together' (IV:144),[3] and with the writing of *The Son of a Servant* he discerns, in what in *The Roofing Feast* he will call 'this patchwork canvas of upbringing, textbooks, people, newspapers' (44:79), the script of a written corpus in which the self appears to be a veritable mosaic of quotations from a multitude of familiar and unfamiliar sources. Like Miss Julie and the other major characters, who are 'conglomerations of past and present cultures, scraps from books and newspapers, fragments of people, torn scraps of fine clothing that has become rags, in just the same way that the soul is patched together' (23:104), Johan is the formation of what in the *The Occult Diary* and *Inferno* Strindberg comes to portray as literally the currents that flow through him. A site traversed by forces and events rather than an individuated essence, he emerges as 'a patchwork' encompassing 'a quadroon of romanticism, pietism, realism and naturalism' (18:92), and just as Strindberg's evolutionary methodology encourages him to regard every individual as 'a geological record of all the stages of development through which his ancestors had passed' (19:46), which means that Johan bears the phylogenetic traces of his European past, of Arian ideas of caste, Christian asceticism, Renaissance hedonism, and an enlightened scepticism, so his ontogenetic history reveals him to be the offprint of his 'blood inheritance, temperament, position in society' (19:189), that is to say, as a contemporary article bearing the unique signature of a particular childhood. He is the legatee of a personal inheritance, but an inheritance that is also fostered by the public discourses, religious, social, scientific, philosophical, and artistic, of the period in which he lives, both as they contribute to his formation and as they provide the codes and conventions which establish the parameters within which his life may be represented in an autobiography. For as Michael Sprinker has pointed out, the written self is primarily 'the articulation of an intersubjectivity structured within and around the discourses available to it at any moment in time.'[4]

Since an autobiography is itself an event in the life it relates, a distinction between the way in which contemporary discourses inform the life related and their role in the method of its relation is difficult to maintain. In *The Son of a Servant*, Johan is, as the Narrator observes, 'a mirror which reflected every ray that struck it' (18:127). Consequently, any comprehensive account of this 'history of a soul's development 1849-67' requires not only evidence of his 'inheritance from his mother, father and wet nurse; the situation during pregnancy; the economic circumstances of the family; the attitudes and beliefs of his parents; the nature of his acquaintances, his school and teachers, his friends, his brothers and sisters, and household servants and so on' (18:452), as the Author acknowledges in the preface, but also of his encounters with specific and dispersed currents of nineteenth-century intellectual and political history, as is indeed the case in the later volumes, where Johan reflects in turn the rays emitted by Byron and Kierkegaard, Schopenhauer and von Hartmann, Darwin and Spencer, Rousseau and Marx, as well as the more diffuse but no less penetrating light cast upon him by Pietism, Socialism, or Naturalism. Like many autobiographies from Vico's *Autobiografia* onwards, a large part of *The Son of a Servant* is a text about texts, a book that traces and examines the origins of its own discourse in the discourses of other writers, and hence emphasizes the paradoxical lack of originality in the unique life of its subject. The text would, he told Bonnier, include 'the story of the origin of all my works, including commentaries on the circumstances in which they were written, their milieux, the ideas behind them, and their execution' (VI:18). Thus it also includes an account of the works that generated the discursive practice now known as 'Strindbergian'. But as the narrative converges upon the present of its narration, it becomes evident that these formative influences also constitute the same texts which the autobiographer has at his disposal to contrive the reconstruction of his life. It is by their light that he reads and writes his life; as he informs Bonnier once again: 'I have simply taken the corpse of the person I know best, and made readings in anatomy, physiology, psychology, history on the carcass' (V:344).

Moreover, in the projections which the individual writers make available, and especially in the scripts to be discovered in Myth, Literature, History, Psychology, Religion, and Superstition, Strindberg has access to an abundance of blue-prints for his own recovery. Literary or other models, which facilitate the perception and creation of character, offer a multiplicity of parts in which to find himself as the appropriate hero of a Case History ('after having read Maudsley's *Maladies de l'Esprit* I have a complete diagnosis of myself' (V333), he writes enthusiastically, in 1886) of a *Bildungsroman*, a Drama of Redemption, or as the agent (or victim) of Nemesis. Even single words such as 'calling', 'sacrifice', or 'suffering' function as metaphorical projections that help him to organize his experience within a narrative framework that lends purpose and consequence to the succession of his acts, and from his conception within the defining ideology of the patriarchal family, which imprints upon him the lineaments of his own family romance, and which he later acknowledges is a plot that went awry ('I was born for family life and a mate - and look what happened', he notes in the diary, 6 September 1901), to the Pietist text which promises him the chance of being born again, to Kierkegaard's dialectical notion of 'Stages on Life's Way', to the history countenanced by current evolutionary theory, and finally in the destiny implicit in the eschatology of Swedenborg and the infernal topographies of other authors (for to ascertain where one is may establish a narrative system, incorporating notions of guilt and atonement, and suffering and punishment, which extends not only to the facts of his own life but to the lives of those among whom he lives), Strindberg has on hand a series of more copious intellectual paradigms. They offer elementary modes of coherence, cultural models that form part of his birthright and endow him with a number of *a priori* plots by means of which he can examine the data of his experience under a series of titles ('The Son of a Servant', 'Inferno', 'To Damascus') that already possess the ability to intend what follows. Determined to discover 'the whole equation in which my life can be solved' (XII:324), he tries on different views and vocabularies, and experiments with diverse ways of seeing, an approach for which he finds authority and a terminology in Kierkegaard, but which is fostered by his own questing temperament. He constantly betrays a tendency to see his life as a journey, and to interpret it in terms of stages, phases, or epochs. 'Thanks for good company on this stretch of the way, and be happy if you can' (VII:92) is his leave-taking from the poet, Verner von Heidenstam, one in a succession of correspondents in whom he confides his progress, for he is embarking upon 'new phases of my fragmentary life' (VII:72), 'new stages on life's way' (VII:108) and will now be travelling in different company. Meanwhile, many years later, in a remark that also conveys his conviction that the writer must have experienced all of life in order to portray it, he explains to his translator, Schering, that he is 'nur ein Dichter der sein Pilgerfart durch alle Stationen Menschlicher Entwickelung lebe um Menschen schildern zu können!' (XIII:262). And it is in this context that he regards himself as a 'scrupulous researcher' who undertakes 'experiments' (40:45) in which he uses his own life as the field of his research. 'I want to test everything, but not to retain it all' (X:154), he tells Hedlund in 1894, and like Voltaire, whom he praises because he 'experimented poetically with every problem' (17:277), he sees writing as an opportunity to examine and project different points of view. 'After having experimented my way through socialism' (VI:162), he adopts the aristocratic radicalism which he associates with Nietzsche ('I intend to experiment poetically with it for ten years' (VIII:32) he tells a correspondent in 1890), ultimately abandons his atheism as 'an intellectual experiment which promptly failed' (XII:324), and then recommends his readers to 'Leave your own self, if you have the strength, and adopt the point of view of a believer; pretend that you believe, and then test that belief to see if it corresponds with your experiences' (46:21).

Moreover, whereas he often claims that 'the contradictions in my writing are a result of my having adopted different points of view in order to be able to see the question from many sides' (VII:92), he also stresses the historical relativity of truth, 'of truth as something in the process of eternal development' (19:28), from the application of his enthusiastic early reading of T.H. Buckle's *History of Civilisation in England*, in *Master Olof*, to the Hegelian account of Pater Uriel's life in *To Damascus III*. Thus he notes that an author's career ought to be responsive to the pressures of his time, a whole of several aspects: 'A writer should be an adequate expression of his age; if he lives in -through - several epochs he will have several physiognomies.'[5] Hence any coherence in the material he collects and analyses depends upon the model with which he is currently working, and upon 'the desire for order of the mental apparatus' (19:180), and either in their most extended form, as the projection of a comprehensive destiny indited by Nemesis, or the laws of Nature, or the hand of God, or only as mere taxonomies of order, such as he discovers in the Tarot pack or the *Kabbala*,[6] each positional reading that this tireless observer and indefatigable interpreter makes of his career derives its authority from the text against which it is being read. Indeed, the bibliomancy to which he sometimes resorts, particularly after 1895, is ultimately only a specific mode of his characteristic search for textual authority, one that will reveal (or so he hopes) the definitive plot of his life. 'Read Isaiah Chapter 54, opened at random, which seemed as if it had been written especially for me' (XI:274), he confides to Hedlund. In what he reads he finds himself and his destiny: as he frequently remarks, of his experience: 'it was written' (XII:135).[7]

But if the assumption behind much of his later writing (namely that 'in old age, when the eye can finally see, one discovers that all the little curlicues form a design, a monogram, an ornament, an hieroglyph, which one can now read for the first time: this is [your] life' (45:97)), is not one in which Strindberg has sufficient confidence in practice to withstand the temptation of continually supplementing his earlier accounts, it nevertheless remains possible to perceive in this succession of superimposed images the legend of their author. For underlying all the attempts to revitalize his life is the power of narrative to animate the past in the present of the reader. The paradoxical nature of this reversal is suggested by Sartre in *La Nausée*, where the biographer and historian Roquentin defines living as 'une addition interminable et monotone'.[8] In life, he argues, days are tacked on to days in a succession without point or purpose, as a brute accumulation of accident and circumstance. Occasionally, a particular event or the sense that one phase of life has ended may encourage the subject to interrupt the onward flow, to pause in order to estimate his position and take a temporary reading of the situation. But it is only the extended practice of narrative that transforms duration into orientated and meaningful time and endows life with a sensible coherence. According to Roquentin, narrative is a universal characteristic of man: 'un homme, c'est toujours un conteur d'histoires, il vit entouré de ses histoires et des histoires d'autrui, il voit tout ce qui lui arrive à travers elles; et il cherche à vivre sa vie comme s'il la racontait.'[9] But the writer, with his professional awareness of the available plots and the devices and subtleties of storytelling, is particularly adept both at finding himself and his destiny already described in the pages of literature and myth, and of seeing his life in terms of writing at the moment of experience, as well as in retrospect.

That literature, and novels in particular, contribute substantially to the way in which life is understood (or, Cervantes and Flaubert might argue, how it is readily misunderstood) is a point that has recently been made with great eloquence by Philippe Sollers:

LA ROMAN EST LA MANIERE DONT CETTE SOCIETE SE PARLE; la manière dont l'individu DOIT SE VIVRE pour y être accepté...Notre *identité* en dépend, ce qu'on pense de nous, ce que nous pensons de nous-mêmes, la façon dont notre vie est insensiblement amenée à composition. Qui reconnaît-on en nous sinon un personnage de roman? (Qui reconnaissez-vous en moi qui vous parle sinon un personnage de roman?)...Le roman, avec le mutisme de la science, est la *valeur* de notre époque, autrement dit son code de référence instinctif, l'exercice de son pouvoir, la clef de son inconscience quotidienne, mécanique, fermée.[10]

Through novels the individual can discover something of the complexity and multiplicity of life, may recognize himself and his contemporaries, and find the technical means to frame and articulate his own story. But more specifically: in the nineteenth century the conception of the world as a network of signatures, as what Strindberg once called a 'cryptographie céleste' (27:436) in the handwriting of God, had been largely superceded by a world in print, a world, moreover, that was rendered visible and made comprehensible through the very novels which helped produce the situation to which Sollers refers. If the realistic novel in general aspired to the accurate reproduction of the world it frequently claimed to mirror, both Balzac, in *Illusions perdues*, and Strindberg, in *Black Banners* and *The Red Room*, depicted the manner of its writing, the way in which works were transformed into products and personal experience immediately written up in literary form. And even after he had returned to the belief 'that the whole of creation is planned and sometimes expressed in a kind of code' (46:272) which is visible in nature, Strindberg not only retained the view advanced in the Foreword to *The Son of a Servant*, that all notions of the other are fictional in so far as 'character only exists as representations of other people', and hence requires the same combination of deduction and imaginative speculation that gives life to characters in literature, but also continued to approach his own experience in terms of fiction and drama since they, too, are a major source of information about his own life. For his stance is continually interrogative ('I still ask: how the hell did I get here? And what am I doing here? (XI:313)) and literature the ground upon which he prosecutes his inquiry. 'What's behind all this?' he wonders, in a letter to Pehr Staaff during his eventful stay on the Frankenau estate at Skovlyst in 1888. 'I don't know, but I will try to sort it out in a novel' (VII:131). Moreover, having translated his perplexity into a text (in this instance the story 'Tschandala'), the implication is that he can then interpret the meaning of his experience, although (as an entry in *The Occult Diary* for 7 May 1904 indicates) the intelligence the text communicates is not always entirely clear: 'Have read *Inferno* and *Legends* again in a reverent frame of mind, but I still don't understand the intentions of Providence - if we are to suffer in order to learn or if we are to be punished and frightened off.'

A persistent problem, therefore, and not only in the period after 1895, when its solution is pursued more urgently, is to what extent he figures in an already prepared script composed by God or by Nemesis, or whether (if it is not merely an accumulation of events amassed by chance) he is the author of his own life. Regarding his contemporaries, it sometimes seems to him as if 'there was a consequence and an order in their lives' (37:60) whereas it is only by writing that he can achieve 'an impression of an intended design' (38:192) in his own. Occasionally, his reading reveals his life already accommodated by a pre-existing plot. He finds himself and his second wife, Frida, in the text of *Louis Lambert*, for example ('das Buch ist für mich und Frida-Mama geschrieben, oder *von* uns Beide' (XII:28) he tells their daughter), and again in Bulwer-Lytton's novel, *Zanoni*:

> Lese jetzt Bulwers Zanoni! mit Entsetzen! Alles is da: Ich, Frida, Mädi. Und noch: der Dämon verfolgt den Armen Zanoni (eine Reincarnation) jede Moment wenn Er sich aus der Materie heben will und in der Einsamkeit sich in frommen Gedanken versenkt. Geht Er aber in lustigem Gesellschaft, da flieht der Dämon! So genau mein Fall!
>
> Und Zanoni hat ein ockultes Kind, der ihn immer anschauet mit ihren grossen ruhigen Augen. Und ihre Mama flieht den Zanoni aus Furcht für 'das Unbekannte' in seiner Person. Er ist Rosenkreutzer, macht Gold, ist zwei tausen Jahre 'jung', kann nicht sterben weil er die Lebens-elixir getrunken! Er sucht immer seine Viola, und die flieht obschon Sie ihn liebt! Les' mir das Buch!
>
> Fillide (Aspasia) ist auch da! (XII:80)

Usually, however, he is the plotter of his own destiny and can sometimes be observed creating a situation in his life that conforms to his current standpoint on, for example, the nature of woman, her rights, and the institution of marriage, and then (as in *A Madman's Defence*) reproducing the text he has prompted in a book.

Moreover, once a text is written life expectantly follows the course it predicates. This is particularly the case with the interaction between certain plays and the autobiographical works which they follow or precede, until in the mind of the author, as in the eyes of the reader or spectator, any clear distinction between invention and a record of events, is erased. For as an enlightened reviewer of *The Father* commented in the satirical journal *Figaro* shortly after the play appeared in 1888, for its author, reality was one with the construction of his imagination:

> Nevertheless the book certainly makes a gripping if not very satisfying and hardly truthful impression. Although we feel that the writer has curiously enough experienced or, it is perhaps more correct to say, believed he has experienced what he has portrayed. Although - even stranger - he seems first to have portrayed it and then believed he has found its image in reality.[11]

Strindberg, the reviewer observed, had difficulty determining whether life or literature took precedence, a problem which his own comments on the play in the testimentary letter to Lundegård reveal, and a detailed analysis of the rapid succession of naturalist works during this period would indicate how *The Father* elaborates upon its author's 'personal circumstances' (VI:141) and then, once written, constitutes an image of the past that superimposes itself upon the present and influences the distribution of roles in subsequent works, the wife he portrays in *A*

Madman's Defence, for example, being a refraction of the image of Laura, and of Berthe in *Comrades*.

Similarly, the confusion of categories to which *Figaro's* reviewer alludes becomes especially acute with Harriet Bosse's almost simultaneous assumption of the role of The Lady in *To Damascus* on stage and, by marriage, in its author's life. The situation is full of intrigue. Harriet enters a dramatic text in which she repeats lines that evoke, on one level, the period of Strindberg's second marriage to Frida Uhl. But the events which this text encompasses were, as Frida Uhl herself observed, themselves adapted from a previous script. In her memoirs she recalls how her life with Strindberg seemed to follow an already developed scenario in which (and the prohibition which he placed on each of his wives regarding their reading his books, from the fourth volume of *The Son of a Servant* onwards (VI:103), suggests that he was not unaware of the predictive, anticipatory nature of certain texts):

> The past swallowed up the present, the shadow ate up the reality. Sometimes Strindberg assumed situations between us which did not exist, and which could not. But for him they were real, exactly as they occurred in his dreams. Then he could say to me something which I had already read and recognized. In his eyes I was wearing his first wife's clothes and acted, according to him, exactly as she would have acted.[12]

With Harriet's entrance, however, the drama of *To Damascus* was no longer only a formation of the past, with one level superimposed upon the other, but something lived forward from day to day by the playwright and the actress who animated a figure of the dramatic text. Indeed, with his appeal to her that she decide the fate of The Unknown in the as yet uncompleted third part of the play in progress, Strindberg in fact temporarily relinquished the denouement to her since she was asked by Strindberg to decide whether the hero married, died, or entered a monastery. And as an accomplished actress, she (like Frida) appreciated her role - at least upon the everyday, if not the astral, plane which also engrossed Strindberg. As Guy Vogelweith has observed, Harriet's presence meant that

> L'auteur va donc vivre dans la réalité le dénouement d'un drama qu'il avait commencé d'écrire. Il va le faire selon l'inspiration d'une femme qui aura joué le rôle de la Dame et qui accepte maintenant de devenir son épouse. Il y a là comme une rencontre insepérée des possibilités sans nombre que promet une réalité encore neuve et des ressources si imprévisibles de la création littéraire.[13]

For it was always the writing of literature that mattered most to Strindberg, and from the outset he protected himself against the possibility of a debacle in life by erasing the distinction between dream and reality and emphasizing the value of any experience as matter for literature. 'Suppose it is all make-believe (*dikt*), and remains so?' he muses, of his relationship with Harriet, in *The Occult Diary* (1 March 1901), 'What then? Then I shall write a poem (*dikt*), which will be beautiful!'

The notion that life is already literature, or that it naturally composes itself into novels and dramas, is therefore one that Strindberg often entertains. He is always alert to the appearance of 'new novels in reality' (IX:93), and complementing his own unremitting self-scrutiny there is a constant inclination to view any episode in which he plays a part in literary terms. Detaching himself from centre stage for once, he spends much of 1893 following what he calls 'the story of Aspasia' (IX:202), his name for the events surrounding the turbulent career of the Norwegian, Dagny Juel, among the writers and artists in the circle around Strindberg and Edvard Munch at the Ferkel tavern in Berlin. 'Oh, it is a novel! She lays waste families and men' (IX:188), he exclaims delightedly, as Dagny passes from one man to another. But shortly afterwards, it is the theatrical possibilities that attract him in what he observes: 'I think you ought to introduce Heiberg right now in the fifth act to resolve the Aspasia drama' (IX:199), he suggests to Adolf Paul, who plays the role of dramaturge, just as he shortly recommends the arrest of Dagny Juel for prostitution as an apt *coup de théâtre* (IX:352), one that remains unused, however, until he employs it himself in the third act of *Crimes and Crimes*. Nevertheless, in fresh information about Dagny's further circulation among the Ferkel group, the eventual author of *To Damascus*, in which the final scene of part one repeats the location of the first by way of all the other settings through which the protagonists have passed in the early scenes of the play, recognizes a masterly finale to the structure of life's events: 'This ending satisfies me completely. Chapter I: Munch-Juel in the Ferkel...Chapter XII Munch-Juel in the Ferkel...(end!?)' (IX:347).

And after 1895 in particular, he continually stresses the theatrical dimension of his experience, sometimes assuming the one role he fills with complete assurance, that of the dramatist ('The poet sits and sees himself in certain scenes. Discovers that he has been given roles'),[14] at others pausing only to speculate on the intentions of the dramatist in whose plot he finds himself. 'Who stages these scenes for us, and with what purpose?' (XII:273), he wonders, in 1898; 'Is it possible that everything terrible I have experienced has been staged for me?' on 24 January 1901; while in *Black Banners*, Falkenström observes that 'It has actually seemed to me from an early age that my life was staged before me so that I would be able to observe all its facets' (41:196). Frequently, he recognizes the stage setting before the event occurs (thus, on arriving in Lund he recognizes it as his Canossa and realizes 'it is here I have to drain my cup to the dregs' (28:180)), and whatever the occasion, the laws of life and those of drama appear to him as one. As he writes to his daughter, Kerstin: 'Scenesveränderung kommt in allen Dramen vor, Personenwechsel auch aber im letzten Akt kommen doch Alle zum Vorschein und der Verfasser darf keinen Einzigen vergessen. So ist das ewige Gesetz des Dramas und des Lebens!' (XIV:41). And it is, finally, this sense of life as both a series of scenes and as 'staged' (*satt i scen*) for him, as something in which he acts but at which he also spectates, that facilitates the accomplishment of the dramatic form of *To Damascus*, a vehicle of self-scrutiny and a pilgrim's drama in which the familiar scenes are repeated, a vehicle which is capacious and supple enough, moreover, to accommodate additional episodes as the drama of his life continues to unfold beyond the point at which the first part concludes.

II

If this characteristic erasure of the boundary between the written and the existential self enables Strindberg to suggest that the ego is an imaginary construct composed of multiple projections and introjections and apprehended as a character in the literature which affords it so many of its incarnations, the text which perhaps illustrates most clearly how life assumes the guise of literature, and how it is domiciled by the ensemble of symbolic systems with which its culture provides him, is the epistolary novel *He and She*. More immediately than most texts, it exemplifies the complex intertextuality of Strindberg's experience into the written text of his life, which is already perceived in terms of literature. Moreover, as he points out to Bonnier in 1886, that year was not the first occasion he had contemplated publishing the letters written by the protagonists of the marital drama which followed rapidly upon his first meeting with Siri von Essen and Carl Gustaf Wrangel: 'For our own sakes, and for the sake of our children, my wife and I have often thought of publishing our correspondence during the rupture in 1876, anonymously and with no names, under the title, *He and She*' (V:356).

In arguing the prompt publication of *He and She* as part of the 'famous portrait of my career while I'm on the go and interested' (V:356), Strindberg described the projected volume as 'an intimate novel (*själsroman*), not invented and arranged, however, but lived' (V:357). The remark indicates the blurring of categories at which the book contrives, and the uncertainty which surrounds its genre and the domain (whether fact or fiction, public or private) to which it belongs. These are all matters which preoccupied Strindberg when, in 1886, he considered the propriety of including the letters concerning his early acquaintance with Siri von Essen within the general framework of *The Son of a Servant*, where they had a natural place after the third volume, 'In the Red Room'.

When he first broaches the idea, he points out to Bonnier that life itself connives at a dramatic plot ('Part 3 runs from 72 to 75 and ends with the fatal chance which sent the hero, then Royal Secretary and extraordinary amanuensis to Norrtullsgatan 12, where he saw his future wife' in the context of his childhood home) and therefore what he now terms 'the so unusual and high romantic drama' (V:356) ought to assume its rightful chronological place in the text to which it belongs. Furthermore, this idea is given immediate encouragement by the discovery that in 'these remarkable documents' he has on hand 'a whole volume' (V:357) virtually ready and waiting for the press. The letters emerge as an example of his thrifty literary housekeeping, and any suggestion of opportunism in his purpose is conveniently disarmed not only by the theoretical standpoint from which he regarded the writing of imaginative literature in the mid 1880s, but also in the categorical '*A writer is only a reporter of what he has lived* (I:190) in the highly contrived discourse on writing with which he had initiated his correspondence with Siri von Essen in 1876, and which was originally intended to form the opening section of *He and She*. Anticipating Bonnier's objections, and the suggestion that he veil the material by recasting it as fiction, he maintains that were he to 'construct a novel now, it would be coloured by new points of view and become untruthful' (V:357). And while he concedes that publication would entail an intrusion upon the privacy of other people ('but, unfortunately, one does not possess one's experience in isolation'), he regards the scientific nature of his project as a value that transcends the personal: 'The question arises, however, if the interests of a number of private individuals should not be set aside in order that such an important matter as the truthful account of the whole of a man's life may for once see the light of day' (V:356). Or as he develops both points a few weeks later, when Bonnier's disapproval of the scheme was plain:

> Apart from that [encroaching upon the privacy of others] the collection of letters has great psychological interest and, to put it bluntly, seems to me better than any novel. A novel would always look like self-defence and would occasion contradictions, misinterpretations, and not be in keeping with the grand and unique work I have now accomplished. A man's life in 5 vols. (VI:17-18)

In the light of *A Madman's Defence*, which would eventually absorb so much of the material whose publication Bonnier would not now countenance unvarnished, in the form of letters, the idea of a novel as a form of self-defence is an example of prescient self-criticism. But even in the text of the letters which Strindberg prepared for publication in 1886 (and which only appeared posthumously in 1919, after he had stubbornly continued to insist on their essential place in his *œuvre* in the contract for his Collected Works, which he drew up with another Bonnier, a year before he died) the issue is not without ambiguity. If the implications of his overtures to Bonnier are that the letters should therefore appear unaltered, then even the suggestion that they be published anonymously, or as he later proposes, with asterisks replacing the names of the correspondents, is itself a significant concession to a fictional mode: as he remarks, 'One can of course believe they are fabricated letters' (VI:17). In fact, as in 'The Quarantine Master's Second Story', that other hasty adaptation of an autobiographical text into a fictional guise, the published version of *He and She* is full of inconsistencies in nomination and detail. Since the correspondence is to form part of *The Son of a Servant*, the letters originally written by Strindberg himself are allotted to Johan. Meanwhile, Sofia In de Betou, Siri's cousin, who was cast in the role of the other woman in the Wrangel household by the more than affectionately familial feelings she aroused in Carl Gustaf, is dubbed 'Mathilde' in the correspondence, as she will be in *A Madman's Defence*, a detail which prompted the editor of Strindberg's collected works, John Landquist, to christen the other two, hitherto unnamed protagonists, Gustav and Maria, when he prepared the manuscript of *He and She* for publication. Even so, identification is not so much obscured as merely confused (and as Strindberg suggested, 'the public ought to be kept in ignorance as to whether it is a matter of actual events or mystification' (VI:74)). Sometimes asterisks give way to authentic initials ('The Honourable Lady E.v.E.' (55:146) indicates Siri-Maria's mother, Elisabeth von Essen, for example, while on page 206, best wishes are sent to 'A. and H.', Strindberg's sister Anna and her husband, Hugo von Philp), at others there is a marginal displacement in their attribution (thus Algot Lange becomes 'Herr A'). But in any case, the mention at intervals of *Master Olof* and 'Uncle Augis' (55:64) would have dispelled most contemporary doubts as to the identity of author and hero.

What he achieves, therefore, is an uneasy blend of document and epistolary novel, carelessly prepared and uncertain of purpose. By the addition of a title, a subtitle, and several chapter headings ('Under fire', 'Unsuccessful Flight', 'A Fly in the Ointment', 'On Fire', 'Men of Honour', 'Separation', and 'Beautiful Weather') which pace events from suspense, to climax, and on to resolution, the published text displays a narrative shape hardly discernible in the short term composition of the successive letters, a shape, moreover, and a title which evokes a specific literary model. For if, in his first letter to Bonnier regarding the correspondence, Strindberg referred in passing to George Sand and Sandeau as an earlier instance of the publication of such intimate material, the text itself makes clear that, even at the time of their original composition, it was George Sand's relationship with de Musset, as imaginatively chronicled in the epistolary novel, *Elle et lui*, that he had in mind both in writing and arranging these letters, the deft reversal of precedence in his title, along the lines of Paul de Musset's rejoinder, *Lui et elle*, notwithstanding.

In this way, a series of private communicative acts, at first sight apparently unrelated to the organized text of a literary work (but which were nevertheless conceived in the light of an already published correspondence) are transformed into a printed book, to be bought and sold as one among the many articles produced over the signature of August Strindberg. And even though he shuns ('No foreword and no notes' (VI:17)) the editorial apparatus accorded the epistolary novels of, for example, Richardson and Goethe, the letters are detached from the original circuit of communication in which they appeared and endowed, by their publication in book form as part of a sequence of works displaying characteristics of the dominant marketable literary genre of the day, with the substance and difference of literature. They are cut off from the communicative presence of their authors, who did of course meet in the intervals between letters in order to augment, qualify, and very necessarily clarify their respective texts for each other, and delivered up to the interpretative ingenuity of the reader.

But this ingenuity is severely tested. For even a cursory comparison of the letters as they appear in *He and She* with those written by Strindberg as they are printed in the first volume of Torsten Eklund's scholarly edition of the correspondence, reveals a significant number of variations in order, and many inconsistencies of detail. Thus, on this level alone, the reader is confronted by a degree of confusion and opacity in the text which would be unacceptable were this in fact a contrived novel. If, for example, Eklund's arrangement of the sixty surviving letters written by Strindberg to Siri von Essen, her mother, or her husband during the period covered by *He and She* (1 July 1875 to 25 June 1876, that is between letters ninety six and one hundred and sixty seven in Eklund's edition) is taken as correct (and inevitably certain ascriptions of date remain hypothetical even after a close scrutiny of the textual evidence), then putting aside the nine letters which Strindberg purposefully excluded from his compilation, the sequence of the remaining fifty-one in the order established by Eklund emerges as 1, 2, 3, 4, 5, 6, 7, 8, 9, 14, 16, 10, 13, 15, 17, 18, 19, 11, 12, 21, 20, 23, 24, 25, 27, 28, 29, 26, 31, 32, 34, 30, 36, 33, 35, 37, 39, 40, 41, 46, 44, 45, 47, 48, 38, 50, 49, 51, in Strindberg's version, and the possibility of confusion is naturally compounded by similar omissions and relocations in his preparation of Siri von Essen's letters.[15] Thus the reader is not only not in possession of much of the necessary background information to which the writers were privy, and which the author of a genuine epistolary novel would have been obliged to work into the text, either in the form of editorial comment or in the letters themselves; the two main sequences of letters, those which pass between Johan and Maria, do not always even correspond with one another. That the book remains readable at all, therefore, depends firstly upon the nature of the generalized effusions contained in many of the letters, which allow the incorrigible interpreter of texts to comprehend them according to the codes of sense and feeling they nevertheless contain, and secondly because in *He and She* specific allusions and even the precise course of events are to some extent recoverable because the reader also has access to the work of commentators or to Strindberg's own retrieval of the situation in *A Madman's Defence*, which is, however, hardly an unimpeachable source, and one which also depends upon the sequence reconstituted in these letters by his evidently faulty memory.

But if mistakes arise in chronology, despite all the precautions taken by Strindberg in the pencilled comments he appended to both sets of correspondence,[16] the omission of specific letters was certainly intended. These omissions were made in order to point particular aspects of 'the so unusual and high romantic drama' rather than from prudence. For if the removal of several pages devoted to Johan's relationship with a former mistress is a deliberate and to some extent surprising suppression of written evidence by Strindberg (it is excised physically from the letter printed in I:216, too), the deletion of the phrase, 'I never suffered when I lay outside your bedroom - oh yes, once!' (I:288), in one of Johan's letters, avoids a possibly *risqué* association that would confuse the purity of his love with what is portrayed as Gustav's sensual behaviour, behaviour from which, in this letter, as elsewhere in the correspondence, he is concerned to distinguish himself. Similarly, a sequence of three letters (numbers 146 to 148 in Eklund's edition) are unromantic, concerned with practical affairs, and sometimes irritable in their concern to 'put aside all lovers' quarrels' (I:318), and they are thus deleted by Strindberg because, like several of Siri von Essen's letters following her return from the journey to Copenhagen, which marked her initial separation from Wrangel, their inclusion would have complicated as well as deepened the sweep of the romantic drama on which he was focusing. They raise problems beyond those with which the published letters engage. Not until *A Madman's Defence*, for example, was Strindberg prepared to confront or raise in print the possibility that 'She' remained physically close to her husband even after she had declared her love for Strindberg himself, and the way in which her leaving with him compelled her to abandon her first child was (like the death of their own first child in the custody of a nurse, two days after birth) something he also remained unwilling to face. Again, when Johan exclaims, 'What does Providence mean by the enormous sufferings and trials it has imposed upon us?' (55:166), the thrust of his question suggests involvement in a moral predicament that would have been undermined by the accompanying and deleted reference to the actual cause of his distress, namely the unwillingness of his landladies in Kaptensgatan 18 to rent the rooms adjacent to his own to Siri, whereas when he passes over the visiting card on which he has written

> I am coming to you tomorrow at noon, 20 years older - an outlaw -
> disinherited - mother and *father*less - alone in the whole wide world -
> but faithful to my promise still in good spirits - Be indulgent to me! Be
> kind for God's sake even if you have your own sorrows. You are two - I
> am *alone*! (I:270)

he actually sacrifices an opportunity to give substance to the image of Johan as a homeless and accursed wanderer, and hence to relate the later impersonation of 'The Son of a Servant', Ishmael, to the Byronic image which these early letters often project, no doubt because it would introduce the complexities of his troubled relationship with his family (a topic on which the later volumes of the autobiography, and not only *He and She*, are strikingly reticent) into a text in which he wished to focus upon the 'Affaire W-----l'.[17] Thus, while some of the material a reader would expect to see provided as essential to the plot of a fully developed epistolary novel (such as Mathilde's letters to Gustav, for example, which Maria mentions on page 89, and the disturbing letter of Gustav's which is referred to on several occasions (pp. 142, 144, 183) and which causes great disquiet when Johan makes its contents known to others) are not included because Strindberg did not have access to the originals and refrained on aesthetic grounds from invention (and were this a genuine epistolary novel, such letters would have offered an opportunity of developing the parallel plot at which, even so, *He and She* sometimes hints in its allusions to the affair between Gustav and Mathilde),[18] there is considerable editorial, if not authorial, interference in the text that remains.

The domain occupied by this text is therefore difficult to locate with precision. Strindberg operates with uncertainty. Refusing an explicit pact with the reader, he takes advantage of conventions developed in order to give an impression of substance to invented characters by apparently protecting them with a considerate anonymity, and evokes the appearance of invention by masking a real situation with some of the accoutrements of fiction. But if Strindberg's indeterminate practice is ultimately acceptable because the writing and reading of novels has blurred a fine distinction between life and literature, the foundation of his enlacing of fact and fiction has its source not in the editorial work of 1886, but in the writing, and even the living, of the experience the letters record.

The literariness of these letters is, of course, suggested by frequent quotation from, and allusion to, a variety of literary texts. They include passages from Heine, Goethe, Longfellow, Topelius, and Dietrichson, and in their original form, as private communications, the use of quotation was even more copious.[19] It is also stressed by their use for stylistic exercises, whose exuberant virtuosity, at least in Johan's contributions, draws attention to the nature of the letters as writing. That it proved so easy to transform them into something resembling an epistolary novel was facilitated by the opening 'Monologue', dated 1 July 1875, with which Strindberg first introduced himself to the Wrangels in the guise of a conventional, faded Byronic Romanticism. It provides the letters with an introductory self-portrait in which inevitable and dramatic events are prepared for by the image it projects of its writer as one 'who seems born to wreak destruction' (55:5), after having been presented at the font by the Devil himself. By turns playful and self-indulgent, Strindberg cultivates this demonic impression and sustains the tempo with a succession of performances, including letters in French, English, and German like the one written at Dalarö, when he jumped ship to abort his attempted escape to Paris from feelings he could no longer master, which was addressed to 'Herr Jesus von Nazareth! Himmel, Milchstrasse, rechter Hand (von Gott gerechnet!)' (55:28). In such letters he sometimes depicts himself in the third person or takes advantage of the dramatic present which the epistolary form permits, whereby the virtual contemporaneousness of the event and its narration is given a striking immediacy. This is so in the Dalarö letter, where the writer records the effect of drinking absinthe on a fellow guest during the time it takes him to write his letter (and most probably the guest is an imagined reflector in whom the writer's own predicament is projected, as in the obviously more sophisticated use of the Beggar in *To Damascus*), and again in the hurried note to Maria, now on her way to Copenhagen, which is written at 'The Inn in Katrineholm, 5 minutes after the train's departure for Malmö' (55:177).

In composing a diplomatic letter to Maria's mother, meanwhile, Johan includes the parenthetical commentary on his text which Strindberg had originally provided for Maria's benefit and his own delight (55:146f), and within the compass of individual letters he stresses the dynamism of events by the use of a rapid succession of registers. Thus, on the eve of her departure for Denmark, Johan opens with a passage of elevated rhetoric in which he bids Maria 'welcome to the league of those who suffer and struggle and conquer in the name of the Eternal One' (55:174), moves on to dispense practical advice on how she might profit from her stay in Copenhagen, and then, after playfully suggesting he has something distressing to tell her, leads his now captive reader towards the declaration: 'I love you' (55:176).

In the same letter, he also employs literary allusion with great subtlety to a more serious end when he takes one of Kierkegaard's favourite texts, the tale of Abraham and Isaac, which is discussed in *Fear and Trembling*, in order to convince Maria of the virtue of sacrificing her daughter. What the occasion demands, he writes, is 'a sacrifice as great as Abraham's, when he gave his child for the sake of the Lord - Rest assured he demands as little of this sacrifice from you as He demanded it of him. He only wants to try you - chasten you - *see if you are worthy!*' (55:172). The Hand of the Lord, he claims, is implementing His design in their lives; she must not resist, and in return for this sacrifice she will experience 'this wonderful turning inside out of the soul - which is what art demands' (55:173). As for the physical turn their relationship has taken, which is so at odds with the notion of the chaste, non-sensual partnership originally sketched in the letters that distinguish their affair from Gustav's inartistic pursuit of his cousin, this is defused by a conventionally poetic natural image and a further appeal to God. Where Maria had urged, 'let us forget all things earthly' (55:117), and feared that physical contact would 'soil this holy fire, drag what is heavenly in the mire' (55:103), Johan points to 'the swallow which sweeps the gravel when storms approach' and 'God himself' who 'could descend to earth and dwell among us', among those who 'grub and dig in what we call the prose!' (*det vi kalla prosan*, 55:172). Why, then, should they hesitate to abandon the discourse of poetry for prose: 'What belongs to heaven can endure becoming earthly for a moment' (55:172).[20]

But the evident ease with which the letters are transformed into an epistolary novel undoubtedly has its basis in the very events they record. The shaping of the material, however slight, in which Strindberg indulged when preparing the letters for publication, was performed on material recognized from the outset as already on its way from a raw state into literature. The events in themselves constitute a novel *en plein jour*. From the beginning, the protagonists were aware of themselves as participants in a drama, or as characters in a novel. As Anna Philp recalled, 'They suited one another well, with their artistic and literary interests',[21] and the tone and direction of what follows is already set by the letter on writing, entitled 'The Art of Becoming a Writer', with which Strindberg first approached Siri von Essen, and in which he insists repeatedly upon the facility with which experience can be turned into literature: 'He who has lived through something has something to relate, he who has something to relate *is a writer!*' (I:190).

Indeed, Siri reveals herself a competent pupil, both at learning how to find consolation for suffering in literary composition ('I have now truly noticed that when one grieves, the safest method is to let one's sorrow flow away by means of the pen. When I was able to write down my pain, the weight on my breast became lighter' (55:180)),[22] and in recognizing the literary nature of the situation. When Strindberg (who on one occasion compliments Gustav on his 'excellent way of playing your role of martyr in this play' (55:119)) eventually comes to write *A Madman's Defence* he will be implementing an idea that had already occurred to Maria, who remarks, 'someone ought to write a novel about this - if I had the courage to get to grips with it,I would do it' (55:101).[23] Shortly afterwards, meanwhile, the aspiring actress, Siri-Maria, perceives the situation to be a drama of parallel plots and neat exchanges, a contemporary comedy of manners (*pièce rose* rather than *noir*) in which the main participants are all finally united with the partner they desire:

Why should I be so cruel as to deprive him (Gustav) of compensation for the freedom he grants me? You are my betrothed - she is his - also betrothed (nothing else). It is quite charming!!! The situation is superb - he falls still more in love with her - she with him...he will himself *request* his freedom, I - go along with it - we separate as *friends* - and then nothing else remains in order to round it all out properly, than to celebrate our weddings together in complete harmony -on the same evening - and go about together like affectionate brothers and sisters. (55:154)[24]

In fact the attempt to give their story a literary form was hardly delayed. Among the letters in the Royal Library are two drafts in which Siri is seeking to transform one phase of her experience into poetry, the more rhythmical of which reads:

Jag stod vid fönstret ensam, så ensam stod jag der
Fast *han* fans uti rummet, fast barnet var mig nära.
Det hängde på mitt hufvud ett vemodstak - så tungt.
Och tanken den var mattad, men än var...[25]

More pertinent, however, is the intention, encouraged by Strindberg among a profusion of suggestions for translations (of François Coppée's *Le Passant*, and from the Norwegian), a travelogue portraying life in Helsinki, and for articles 'for Dagligt Allehanda on the theatre and other things' (I:319), that Siri write a short novel utilizing events in progress. He had continually encouraged her to write ('Well write then! It is your duty as a woman to give your opinion on questions which men have never been able to express themselves' (I:192)) at the expense of her passion for the stage, from which he sought to wean her, and in 'The Art of Becoming a Writer' he demonstrated precisely how she could usefully transform her experience into literature, firstly by pretending that she was merely writing an intimate letter, and then, whenever necessary, by employing a kind of Stanislavskian transfer of emotion from an event in the past to material in the present, in order to rekindle faltering inspiration. Now, to flesh out the novella in fifteen chapters for which he provides the plan which Karin Smirnoff later published in her account of her mother's marriage to Strindberg, *Strindbergs första hustru*,[26] he discovers an immediate use for the real letters she has already written to him. 'Les lettres - toujours les lettres!' he exclaims, in the outline for a narrative, which, presumably in order to veil and distance the intimate nature of the material, was to be - like *A Madman's Defence* - written in French, the characters rechristened Armand, Cécile, Caroline, Inez. Catching events on the run (for as he reveals, the outcome is as yet unknown because unlived: 'la fin - qui sans doute se fera voir avant que la nouvelle sera achevée'), what he sketches is a romance in the spirit of the letters, 'cette correspondance intime des âmes, ce saint amour, ce feu sacré par lequel le jeune auteur va être guéri de ses erreurs fatales et retourne à la vertu et ses Muses, reconcilié de ses anges dechus, ses idéales cassés, et en croyence sur ce qu'il y a de beau et de bon.'[27]

This redemption of the poet by a woman whom destiny has thrown in his path introduces a motif to which Strindberg will often return, notably in the first part of *To Damascus*, where Maria's role is taken by another Madonna, Eve, whose 'voice sounds like my dead mother's' (29:13), and at whose feet The Unknown, another accursed and homeless writer, like Byron's Cain 'a fugitive and vagabond on earth'[28], also contrives 'to become a child again' (29:23). But in the draft of the novella, as in the letters of *He and She*, the script which Strindberg prepares is not uniquely his own. It is an expression of what in *The Son of a Servant* he calls 'the desperate devil worship of late romanticism, which saw in woman the saviour, the angel' (19:130), and, as Ulf Boethius points out, his specific conception is for 'a story in the spirit of George Sand, both the plot and the ideas recall her novels',[29] most pointedly, *Elle et lui*.

Strindberg had George Sand's epistolary novel on loan from the Royal Library from February to September 1876.[30] It was reading he eagerly shared with Siri von Essen and together (somewhat ominously) with one of the key nineteenth-century texts concerning adultery, Flaubert's *Madame Bovary*,[31] and a medieval Swedish text, the 'Love-letter from Ingrid Persdotter', which he quotes at length in his historical study, *The Swedish People*, and also has in mind in that other reworking of the material of *He and She*, the play specially written for Siri, *Herr Bengt's Wife*, Sand's book forms the immediate literary intertextuality of their correspondence. Indeed, on several occasions it seems to offer a basis for their intrigue. Responding to Sand's account of her relationship with Musset, in which 'elle' (Thérèse) seeks vainly to save the fallen and baneful *poète maudit* 'Lui' (Laurent), whose predicament as a post-Byronic hero he shares, Strindberg uses the letter in which Johan first writes openly of his feelings for Maria to develop a prominent theme from *Elle et lui*, namely the fine distinction between love and friendship. However, he foresees a more fortunate outcome to their own situation than to the one in which the dissipated Laurent finally escapes the tutelage of Thérèse. 'But we have a duty which is greater than love - read *Elle et lui* to the end - do - I am Lui - but you are better than Elle and you can govern me' (55:111), he tells her, addressing her shortly afterwards as 'You who can give this country its greatest writer' (55:115). Meanwhile, her reading of Sand's text prompts Maria to an alternative interpretation, which she puts forward in the course of her own declaration, written at the same time as Johan's (and well before *Miss Julie*!): 'I would trap you in order to arouse wicked passions in you - for the pleasure of seeing you at my feet like a slave and then to play the magnificent and charming woman à la Thérèse!?!' (55:86). In fact, Maria's insight into the self-deluding mechanism of reading and the danger of mistaken identities appears for the moment to be greater than Johan's; as she points out, when the image of the text fails to accord with the woman of the world: 'You had read the book, it was another Thérèse you saw in me' (55:87).[32]

Thus, even if he had not yet achieved the public notoriety of George Sand or Musset, which was the precondition for the transformation of that relationship into common literary coinage,[33] *Elle et lui* provided Strindberg with an early, pre-Naturalist example of the profit to be made from the public exploitation of the private domain as marketable literary merchandise. But where a recent editor refers to *Elle et lui* as 'cette étonnante version hagiographique' of 'l'histoire vraie',[34] what distinguishes Strindberg's book from Sand's is that the letters he uses were not reconstituted after an interval of twenty years, in response to a rival account (Musset's *La Confession d'un enfant du siècle*) but appeared as immediate Romantic transcriptions employing the codes of Sand's novel. Reading *Elle et lui*, itself the distillation of prevailing Romantic attitudes, gives Johan and Maria access to the means of fashioning their own lives. It is there they discover formulations for their own experience and precedents for the situations in which they find themselves, both as regards the collapse of frail and cherished distinctions and the formulae of piety, sophistication, and tact by means of which they gain a purchase on experience and convey it to others. These include a sanction for their rejection of convention in favour of a life in art,[35] for 'She' a role at first chaste as a sister and then as 'une maîtresse tendre comme une mère',[36] and for 'He', the aspect of a divided self, torn between the abyss and childlike innocence, in thrall to Satan ('j'ai rendu à Satan ce qui appartient à Satan, c'est à-dire ma pauvre âme') and reduced at an inn in Florence by 'un accès de fièvre cérébrale'[37] to a condition resembling Johan's on Dalarö, from which Laurent awakens to see Thérèse in the company of the manly Palmer, much as Johan saw Maria with the martial Gustav, standing beside his bed.

With its speculations on 'une mère prudente, un ami sérieux, une première maîtresse sincère',[38] *Elle et lui* is in fact hardly more certain of the roles taken by its protagonists than the actors in *He and She*, where on one occasion a confused Maria addresses Johan as 'My own beloved - own friend - brother - betrothed - or whatever I should call you' (55:163). In writing, at least, the parts of lover and mistress are replaced by other nominations, on a sliding scale of intimacy and responsibility. Once again as in *Elle et lui*, the most common are mother and child ('When I write, I want to be great; otherwise let me be your little child, and you cannot imagine how much you mean to me in every way, as a mother, a sister - anything you like, but not my mistress! Let me be your child' (55:165)) or brother and sister ('fate which has in you sent me the brother I have lacked ever since my childhood' (55:71), Maria tells him, adding later: 'I love you with the devotion of a sister, without coquettish caprices, without anything that could be called a forbidden love' (55:86)),[39] the latter disposition of roles being one which Strindberg later examines in *Creditors*, where another Gustav describes how his wife was stolen from him under cover of an artful nomenclature. When the lovers sense their illegitimate passion awake, he explains:

> ...they become uneasy, their consciences are disturbed, they think of him [the absent husband]. They look for protection and creep behind the fig-leaves, play at being brother and sister, and the more physical their feelings become, the more spiritual are the surroundings they invent for themselves.
> *Adolf*: Brother and sister? How do you know that?
> *Gustav*: I guessed it. Children usually play at mummies and daddies,

> but when they grow up they play brothers and sisters. To hide what
> must be hidden!' - And so they take a vow of chastity - and then they
> play hide-and-seek - until they find one another in a dark corner, where
> they are sure no one can see them! (23:207)

Moreover, just as Gustav's formidable omniscience here and in his suggestion,
shortly afterwards, that the lovers 'feel within themselves that *someone* sees them
through the darkness' (23:207), helps to clarify in retrospect the unease that fosters
the circumlocutions of *He and She* (and in a note omitted from the novel, Strindberg
informs Siri that 'Now there is only You and I and God!' (I:320)),[40] so the parlance
of these letters affords glimpses of other roles that also emerge in many later texts,
notably the poet and his muse, the plebeian and the aristocrat, and the swineherd
and the princess, as they inform *Herr Bengt's Wife, The Father, Miss Julie*, and *A
Madman's Defence*, where we are told: 'The son of the people has conquered the
white skin, the commoner has won a girl of breeding, the swineherd has mixed his
blood with that of the princess' (MD.121).

III

The question of roles, of which part and in what script one appears, is, of course,
complex. How one is regarded by the other may well decide one's own assumption.
Thus, in a letter omitted from *He and She*, Strindberg writes, in some perturbation,
'Answer me! Do you consider me your betrothed or your lover or your friend? I must
know for the sake of my destiny and in order to clarify my unpleasant role!' (I:320).
Usually, however, he is responsible for the distribution of parts, which are generally
legitimized by literary inspiration. Behind his reading of the situation there lies his
reading. For example, Thérèse's final letter to Laurent, in which she concludes:

> Dieu còndamne certains hommes de génie à errer dans la tempête et à
> créer dans la douleur. Je t'ai assez étudié dans tes ombres et dans ta
> lumiére, dans ta grandeur et dans ta faiblesse, pour savoir que tu est la
> victime d'une destinée, et que tu ne dois pas être pesé dans la même
> balance que la plupart des autres hommes. Ta souffrance et ton doute,
> ce que tu appelles ton châtiment, c'est peut-être la condition de ta
> gloire.[41]

'Génie', 'grandeur et faiblesse', and in particular, 'douleur', 'destinée', 'souffrance',
and 'châtiment', are all key terms tantamount to switch words or nodal points of
compressed meaning in the field of discursivity, whether French or Swedish,
whereby Strindberg recovers his life. Among countless other texts, *Elle et lui*
mediates a corpus of Romantic attitudes by means of which the writer identifies
himself, and the experience recounted in these letters substantiates itself according
to expectations that are fostered by the socially given text of the world in which their

writers live, and by means of the general cultural text which enables both Strindberg and Siri to communicate with one another, and, eventually, with a wider literate public.

Moreover, those words about which meaning clusters at its most intense, program or initiate a reading of events that renders experience legible and endow it with coherence and purpose. The letter written on the eve of Maria's departure for Copenhagen is in fact a dense matrix of meaning, employing almost the entire current register of interpretation, which permeates not only this correspondence and Strindberg's early works in general, but recurs throughout his production. Particularly notable is the complex of signification formed by his appeal to the concepts of suffering, as a sign of distinction and elevation, a source of and a spur to achievement, of genius and 'the magnificent halls in the temple of Art' (55:111), of a sacred calling, opposition to which represents 'a sin against the H. Spirit' (I:199), of martyrdom, which is really 'sweet' and 'the reward of genius' (55:114), and of sacrifice, the pain of which validates the pleasure which art affords.[42]

It is not, of course, difficult to trace the provenance of these ideas. Out of a general Romantic inheritance there emerges a familiar compound ghost of influence, embracing Ibsen's treatment of the notion of the poet's calling and the skald's gift of sorrow in *Brand* and *Pretenders*, Kierkegaard, Byron, Schopenhauer, and von Hartmann. In the latter two, for example, with their determination to uncover the inborn error that man exists in order to be happy, Strindberg finds philosophical authority for the intelligence that Byron depicts poetically, namely that

> Sorrow is knowledge; they who know the most
> Must mourn the deepest o'er the fatal truth,
> The Tree of Knowledge is not that of Life.[43]

And this expression of 'the ancient myth of the tree of knowledge' wherein 'conscious life was pain' (19:60), which Strindberg discusses in *The Son of a Servant* and quotes among the preliminary notes for *Inferno* (another text which, like Byron's *Cain*, divides the path of love from the way of knowledge) is also developed, with the encouragement of Kierkegaard, into a belief that the writer represents mankind precisely because of the extent and depth of his suffering. In the passage in *Repetition* in which he dicusses one of Strindberg's principal later identifications, Job, Kierkegaard observes:

> Nowadays people are of the opinion that the natural expression of sorrow, the desperate language of passion, must be left to poets, who as attorneys in a lower court plead the sufferer's cause before the tribunal of human compassion.[44]

This represents a notion that Strindberg stresses both in the letters of *He and She*, where he urges Maria to 'suffer, suffer, so that your heart wants to break; it doesn't break, it merely increases in size! - You must suffer everything if you wish to be an artist' (55:174), and in *A Blue Book*, in the text 'The Poet's Sacrifice'. The writer is thus both 'the representative of the human race' (I:201) and someone for whom life is 'staged before him...in order that [he] should both suffer and describe it' (XV:356).

But the language in which Strindberg presents himself in *He and She* indicates a still more far-reaching dimension to the context in which he reads life. The most persistent incarnation in these letters, and one that is associated with the conception of Nemesis which colours the opening monologue, is the view of himself as one who is 'born to wreak destruction' (55:5). This is expressed to the point of tedium, in the form of a self-consciously melodramatic literary pose which occasionally suggests the element of Romantic titanism in Strindberg's work, an element that reaches its full amplitude in the second part of *To Damascus*, when The Unknown wishes, quite literally, to have the last word:

> I am the destroyer, the annihilator, the world-burner, and when everything lies in ashes I shall wander starving among the ruins and rejoice at the thought: it is I who have done this, I who have written the last page in the history of the world, which can thereby be considered at an end. (29:175)[45]

Besides Cain, The Unknown's antecedents in this established repertoire of roles by now includes Merlin and Robert le Diable; but even the earliest instances of what Brandell follows Strindberg in calling his 'crisis religion'[46] are formulated in terms of recognizable religious and mythical categories. In the Dalarö letter, he already sees himself on the way to Damascus. 'The Lord has struck me', he exclaims, but 'the cry Saul! Saul! never came' (55:33); the defiant and scarred Jacob of the later autobiographical volumes and *To Damascus* is even now a familiar: 'I have rebelled against God - I have blasphemed - I have fought against him like Jacob...but now the tendon of my thigh is paralysed' (I:238), he informs the Wrangels, and again, 'If I meet him I shall wrestle with him, however paralysed I am already in my left side!' (I:238); while in his many references to his 'stony way', 'station after station', and 'the thorns in the wreath pressing into my brow' (I:324-5), he displays an evident readiness to view his life in the light of Christ's.

Writing in an age when Renan had transformed Christ into what Albert Schweitzer described as 'eine lebendige Theaterfigur'[47] it was, as Nils Norman points out, 'a short step' for Strindberg 'not only to associate [events in his life] with episodes in The Gospels but also well-nigh identify himself with Christ.'[48] And he did so not in the spirit of an *imitatio*, but in the terms of a Naturalist identification in which he recreates Christ in his own image. Indeed, throughout his life, Strindberg had occasion to read his experience in this way. As a writer and 'the representative of the human race',he is already 'a kind of Christ' (I:201) and so continually forced to 'empty another chalice' (IV:103). 'Now when I go up to Jerusalem, perhaps my Golgotha, to keep the Passover, alone, without disciples' (VII:37), he writes, on the eve of his return to Stockholm in 1888, and in 1894 he castigates the Judases among the writers of the 1880s who have betrayed him, and advises his old friend

Littmansson: 'If you are really serious, if you wish to make anything of yourself...then take up your cross and follow me' (X:131). 'Soon I shall go to eat the lamb of the Passover at the Ferkel before I go to Golgotha in Plötzensee' (X:7), he tells his irreverent fellow reveller, Bengt Lidforss, while only a year later, in the midst of the Inferno crisis, he adopts a different tone but the same register to inform Hedlund, 'I want to return home again, after I have been up to Jerusalem and spoken to the people' (XI:81). The role, moreover, is one that merges naturally with the projection of himself and the writer in general as a scapegoat who assumes the burden of general suffering, and in particular with the most sustained and comprehensive of his self-images as 'the son of the huts and tenements- The Son of a Servant - Hagar's -the desert's' (XIV:144), with its clear association of his identification both with contemporary impoverishment and the Biblical narrative of Ishmael, in which he habitually found a correlation for his own destiny. For all these roles are associated with the wilderness; each (whether Christ, scapegoat, or Ishmael) is an outcast in the desert to which Strindberg saw himself condemned even before writing the first volume of his autobiography.[49] 'My way leads into the wilderness, without friends, without being permitted to have any friends' (V:110) is a recurrent plaint. It crops up both as a casual image ('je n'étais plus seul dans le desert', he comments, in a letter to *Le Figaro*, after discovering Jollivet Castelot's *La Vie et l'âme de la matière*), and as a carefully primed account of his destiny, as when, in 1900, he writes to Nils Andersson: 'My greetings to Herrlin! Tell him I never attain harmony! But it is in the nature and idea of Desert wandering never to arrive!' (XIII:265).

But whether or not he pauses to make a specific association with Christ or an Old Testament predecessor, the use of these and similar images is typical of the way in which Strindberg promptly sees his experience in terms of myth and legend. In even the most apparently casual statement, as Harry Carlson suggests, what begins as a chance series of associations immediately assumes a form and a context. The symbol develops into myth and the myth into cosmogony within the space of a few lines.[50] Or at least, the identification appears spontaneous because, as the bearer of the appropriate cultural information, and having already allotted himself a role, his surroundings and the people he encounters are rapidly composed into the context he expects. With his mind on matters infernal, it is not surprising that the landscape around Klam in Austria, where he is staying with his parents-in-law, should remind him of Dante's Inferno or that the dog discovered on the threshold of Munch's house in Paris suggested Cerberus to him. And in many of the notes preserved in the Royal Library, it is possible to observe how he enlists a number of interrelated identifications in order to explore and ascertain his situation. Thus in the drafts for a play entitled 'Mäster Ensam' (Master Alone), he tried on a number of familiar guises he had used elsewhere in his plays (Merlin, Robert of Normandie, Hercules, Socrates), before, in a typical instance of cross-fertilization, he settled momentarily upon 'Socrates and Omphale' and proceeded to apply it to current matters:

Socrates against a disorderly world. However he behaves, he is criticised. If he lives with a woman, he is tormented; if he is loving towards her, he is called sensual; if he is as restrained as he would like to be, he is mocked as decrepit. If he lives alone, chaste, he is called depraved. If he goes to women, he is called lecherous. If he is indifferent as regards religion, he is called a godless blasphemer; if he is religious, he is called a hypocrite when he cannot bring his life and faith into harmony (which is an impossibility.) The envious commit wrongs against him and when he does not want to suffer wrongs even against himself, he is called envious.[51]

Thus, as Carlson again remarks, 'Thinking mythopoeically was not a momentary, periodically recurrent aberration, it was as natural for him as thinking dramatically,'[52] and alongside the correlations which he fashions for himself, those with whom he lives are also alloted roles into which they, too, disappear, or are raised, like Strindberg in his own particular assumptions, to the status either of 'dramatic personae', such as Yeats also described in a volume of his *Autobiographies*, or of participants in a mythical or literary text from which, as Omphale, Beatrice, or Cinnober, they cannot escape.

Having made the identification, however, Strindberg then builds upon it with great care and industry. His description of the landscape around Dornach and Klam leads him by means of etymological speculation and association ('törnetagg', 'törne', 'törnestigen' - prickle, thorn, way of thorns) to recall the wood of the suicides in the *Inferno* and so confirm a link with Dante's poem, while in general terms it evokes both the crown of thorns and 'the field of thorns' (28:176) to which his destiny appears to have condemned him. Moreover, the *document humain, Inferno*, is - as Eric Johannesson suggests - perhaps the most literary of all hells,[53] the outcome of assiduous research in which Strindberg ransacked not only Dante but also Virgil, Swedenborg, Byron, Hesiod, the *Rigveda*, Viktor Rydberg's *Undersökningar i germanisk mytologi* and *Medeltidens magi* as well as Balzac, Wagner, and Péladan, in order to confirm, and to confer shape on, his own infernal experiences. The metaphor of hell controls the narrative, accounts for what material is developed and what is omitted, and governs the course of events. Incidents that are insignificant in themselves gain in substance and meaning only by the narrative in which they are placed, where they are worked over and written up as events plotted and paced with conscious literary intention. The title and chapter headings indicate this procedure, of course, but two minor and amusing instances may exemplify Strindberg's practice. One is the dramatic irony at which he connives when the goldmaker is reduced to beggary; another occurs in the retouching in which he indulges in the description of the scenery around Dornach. Along with such infernal trappings as the remorseless mill, the goat's horn, a sinister broom, and the miller's boys, 'as white as the false angels' (28:135), he comes across a wooden building of which he writes:

It was a low, oblong shed with six oven doors. ...Ovens!

Good God, where was I?
The image of Dante's hell rose up before me, the coffins with the
sinners being baked red hot - and the six oven doors! (28:134)

This description, with its allusion to Canto 9 of the *Inferno*, is based on an entry in
The Occult Diary for 9 September 1896, which also incorporates a sketch of the
forbidding building (in fact, in commonplace reality a malodorous pig-sty) made at
the time. However, the sketch reveals that initially Strindberg noticed and drew
eight openings. Only afterwards, possibly when composing *Inferno*, were two of
these crossed out to bring it into line both with Dante and with the mystical
interpretation of numbers since, as an insertion beneath the drawing points out, '6 =
a bad number'.

Inferno, however, represents only the culmination of a period of close reading in
which Strindberg scrutinized every occurrence in order to penetrate to the text
which lay beneath the surface. Probably the most striking of the many examples of
the ingenuity with which he pursued his researches, and the detail on which he
founds his reading, is the extraordinary venture into comparative biography which
he conducted in the letters to his daughter Kerstin, *The Occult Diary,* and *Inferno,*
where he traces a network of relationships between himself, Napoleon, and the
Greek hero, Ajax. Initially playful, this speculation becomes an experimental field
of research in which he enlists the resources of history, mythology, etymology,
number magic, and iconography, in order to establish a correspondence that would
also substantiate the eschatology of guilt and suffering on which he is concurrently
working. This whole topic has been studied by Nils Norman in his exemplary
article, 'Strindberg och Napoleon', which demonstrates that 'in Strindberg's
mythical world, however bizarre it might seem, there was a logic of symbols,'[54] and
only the kind of detail in which Norman recovers Strindberg's own minute tracing of
the etymological and mythological correspondences which link the three figures can
adequately convey the reach and precision of his method. But a limited example of
the kind of symptomatic reading in which Strindberg excelled can be seen in a letter
to Hedlund, in which he reads his life according to the text of astrology. Born under
the sign of the ram, and hence predestined to be a scapegoat ('This sign represents
the sacrifice' (XI:281)), he perceives that 'Every success is followed by sufferings;
every trace of happiness is smeared with dirt; every encouragement is a mockery,
every good deed punished with the cross', and that this is a prescription that
establishes the unmistakable contours of his own destiny. But the sign also signifies
renewal, and he gains some encouragement from its Cabbalistic and Biblical
implications. Moreover, in a reference by Manilius to 'The Ram, famous for its
fleece of gold', he discovers not only a correspondence to his current interest in
alchemy, but also to his 'first performed play, *In Rome*, which deals with Jason,
whose statue with the golden fleece was Torwaldsen's first'. Likewise, the jewel
related to this sign is the amethyst, his own favourite, notwithstanding that his is 'in
pawn in Paris for 3 francs', and among other pertinent factors he recognizes in the
Martian provenance of the Ram ('Out of his mouth went the two-edged sword') an

affinity with 'the motto of my first publication [*The Freethinker*] - I am not come to bring peace but the sword'.[55]

It is naturally tempting to regard Strindberg's recourse to myth solely in terms of psychology, either to discern throughout the capacious embrace of the Great Mother, as is unfortunately the case in Harry Carlson's otherwise often stimulating study, *Strindberg and the Poetry of Myth*, or, like Donald Burnham, to stress the purely therapeutic value of his identifications. Burnham maintains, for example, that 'by means of these outer representations [Strindberg] was able to confront, work through, and gradually accept the reinternalization of his conflicts.'[56] It is certainly true that symbols and myths permitted Strindberg to reorganize himself and his relationship to his experience; in *Inferno, Legends,* and *Jacob Wrestles* the use to which he puts the figures of Jacob and Job, allowing the one largely to replace the other as his involvement in events passes from passive suffering to active engagement, provides one obvious example. But the stress placed by Burnham on the therapeutic underestimates a number of other factors, among them the amount of sheer play in his speculations, and - in cases where Strindberg relies on detailed if idiosyncratic research - the purely literary dimension. For it is in literature that the reorganization takes place. Strindberg's use of myth is situated within a recognizable literary tradition, and its primary purpose is to provide him with the means of organizing a literary text rather than the reorganization of the existential, unadulterated text of himself.

Furthermore, many of the identifications he makes, among them the comprehensive image of himself as 'The Son of a Servant', are not so much therapeutic as the means of self-aggrandizement. They confer distinction, elevate him to a singular destiny, and ultimately contribute not to the revelation of his hidden or unknown self but to the screen across which his image flits in one (dis)-guise or another. They are, as Gunnar Brandell has indicated, 'conceptions to which Strindberg has recourse for self-defence when his situation appears unendurable',[57] and the fear that the assumption of many roles might deprive him of his own identity, that he would become featureless, like the figure of his story, 'Jubal Without an I', was not without foundation. The multitude of incarnations in which he deposits some aspect of his experience, from Ahasverus, Asmodeus, Christ, Hercules, Jacob, Job, Jonah, and Joseph, to Tobias, The Flying Dutchman, Loke, Starkodd, Svarte Balder, or An, Cain, Ishmael, Merlin, Napoleon, Robert le Diable, and Satan, are components of a multiple image, the contents of what amounts to a theatrical wardrobe composed in language and providing a looking glass in which, somewhat in the manner of the experiments with superimposed photographic images of his contemporary, Francis Galton, to which Strindberg alludes on the first page of *The Occult Diary*, an ur-image might be perceived. But if this is the promise, the example of *To Damascus* is salutary. Caught up in the median order of symbols, he confronts himself as 'The Unknown'. The final signified eludes him because it belongs not to literature but to the real. 'We all travel incognito' (51:30), the Hunter admits in *The Great Highway*, and the epitaph with which the play concludes, 'a cursory inscription' (51:100) written in the snow, is only a final gesture, one more version of the myth with which, above all others, Strindberg has been engaged, the myth of himself.

For the remarkably consistent portrait which emerges in the successive representations of himself throughout his life is a personal myth, based upon a system of private associations. In the biography he evolves for himself, he frames a portrait in order to represent himself in the form in which he wishes to be regarded, both by himself and by others. The act of symbolization removes him from direct participation in the events he records. If it facilitates his reorganization, it also places him at a distance; that is, it replaces the event with an account of it in which it enters the domain of the imagination. To quote Lacan:

> The drama of the subject in the verb is that he faces the test of his lack of being. It is because it fends off this moment of lack that an image moves into position to support the whole worth of desire: projection, a function of the Imaginary.[58]

Moreover, since he is neither the creator of the symbols nor the founder of the myths which he employs to convey this image, but their inheritor, in using them, he is formed by them. Wherever he finds himself, he discovers precedents, from Joseph in Potiphar's house in several of the naturalist novels and plays, to Saul on the road to Damascus, and thus, as Ernst Cassirer writes

> The more richly and energetically the human spirit engages in its formative activity, the farther this very activity seems to remove it from the primal source of its own being. More and more, it appears to be imprisoned in its own creations - in the words of language, in the images of myth or art, in the intellectual symbols of cognition, which cover it like a delicate and transparent, but unbreachable veil.[59]

In the versions of himself which Strindberg transcribes, he sees therefore not himself but his reflection as it is fashioned by his desires and his regrets. In short, he is a prisoner of the mirror in which he regards himself.

CHAPTER FIVE

Publishing the Private
or The Economics of Experience

Sometimes it has occurred to me that a man should not live more than he can record, as a farmer should not have a larger crop than he can gather in.

- Boswell: The Hypochondriack

Though the earth and all inferior creatures be common to all men, yet every man has a property in his own person; this nobody has any right to but himself.

- Locke: Second Treatise on Civil Government

I

In a finely tempered and persuasive record of her encounters with Strindberg in Switzerland in 1884, Hélène Welinder recalls a conversation in which his young compatriot's sympathetic concern prompted the tired and harassed writer to describe the condition of almost permanent literary production in which he lived with unusual clarity. 'I cannot rest, even if I would like to,' he is reported as saying:

I have to write for my daily bread, to maintain my wife and children, and in other respects, too, I cannot leave it alone. If I am travelling by train or whatever I'm doing, my mind works without ceasing, it grinds and grinds like a mill, and I cannot stop it. I get no peace before I have put it down on paper, but then I begin all over again, and so the misery goes on.[1]

Whether or not the image of the remorseless and insatiable mill reached this quotation as a direct transcription of Strindberg's words is, of course, open to question. Nevertheless, even if it belongs entirely to Welinder's reconstruction, it is apposite, for it not only features frequently in Strindberg's later work as an image for the treadmill of conscience and the tenacity with which the past clings to the present;[2] it also encompasses the suggestion that to write out what experience provides affords at best only temporary relief. But there is an additional complication at which it also hints, and which is inseparable from the publication of such writing, namely that in relieving himself of what he has lived, the professional writer consumes his experience and hence needs constantly to renew his primary material if he is not to become, or appear to become, 'written out'.

This tension between the pressures of 'writing out' and becoming 'written out' highlights a polarity which informs the whole of Strindberg's career. He is caught between the subjective drive which compels him to write ('and in other respects, too, I cannot leave it alone') and the inescapable exigencies of a market with which his inspiration and his fund of material may be out of step, and which either devours what he offers it and then demands more, or rejects his products as unsaleable. The law of supply and demand enters into an uneasy partnership with the fluctuations of inspiration, which sometimes floods the market when the latter is slack (and no market could accommodate the extraordinary series of sixteen plays, including *To Damascus* I and II, *The Dance of Death, Erik XIV,* and *A Dream Play,* which the prodigal Strindberg produced between 1898 and 1901) or remains unresponsive to its seasonal needs, or to specific commercial advantages as regards length, genre, style, and material.

A few weeks in the spring of 1888 are typical. Forced to produce a quantity of what he considers inferior material 'which could be sold as summer reading' (VII:80) merely in order to live, and speculating privately over the sale of several older works in manuscript to earn some ready money,[3] Strindberg fears for his talent. He is casting about for an alternative source of income in order to escape the deleterious effects of overproduction 'in this age of specialists and the division of labour' (VII:82) when suddenly 'a narrative set in upper Sörmland (150 pages perhaps) called *The Sexton in Vidala'* (VII:89) erupts into a publishing schedule which is geared to the short pieces of *Life in the Skerries (Skärkarlsliv)*,[4] and it is only with some violence to the text in hand that the one can be reconciled with the other. Indeed, the new narrative, which becomes 'The Romantic Organist of Rånö', rapidly outgrows Strindberg's expectations: 'It was intended to be a trivial sketch of an uninteresting organist fellow,' he tells Bonnier, 'but has turned into something much more than that' (VII:103). Meanwhile another text is taking shape in events at Skovlyst where Strindberg is for the moment impecuniously and precariously lodged ('This will be a novel later' (VII:112) is his ominous comment to Edvard Brandes, when he sends him an interim report), and *Miss Julie,* which he shrewdly estimates is a work 'which will go down in history' (VII:104), remains unpublished even though he relinquishes every pretension to a reward which would be commensurate with what he recognizes is 'the flower of my production and of Swedish drama' (VII:106), and asks of Bonnier only the most meagre of returns, its labour cost at a subsistence rate of pay: 'My conditions are only the production costs for the manual labour (= one month of life)' (VII:104).

Strindberg was, of course, aware that the reach of his talent and his productivity were too capacious and versatile for the restricted Swedish market, and he recognized a more appropriate stage for his labours in Berlin or Paris. 'My enormous productive urge (and the word Strindberg uses, *produktionsdrift,* indicates both an innate urge and its actual marketing) requires the book markets of several countries' (VI:80), he told the dubious Bonnier in 1886, and even if it meant forsaking his native language, he had frequently to live and to write accordingly. With a majority of his recent plays either unpublished or unperformed in Sweden, an essential aspect of his departure for the continent in 1892 was the need to discover new outlets for his work. 'After trying for so many years to live as a Swedish writer, I have realized it is impossible and am at crisis point' (IX:5), he informed a colleague earlier that year, and in the period which followed many works, among them *Inferno*, were fashioned and written either wholly or in part with a foreign public in mind, as he found himself once again a (not so) young man from the provinces laying siege once more to 'die Hauptstadt des XIX. Jahrhunderts'. And he knew enough not to arrive empty handed. 'Am bringing 100 pages of a feuilleton in French with me', he told his contact in the city, Littmansson. 'Will start straight away with some sensational articles so that Paris will be astounded' (X:225). Worldly wise at least in this, he knew by now that the writer is his own product and must display himself spectacularly.

For his predicament was by no means unusual during a period in which the writer was generally confronted by what Goldsmith, a century earlier, had described as 'That Fatal Revolution whereby Writing is converted to a Mechanic Trade.'[5] Produced in private for an anonymous and dispersed public, and increasingly dependent upon the author's subjectivity for its matter (and the shift which Georg Lukács detects from the multifaceted participation in society of Goethe, Stendhal, and Tolstoy, to the writer's confinement to the specialism of his trade in keeping with the capitalist division of labour, is an essential element of Strindberg's career),[6] writing in Europe becomes capitalized in the nineteenth-century: that is to say, as patronage recedes and it becomes impossible for literature to escape the general division of labour, the writer who seeks a living by his pen alone, puts his thoughts and feelings into circulation on the open market, where the work of art in which they are rendered purchasable, becomes another commodity, in competition with all the others.

This is a mill to which all is grist, but the process has rarely been so clearly expressed as in a letter from Balzac to his publisher, Mame, after a visit to the Grand Chartreuse. The experience had, he maintains, been profound and uplifting, but within a week he is writing:

Redoublez d'attention Maître Mame
J'ai été, depuis longtemps frappé et désireux de la gloire populaire qui consiste à faire vendre à des milliers incommensurables d'exemplaires, un petit volume in - 18 comme *Atala, Paul et Virginie, le Vicaire de Vakefield, Manon Lescaut, Perrault,* etc
    La multiplicité des éditions compense le défaut du nombre de volumes; mais, il faut que le livre puisse aller en *toutes* les mains, celles de la jeune fille, celles de l'enfant, celles du vieillard et même celles de la dévote. Alors, une fois le livre connu, ce qui est long ou bref, selon le talent de l'auteur et (celui) du libraire, ce livre devient une affaire importante, exemple, les *Méditations* de Lamartine à 40 000 ex(emplaires) et les *Ruines* de Volney, etc.
    Mon livre est donc un livre conçu dans cet esprit, un livre que la

> portière et la grande dame puissent lire. J'ai pris l'Evangile et le
> Catéchisme pour modèles, deux livres d'excellent débit, et j'ai fait le mien.
> J'ai mis la scène au village, et, du reste, vous le lirez *en entier*, chose rare
> avec moi.

In thus describing an as yet unwritten book (but which eventually appears as *Le Médecin de campagne*) Balzac promptly transforms a moving spiritual experience into an item for sale, citing the prolifically selling New Testament as one of his models and outlining the type of public at which it is aimed. And while, as a professional writer, he is immediately able to place it in terms of genre and style, and is certainly in no doubt that he can write this instrument of his 'gloire populaire' when he chooses so to do, as a businessman he can also gauge its sales potential and see it will prove a sound investment.

Throughout the Inferno period, it is clear that Strindberg is also constantly examining his experiences with a similar view to publication. From the outset he is intent on producing 'my book about everything I have "seen" and experienced since last December' (XI:193), and while he occasionally considers reverting to an earlier, pre-capitalist mode of publication by allowing the book to circulate only in manuscript (XI:323), his more practical schemes fluctuate between the novel and autobiography, the *document humain* and a work of speculative natural science. Moreover, however alarming the experiences he is monitoring become, there is no doubt that in seeking to interpret the enigmatic script of what he terms *makterna*, the capricious powers who seem to him in turn to be monitoring his life, he continues to function as an author, accustomed to publishing his experiences on a market that is, in its own way, equally capricious and enigmatic. On one level, the central phase of the Inferno period is inaugurated as a business project in which, with Torsten Hedlund as his agent back home in Göteborg, he secures a period of relative financial stability that allows him to conduct the experiments with the data of his own life which will eventually contribute so much to the text of *Inferno*, by ensuring, against various promisory notes of future writing, a privately donated sum of 1,200 kronor paid in monthly instalments by what he gathers is a group of business men, on occasion directly to the locations where the drama of his life is acted out, the Hotel Orfila and Mme Charlotte's Crêmerie (XI:135-8) where he sleeps and takes his meals. 'I propose this consortium as follows', he writes to Hedlund: 'that I write a series of [articles as] letters [for publication in *Göteborgs Handelstidning*], straight from memory and my notes, without taking your paper or its readers into account, but so that every letter can form a chapter in a book which, if you like it, I then offer you [the chance of publishing], and for no honorarium if it does not promise to earn one' (XI:138).

Traces of this plan remain in the letters to Hedlund which Strindberg wrote between 6 and 22 July 1896 on manuscript paper rather than on the ordinary writing paper he used for several other more mundane letters to the same correspondent, paginated consecutively from 1 to 59 across the intervals in their composition.

These letters evidently encompass a provisional attempt to organize the material he later incorporated in the early chapters of *Inferno*, and already betray the ongoing process of artistic rearrangement of lived experience, for example in the account of his discovery of the French chemist Orfila, the instance of bibliomancy connected with the latter's book, and the general description of his predicament at the beginning of July, all of which is similar in tone and effect to the opening pages of *Inferno* (XI:245-6).[8] And even if he claims only to be 'preparing a book in manuscript - which I am writing for myself and *de Enkelte* (Strindberg uses the Kierkegaardian term); without bothering about publishers, newspapers, old maids or the magistrate's court' (XI:388), he nevertheless also knew precisely when it was opportune 'to re-establish contact with life' (XI:310) and resume the profitable exploitation of his experiences in literature, once he had accumulated the necessary experience. Indeed, both the beginning and the end of the Inferno process as a whole demonstrate a remarkable combination of self-awareness and business acumen. The letter in which Strindberg initially reopened contact with Hedlund as the possible intermediary his future project would require, was written the day after he had sent his current intimate, Littmansson, the retrospectively significant information, 'What destiny now awaits me I do not know, but I feel 'The Hand of the Lord' resting upon me. It heralds a change upwards, or straight down to the centre of the earth, who knows!' (X:152),[9] a clear sign that he intended a new departure, and it was followed by another in which he refers to his need for 'raw material in large quantities, observation, preferably my own, for I cannot depend upon other people's' (X:206-7). And having thus primed what proved to be an effective avenue to the support he needed, he was equally astute some two years later in recognizing when 'the period of grace' (XI:304) afforded him by his backers was over and he had to 'take up the yoke again and work for my bread' (XI:303) by recommencing his literary career. Moreover, he revealed a similarly astute awareness of when this material had been fully exploited. In a letter to Gustaf af Geijerstam in March 1898, he admits what is so often the case with his projects, namely that he 'has miscalculated the extent of the manuscript' (XII:271) he has on hand. Although his current work, *Jacob Wrestles*, was not yet finished, he considered 'my religious conflicts at an end, and the whole Inferno saga over' (XII:271), and a few days later, impatient now to continue the playwrighting he has resumed in *To Damascus*, he contemplates a solution to the problem of his scanty copy which is no less mercenary in its implications than Balzac's plans for *Le Médecin de campagne*. Writing from Paris, he suggests:

A new plan!
On my journey to Lund (or Copenhagen) sometime early in April, depending on the money, I might stop off for a few days in a Benedictine monastery in Belgium to which I have been invited. I want to describe my impressions in Inferno II.
You can see that this will be a 'clou'.
So: a delay!

Why have a fiasco of a book, when we could have a success! To bore the public by reappearing with Part III in the autumn won't do! Two stout blows, and then full stop. (XII:278)

Thus as Lukács remarks, when discussing the novel in which this process is depicted most comprehensively, Balzac's *Illusions perdues*: 'From the writer's ideas, emotions, and convictions, to the paper on which he writes them down, everything is turned into a commodity that can be bought and sold.'[10] Or to quote Arne Melberg, whose language permits the point to be made very neatly indeed, literature is now a fusion of work and commodity, or *verk* and *vara*:

> the nature of literature as *work* is determined by conditions in the sphere of circulation, where it also becomes an object and *commodity*. And the work (*verket*), as an aesthetic and meaningful unity (*enhet*), emerges as precisely a closed totality (*helhet*) in consequence of the market where it is forced to circulate as a commodity (*vara*).[11]

Melberg's formulation aptly indicates both the context in which the professional writer may produce his works under contract, to a specific length, and at so many words a day, in order to earn the going rate per page or column (and as Strindberg discovers, when he negotiates the asking price per sheet according to the number of spaces per line with his publisher and compares his rate with the fees several of his contemporaries can command, not all writers or subjects realize the same rate (III:288)), and the attempt by a minority of writers, like Baudelaire and Mallarmé, to detach the work of art from market forces by disclaiming its utility value. And yet, as Roland Barthes has pointed out, it is precisely in order to preserve the work of art from the rough and tumble of the market place that such writers are also drawn to stress the labour involved in writing as a value in itself. Gautier, Flaubert, or Gide, Barthes observed, 'substituer à la valeur-usage de l'écriture, une valeur-travail...L'écriture sera sauvée non pas en vertu de sa destination, mais grâce au travail qu'elle aura coûté. Alors commence à s'élaborer une imagerie de l'écrivain-artisan qui s'enferme dans un lieu légendaire, comme un ouvrier en chambre ...passant à ce travail des heures régulières de solitude et d'effort.'[12]

The consequences of this situation are far-reaching. Whether it is shrouded in the notion of *impassibilité* or shamelessly solicits attention by parading the author's personality in public, the work in which the writer disposes of his qualities and abilities, as if they were objects he could give away, diminishes and impoverishes him. 'L'homme n'est rien, l'œuvre tout', Flaubert asserts,[13] and from 'Le Chef d'œuvre inconnu' to *L'Oeuvre* and *When We Dead Awaken* or Mallarmé's 'Herodiade', numerous nineteenth-century works maintain that when the product is imbued with life, its creator dies to life. Once completed it enters upon a life of its own, and into a series of relationships with other texts and other men, in keeping with the ideas developed by Marx in the section on estranged labour in *The Economic and Philosophic Manuscripts*, where the dehumanizing consequences of the product's domination of its producer are so eloquently described. 'The more the worker produces', Marx writes, 'the less he has to consume; the more values he creates, the more worthless he becomes; the more his product is shaped, the more misshapen the worker; the more civilized his object, the more barbarous the worker', and deprived of direct, immediate contact with his audience, the writer, too, is plundered by his creation and deformed by his revelations. As Marx goes on to write, in words that have a particular poignance where the autobiographer is concerned:

> The worker places his life in the object; but now it no longer belongs to him, but to the object... What the product of his labour is, he is not. Therefore, the greater this product, the less he is himself. The externalization of the worker in his product means not only that his labour becomes an object, an *external* existence, but that it exists *outside him*, independently of him and alien to him, and begins to confront him as an autonomous power; that the life which he has bestowed on the object confronts him as hostile and alien.[14]

Dispossessed of his identity by the initial estranging transfer of the self he seeks into the language in which it is sought, the autobiographer thus confronts himself in the work as an alien figure whose life resembles but is no longer his own, and as the market on which he is launched becomes more impersonal and his readership more dispersed, so there is a complementary tendency for the writer to grow more intimate and his books to become the increasingly personal explorations of private experience. On the one hand, there is the inhospitable, strange, and alien world dominated by the impersonal powers of the market, in which the imperilled self (and this is a theme in Jacobsen's *Niels Lyhne* and Hamsun's *Hunger* as well as of *By the Open Sea* and *Inferno*) lives as it were with no fixed abode, while on the other, the diminished social role to which he is restricted by specialization, hands the writer over to self-reflection and self-projection.

In part, this has to do with the role subjectivity plays in the competitive struggle for the attention of a public the writer has to woo. A form of self-advertisement, it is a way of marketing his product: the individual consciousness seeks to distinguish itself, to affirm its incomparable originality and uniqueness. And if the style is the man, the man is what he produces. He develops, and the public purchases, a work that is identifiable with the name of its producer, a name that becomes associated with what he produces. He seeks to be unmistakable, and beyond a characteristic style, a personal matter is one means by which the literary work identifies its progenitor, selects its readership, and demarcates the boundary separating the property of one author from another. Thus, dependent as he is for his livelihood on the interest of the public, attention devolves upon the person of the author, upon the image of himself that his works project, either in the form of a direct and strident self-exposure, in which he lives shamelessly in the eyes of the public, or through the creation of biographical images within the work whereby, as 'The Son of a Servant' or 'Joseph K', the writer is identified. The art of scandal and provocation is therefore linked with the other arresting images of the writer, including what could be termed the canonical set of actions which a culture expects him to carry out, and the legend of himself which the writer creates is thus itself a literary fact, a constituent part of the work for sale, and one which plays a structural role in the formation of the text.

This notion of self-reflection and self-projection is central. Where a previous generation (and in Sweden it is the group of writers known as *Signaturerna* who 'are the last representatives within Swedish belles-lettres who exist as a literary grouping outside a literary institution that is determined by the demands of the market place')[15] could write without attending to themselves (as Stig Torsslow suggests, 'they did not dream of being themselves - they did not even understand what that meant - but strove to write what criticism expected of them'),[16] Strindberg is brought by what he once termed 'the application of mercantilism to literature' (4:206) to place the author's own tribulations and possibilities at the centre even of what is ostensibly an historical drama, *Master Olof.*[17] Freed by private resources, a position at the university, or a civil service post, from the need to publicize themselves, the writers of the *Signatur* group were, according to their spokesman, Carl David af Wirsén, the Secretary of the Swedish Academy and Strindberg's long-standing opponent, preserved from the demoralizing effects of the professional writer's life, and not least from that loss of character for which Strindberg in all his provocative variousness and apparent instability, was so often accused, not least by Wirsén himself:

> Being employed upon precise tasks in the service of the state has given character a healthy firmness, and the muses, whose appearance is as fleeting and unpredictable as it is sweet, have thus come unbidden and, as they love, shown their favours without having been troubled by importunate and indelicate requests to be present at all times.[18]

As he strove to establish himself as an independent man of letters, however, Strindberg recognized that 'even when he is recognized a writer is nothing in himself, but everything by virtue of the opinion others have of his talent' (37:151), and he therefore claimed that writers had 'always worked with a great deal of noise; if they have not succeeded in making that quantity of *bruit* at which they have aimed, they have once again vanished into the eternal silence.'[19] 'Rien n'est si désagréable que d'être pendu obscurément', as he was tempted to add to the title page of *The Red Room*;[20] and hence the writer, if he is at all well known, becomes a kind of public property, even a public spectacle:

> The writer is a person who appears in public. The public follows his apprenticeship and watches his progress. The newspapers follow his work both with affectionate care and microscopic attention. He walks a tightrope over a waterfall. As long as he goes elegantly, no one dares whistle. On the contrary, people outdo each other in their applause to show they have taste. But as a public, they cannot avoid feeling a certain, why not say pleasure, if he falls. (16:53)[21]

Thus, when he threatened 'to travel around in Sweden and show [him]self for money' (V:272, but the idea recurs, and finally as a metaphor for his career as a writer in the late prose text, 'The Inevitable' (46:71)), it was only an extension of this primary appearance before the public that Strindberg had in mind. Had he not already sought to exhibit himself in language, there would have been no question of this physical spectacle.

When, however, it is ostensibly the writer himself, or his pseudonymous representative, who is repeatedly launched upon the market, the situation wherein the writer makes a business out of his inner life becomes particularly transparent, especially when retailed with the nakedness with which Strindberg appears to display himself.[22] Indeed, Strindberg generally regards private experience as a form of primary capital, to be accumulated and then invested in language. 'Better, however, an unhappy marriage than none at all. One goes through it and comes out more experienced than before, and experience is capital' (41:290), the literary entrepreneur, Smartman, maintains, at the close of *Black Banners*, and Strindberg, too, evidently considered the events he sometimes instigates in order to acquire the material he needs for his work as *kapital* (capital) to be transformed into *kapitel* (chapters). 'Well, I got a new chapter out of it' (I:151), he remarks, after parting from an early mistress, much as when the hero of the late autobiographical novel, *The Cloister*, salvages his sinking courage on the way to meet his estranged wife's family by adopting 'as usual the writer's point of view: "If I don't come out of this with honour, I shall at least get a chapter for my novel!"' (C.92). Or as he observes again, some five pages later, when he relates how he 'went out to botanize and look at the landscape, and worked himself up into an irresponsible creative mood in which he thought about the piquant aspects of the situation: "This is a scene which no one has experienced before! It is mine, even if it's going to make my skin smart"' (C:97).

It is such 'collections of experienced material' (18:274 -*materialsamlingar av erfarenheter*), as he calls them, which form the basis of his production, and either immediately or in due course, they are turned to his account by a talent which authorizes the accumulation of experience irrespective of the cost to others which its exploitation occasions. 'He considered his talent was also a kind of capital; even if it brought no profit now, it gave him the right and duty to live whatever the cost' (19:27), he explains in *The Son of a Servant*, just as he later confesses that 'for me life is only material for dramatic works',[23] and acknowledges in a diary entry for 25 January 1901 that 'if my life had passed calmly and quietly, I would not have had anything to relate.' Moreover, as a practising author he prides himself on the ability to perceive not only what is valuable in experience, but also how it should best be utilized. Hence the delight with which he realizes that some events, for example Dagny Juel's appearance in Berlin, come ready cut and trimmed (*klippt och skuret*) for literature ('Oh it's a novel!' (IX:188) he exclaims, with relish) or fall into the appropriate literary form when exposed to a tutored ear. In the Vivisection 'La Genese d'une Aspasie', the accomplished man of letters instructs the novice: 'Installé dans la même maison le maître dédie une éducatiυn complète au petit, le fait narrer sa vie, lui indique où gisent les motifs avantageux. "C'est du théâtre, lui enseigne-t-il; voici une nouvelle; voilà un roman"' (VR:22)

The experience behind such mastery is intimated early in *The Cloister*, which opens with the writer reflecting upon recent events: 'By lying in bed and chewing over his experiences like this, he converted them into literary currency, and thus engraved or riveted them so securely on his mind that he could draw on them for future use as safely as if they were funds deposited in a bank' (C:14). Again the image is characteristic. Nothing may be squandered: the trace of every event is jealously guarded and, his spendthrift inspiration notwithstanding, Strindberg frequently refers to this steadily augmented basic capital in terms of prudent literary house-keeping. For the question is often how much he has in his current account and how much is deposited for the future or lying unused or unexploited in the form of already written but unpublished or out of print works that represent 'dead capital' (V:278) on which he demands the 'interest' (IX:205) due to him. Thus when writing *The Son of a Servant* he deliberately leaves certain motifs on the shelf. This is particularly the case with his experiences on the island of Kymmendö in the Stockholm archipelago, and with the history of his first marriage. For the time being both are allowed to gather interest, but in May 1886 he tells Bonnier that 'when I have finished part II, I have been thinking of writing a little book of Swedish idylls for the Christmas trade...These are savings (*sparpenningar*) from *The Son of a Servant*, in which the scenery has been intentionally neglected' (V:320), and some six months later he already sees their realisation in 'a Swedish rural novel in which I shall invest my large reserve fund from Kymmendö, which I have not used as long as I had hopes of returning there again', adding, with a rare and passing tolerance: 'To be sure, young Geijerstam has drawn a small compulsory loan on my fund, but I have seven years' savings and so many feathers left that I can donate a little down to the goslings' (VI:122). As for the history of his marriage, he merely remarks, darkly: 'We'll come back to the matter'.

This attitude to the relationship between the writer's work and his lived experience is not, of course, unique to Strindberg. At about the same time, Victoria Benedictsson wrote to Axel Lundegård that 'we writers have no other capital to draw on than our knowledge of human nature. This is therefore the capital which we must accumulate',[24] and Béatrice Didier has recently written persuasively of the way in which the intimate journal becomes a deposit account for 'le capital fondamental: le moi'[25] as it is augmented or misspent from day to day. But in Strindberg's case, rooted as it so firmly is in the spirit of Protestantism to which Didier often alludes in her analysis, it is exacerbated by his pronounced sense of property rights, both as regards his own person and the ideas he entertains. Writing, which acts as a daily inventory in which he monitors the debit and credit of his account with the world, is also entrusted (and not only in the period when he was preoccupied with the notion of a 'battle of the brains') with the preservation of the writer's intellectual domain. 'It is surely the case', he argues, in the late essay, 'The Mysticism of World History'

> that when someone has adopted an opinion or viewpoint, it is somehow assimilated into their person and becomes a property which at first

requires defending, and then that one goes on to the attack in order to increase it, like any other type of property. To surrender one's opinion to another's is really like being conquered, becoming another man's slave, and one does not want that to happen. (54:370)

Thus the intensity with which Strindberg maintained the principle that 'what one has oneself experienced is of course one's own, and he who wishes to take it away from one is a thief' (X:216), and hence the lasting aggravation to which he was provoked by an embezzler of other people's experience such as Gustaf af Geijerstam, whom he repeatedly accused of filching his material.[26] For if, as The Unknown declares, 'what I have lived through is mine and no one else's', then 'what I have read has (also) become mine, because I broke it in pieces like glass, melted it down, and out of the shapeless mass blew new glass in new forms' (29:322), and Strindberg consequently resents all interference with his script since, once written, it has the creditworthiness of any more orthodox financial transaction: 'Altering a text which is signed by an author ought really to be considered tantamount to altering the value of an accepted bill of exchange'(54:236).

However, the kind of conspicuous consumption of private experience in which Strindberg engages is ultimately a form of self-consumption. Paradoxically, in displaying his riches so generously, he periodically impoverishes himself and needs to replenish his resources. 'My purpose in travelling to Berlin', he informs Schering, 'is for study and to get some new ideas, for here the sleep of winter prevails all the year round, and I have lived up the whole of my stock which I brought back from abroad the last time' (XIV:220). For the kind of primary capital accumulated in lived experience or drawn from other books (and topping up experience could be expensive, as Strindberg indicated to Bonnier apropos the story 'Rebuilding' (*Nybyggnad*): 'the novella is composed, studied (I have read 100 francs worth of books)' (V:8)) is rapidly exhausted, and a professional writer such as Strindberg elected to be, is forced, as Walter Berendsohn once pointed out, continually to

> *look about him for a new motif*, which stimulated and attracted him,
> but which also saved him from repeating himself and boring his readers.
> Originality, not to come again with the same thing, to be new and in the
> vanguard of intellectual development, are clearly conscious demands,
> which he placed upon himself and his creativity.[27]

Always afraid of 'falling behind' (V:343 - *att bli på efterkälken*) in the advance of contemporary ideas, this is one reason for the apparent inconsistency of Strindberg's work, its frequent shifts in direction, the rapid introduction of new subjects, styles, and genres, the continual enticement to experiment with fresh standpoints, to change his mind, his place of residence, or even his wife, in accordance with the modernist doctrine that Baudelaire formulated so succinctly:

> Plonger au fond du gouffre, Enfer ou Ciel qu'importe?
> Au fond de l'inconnu pour trouver du *nouveau*![28]

As the autobiographical persona of the barely fictional narrative "Sequestration Journey" (*Kvarstadsresan*) points out, 'All my work is only a matter of changing opinions' (17:18), in part because - as Strindberg once expostulated to Littmansson - 'It must be new! New!' (X:189), and the consequences of such an attitude are to be found in *A Madman's Defence*, fruit of 'an experimental psychological investigation' that is ostensibly undertaken 'merely to enrich my literary fund' (VI:242), in *The Cloister*, where Axel has 'consumed most of his experiences' (C:73) and therefore sets out to replenish his stocks by finding what Strindberg at the time liked to call 'novels in reality' (IX:104), or in *Inferno* where, already adept at cultivating sickness and passion in himself in pursuit of the truthfully observed motif, he commences his return to literature by adopting the mood of deceptively casual receptivity that he attributes to Axel in *The Cloister*.

> I have no opinions, only impromptues, and life would become pretty monotonous if one were to think and to say the same thing every day. It must be new; the whole of life is after all only a poem, and it is much more amusing to float over the swamp than to stick one's feet down and search for firm ground, where none exists. (C:58)

On occasion, at least, this was the spirit in which he embarked for the continent in 1892 to fill what became known as 'Gröna säcken', the green canvas bag into which he put his notes and scientific records, and the seemingly directionless period in Berlin, his short second marriage included, emerges as a time in which Strindberg accumulates the capital of experience without at first knowing how to make use of it in literature. It offers an image of Strindberg as the plaything of chance, at drift, allowing events to happen to him ('I feel liberated, drifting on the surface of a sea' (28:10), he recapitulates this mood later) but trawling fresh matter to replace his exhausted copy. 'I act by improvising; that makes life more amusing' (28:78), he explains, and while his striving for some kind of transmutation certainly retains a role for the improvident goldmaker with which his existence during this period is most dramatically associated, it is pertinent to notice that the immediate crisis is artistic, a combination of factors to which Strindberg, with his acute feeling for the pulse of literary history, was especially sensitive.[29] Sensing that 'the naturalistic period...has now come to an end' (28:182), and in any case no longer wishing to locate himself in a moral and intellectual framework with which he had never been entirely at ease; responsive to the challenge which Verner von Heidenstam's literary manifesto, *Renässans*, directed against his already eroded standing in Sweden;[30] encouraged by the example of Przybyszewski's and Munch's artistic experiments in Berlin and his acquaintance with Gauguin and the Symbolists in Paris, where he discovered an art that was alert to 'l'inépuisable fond de l'universelle analogie'[31] and not prostrate before the superficial transcription of external reality (and as he told Hedlund: 'I abandoned writing literature to avoid being superficial' (XI:138)), he 'commence aussi à sentir un besoin immense de devenir sauvage et de créer un monde nouveau'.[32] In short, he recognizes the need to renew a genre which he had himself brought to fruition in *Miss Julie* and *Creditors*, and his 'Inferno Crisis', with its issue in the achievement of *To Damascus* and *A Dream Play*, is thus undoubtedly best apprehended in the light of Boris Eichenbaum's shrewd judgement upon an analogous and contemporary case: 'At the core of all Tolstoy's crises lies the search for new artistic forms and for their new rationale.'[33] And if this new rationale is to be seen as fundamentally 'mystic', as is now sometimes the case, then it is worth remembering that, as A. G. Lehmann wisely points out in his study of Strindberg's French contemporaries: 'mysticism affects aesthetic theory not by enabling its adepts to 'believe anything', but by giving them, or attempting to give them, an explanation why they find art valuable at all.'[34]

For the process of self-consumption inherent in his Naturalist aesthetic frequently overwhelms Strindberg with feelings of disgust that extend to his practice as a writer in general. In a letter of 1898 he described himself as someone who 'gehe...wie ein Menschenfresser und Henker herum. Welch' ein Lebensberuf Schriftsteller zu sein: wie ein Fleischhauer töten und verkaufen' (XII:342), a description in which the characteristic conflation of text and flesh recalls both the famous quatrain from his volume of poetry, *Sleepwalking Nights*:

Där hänger på boklådsfönstret
en tunnklädd liten bok.
Det är ett urtaget hjärta
som dinglar där på sin krok. (13:209)

(There hangs in the bookshop window / a thinly clad little book. It is a gutted heart / which dangles there on its hook.)

and the even earlier critical observation on another writer from 1876: 'A writer is not a writer just because he has written a book, for he has not had the courage to give his own blood, give a piece of his own inner life, instead of those events he has only encountered by chance. It is a grisly task to place one's heart on a *montre*. It is the cruelest kind of sacrifice to be a writer - but that is how it is!'[35] And these doubts, shored up as they are by the notion of self-sacrifice, are only compounded when he recognizes the impossibility of writing openly of himself without encroaching upon the property of those about him, an anxiety which informs the account of the writer's life presented in *The Cloister*, where Axel's consumption of his outstanding experiences reveals (if somewhat disingenuously, since the book implicitly in question, *A Madman's Defence*, had in fact been written by Strindberg some years earlier and in different circumstances to those in this retrospective reconstruction of his life) how exhaustion and poverty compel him to encroach upon a proscribed domain:

Approaching penury had forced him to sit down unwillingly to write, but as he had consumed most of his experiences he was obliged to misappropriate a subject that was really proscribed. He suppressed his own feelings, overcame all discretion, and began. (C:73-4)

The irony of the situation, in which the writer who preys upon himself and offers up his flesh for others to consume also battens upon those close to him and devours them like a cannibal or vampire, is in this case multiple. In order to provide both for his previous wife and children, and for his new attachment, the only narrative he has on hand is 'the merciless portrait of his first marriage' (C:75). Unable to produce a new work, in part because the already written account of this marriage so disgusts him, and quite unable, too, to invent or imagine a text with no basis in his experience, the unpublished book is nevertheless his only immediate means of support. And yet, by publishing it, his revulsion at his trade as a writer becomes too great even for the role of scientific vivisector which he evolved during the 1880s to exonerate him from writing as he does so explicitly of others. Torn between the morality of telling what he regards as the truth and the immorality of publishing the private (or put another way: unable to reconcile himself to satisfying the demands of a voracious market by continuing to prey upon himself and others), he now experiences how

> ...the increasing distaste which he had for some time felt for his profession as a writer developed into an abhorence.
>
> What an occupation: to sit and flay one's fellow human beings and then offer their skins for sale and expect they should buy them. To be like the hunter who in his hunger hacks off his dog's tail, eats the flesh himself and gives the dog the bones, his own bones. To go about spying out people's secrets, to betray one's best friend's birthmark, use one's wife as a guinea pig (*vivisektionskanin*), behave like a Croat, chop down, defile, burn and sell. (C:130-1)[36]

Thus it is that when Strindberg attempts to recapture the spirit and ideas of the years leading up to his Inferno crisis, in a narrative that is inevitably coloured by his later experiences, his representative in the book, Axel, is already depicted as trying consciously 'to purge himself from the leaven of Naturalism' (C:20) which produced so brutal a book as *A Madman's Defence*, at the same time as he is shown up as the unwilling writer of such a book because unlike Strindberg when he came to review these years, he has not yet developed an alternative way of seeing the world.

II

Whatever the anachronistic obscurities of *The Cloister*, however, it is not surprising that as the most transparent and far-reaching example of his naturalistic art, *A Madman's Defence* should so compel Strindberg's attention. Of all his works, it is the one which disturbs him most, and it intrudes into many other texts besides *The Cloister*, where he claims it was 'written in self-defence and as a testament, because in finishing it [he] intended to take his own life' (C:79). Obliquely, its presence is already felt in *Creditors*, where Tekla uneasily deflects discussion of the book she has written about her first marriage (23:253); it reappears, unexpectedly but appropriately, in *Black Banners*, in Zachris's plans for the publication of a similar story in Germany 'if pressed by necessity' (41:214 - *A Madman's Defence* was, of course, first published in Germany as *Die Beichte eines Thoren*); and it is also a central motif in *To Damascus I* where, as the embodiment of his guilt and of his misused talent, it relates The Unknown's situation in the first scene to the hiatus in his literary career which comes to light when he admits 'I am bankrupt, for I have lost the ability to create' (29:101) partly as a result of his most recent book, the account of a previous marriage which he forbids his companion to read. It is only when he acknowledges this link between his guilt and his literary impotence that he begins his progress along the road to Damascus, and towards the rationale which provides him with the basis of a new art.

Moreover, Strindberg's often contradictory and perplexing, sometimes ingenious, and on occasion deliberately misleading comments on the book between 1887 and 1894, indicate the continual disquiet, embarrassment, and uncertainty it caused him, not only as regards the propriety of what he had done in writing so intimately and with such venom of the private life he shared with others (and here the barbarous deformation of the producer referred to by Marx in his account of alienated commodity production is again a relevant factor), but also as to what kind of writing the book represents, to which domain, public or private, it belongs, its genre, who should read it, where, and in what language and what form. For beyond what the book reveals of Strindberg and his intimate life is what it conveys of the nineteenth-century literary institution, of the writer's confinement to a largely private sphere of existence, and the conflict between the exploitation in literature of private material and the economic necessity of its publication, a conflict accomplished by a shift in public expectations, which now anticipate the lineaments of the author in every kind of literary text.

If combining what Zola terms 'une méthode chirurgicale, s'appuyant sur la science, aidant la science'[37] with a Kierkegaardian sense of duty seems to sanction his right as a writer 'to intervene with his time-honoured freedom in human lives and destinies, as a calling and a duty' (37:108), and thereby to satisfy 'the spirit of the time [in its challenge] to write about the living and not the dead' (VI:191), then Strindberg feels justified in overturning the reticence of a previous generation (and the shift can be observed in a comparison with Trollope's remark in his autobiography: 'My marriage was like the marriage of other people, and of no special interest to anyone except my wife')[38] and publishing what he originally called the 'Histoire de mon marriage', a work he claimed was 'plus sincère que toute le reste' (X:86) and warranted because 'it is my story stark naked. . .It is a terrible book, but it is a true one' (VIII:188). Initially he regarded it as 'a whole original novel in French' (VI:381) which, with Zola in mind, he often called his 'Oeuvre',[39] and in March 1888 he was already sounding out Hans Österling with a view to publication. His approach even hints at the category into which the work might fall: 'Do you dare take a French novel, set in Sweden, as indiscreet as [Hans Jæger's *Fra*] *Kristiania-Bohèmen*, but tremendously good, and which cannot or may not ever be published in a Scandinavian language' (VII:33)?[40] But the proviso already indicates a reservation. If, as Sven Rinman infers,[41] a foreign language gave him an essential, uninhibiting distance to his material which enabled him to write the book in the first place, Strindberg also wrote in French because he knew that 'when a work creates a scandal in its country of origin, it only has to cross the frontier where one no longer knows the "local circumstances" and it becomes literature'(16:48).[42]

But while a foreign language might suggest a wish to shield the feelings of those about whom he wrote, it also had practical advantages. As he explained to his cousin, the manuscript 'consists of 350 quarto pages, in French, for the dual purpose of keeping completely unauthorized people out of the matter, and so that it may not come under the heading of a Swedish manuscript, which according to certain contracts would fall to my publisher' (VII:43). And when he tried to interest the French publisher, Albert Savine, in the book, it was certainly not least this Scandinavian public that he envisaged among its potential readership: 'D'ailleurs et pour fixer le nombre des exemplaires à imprimer, il faut vous dire que vous pouvez compter sur mon public entier en Suède, Norvège, Danemark et Finland, en égard à ce qu'une édition en langue Scandinave ne sera jamais publiée' (VIII:371). While he continued to describe *A Madman's Defence* as a novel when expedient, however, the very fragility of its almost diaphanous fictional guise caused him to contemplate an alternative future for the text by playing down its literariness and stressing its documentary, even its testamentary, character as an 'Ehrenrettung' (VII:42), composed 'in the face of death' to claim his own redress, repudiate 'the fable that I was mad' (VII:48), and correct his strategy in texts such as *The Father*, in which he maintained he had 'lead opinion astray on purpose in order to conceal the real situation' (VII:47). 'Ce n'est pas un roman,' he told an unknown correspondent in 1893, 'ni un livre dans le sens propre de ce mot, c'est plutôt un fragment d'une vie agitée, et ce volume, écrit devant la mort; déposé chez des parents sous le sçeau pendant deux ans il fut destiné à servir comme document de famille pour l'avenir, je n'avais jamais l'intention de le faire imprimer' (IX:339), and in fact, three days after his letter to Österling of March 1888, he had already informed Edvard Brandes that he was working on 'my history, which will never be published, but will be read in manuscript by my surviving [relatives]' (VII:36). Moreover, when he took the extraordinary precaution of sending the book in manuscript to his cousin, Johan, and (thereby covering himself against misreport, and the text against misrepresentation) also to Heidenstam, the accompanying letters described it as 'a document to be deposited in the family archives... to enlighten posterity about the situation, provided that violent measures do not compel me to disclose everything immediately to my contemporaries' (VII:43). And such was the uncertainty surrounding the domain of this text in the minds of Strindberg's contemporaries as well as in his own, that as a submission for the defence in the mysterious prosecution brought against the book in Germany, this family letter was indeed accepted as evidence that it was neither a novel nor intended for publication.

Whatever the purpose he attributed to the book, however, the moral dilemma in writing and publishing *A Madman's Defence* was certainly instrumental in provoking the revaluation of personal values during the Inferno period, when Strindberg largely abandoned literature for science and painting. In the former he escapes into a neutral language of chemical formulae and mathematical symbols that precludes identification save eventually of the 'calculating...measuring...master builder' (27:494) whose signature he came to recognize in the recurring forms of nature; in the latter, he abandons himself to 'the teleology of chance' (X:215) and carries painting to the verge of non-representation, to the point at which the subject vanishes. Thus in both cases he avoids the type of compromising identifications of the Naturalist period and also, as Göran Söderström has suggested, transforms the visible world into a *skogssnufvistisk* (or modernist) work of art, evolved by a creator whose artistic rationale resembles nothing so much as Strindberg's own.[43] From the too naked exposure of Naturalist writing *à clef*, with its merciless treatment of those surrounding his own central figure, he therefore works towards the rehabilitation of fantasy and an art that yields its innermost secrets only to those initiated into the mysticism of everyday life, where 'banal facts' (XI:263) and 'strange chance occurences' are transposed by analogy into meaningful events and a moral order wherein man is no longer, as in Naturalism, continuous with a determining nature that seems to preclude either a basis for personal responsibility or a rationale for pain and suffering, but part of a planned cosmology, in which the earth resembles a place of correction for crimes committed before birth, and men and women are merely one another's tormentors: 'If this existence is already purgatory or an inferno for crimes we have previously committed we are all demons, here to torment each other, and when we are driven against our will to do evil, we are only doing our duty, but suffer all the same from the fact that we have done wrong. This is the double curse of existence. No one has the opportunity of tormenting one another as thoroughly as a man and woman, who love each other (= hate each other)'.[44]

Thus his return to literature and to the continuing exposure of himself and others is again authorised, for he is now able to see his own life in its emblematic form as an *exemplum* or 'warning to others' (28:6) which he considers it his duty to make public, and in place of the no longer tenable role of vivisector he can, as the interpreter of this rediscovered moral order, recognize it as his duty to chastise others as they, indeed, seem so often to chastise him. And just as he had previously found solace in the idea that he had 'sacrified all the peace of my private life and offered up my whole person for the sheep' (V:356) as 'the preacher, the prophet, the truth teller' (18:313), so the later conception of the writer as a 'scapegoat' is already developed in the confession, 'I struck my own wife, myself! It was a personal sacrifice, which I had to make. But that I struck those who were wretched! That is terrible, but it was perhaps the most essential point of all'. Ultimately, such statements, like the numerous Biblical texts from Ezekiel and Jonah, which come to hand whenever his writer's role perturbs him, serve to ratify his conduct both retrospectively and in later works such as *The Dance of Death* and *Black Banners*, in which on one level of the text at least, his material is no less personal than in the Naturalist novels and plays. For in both public and private matters he continues to expose himself and those about him; it is simply that after the Inferno crisis he works within a framework that mitigates his guilt. As he explains, to the poet Gustaf Fröding, '[I] must go forth and prophesy, in spite of the risk of being disavowed like Jonah' (XII:316); only now, in the economics of experience he has evolved for his craft, he expects to pay in terms of personal suffering for the use he makes of other lives besides his own.

This, then, is the passion of the writer as it appears to Strindberg, and his suffering is without end because, his periodic schemes to combine literature with some other source of income notwithstanding, there is never any serious doubt that he will continue to appear before the public in words. However, as strategems 'to save my talent from overproduction and my children's future from *misère*' (VIII:180), to provide the secure and regular income which writing did not yet afford, and to retain the freedom to write as he chose (and for this reason he also resisted the idea of a writer's stipendium as a form of 'commitment which a writer ought not to take upon himself' (54:235)), all the possibilities that he entertains as regards an alternative career, whether as banker's clerk (VII:76), language teacher, tourist guide (VIII:180), gardener (V:121), lighthouse keeper (VIII:209), secretary and amanuensis to the theatre director August Lindberg (IX:8), or 'secretary, major domo, or head waiter in a large hotel' (VII:79) where, like Jean in *Miss Julie*, he dreams of using his talent for foreign languages , deserve serious consideration both for what they reveal of his general predicament as a writer of exceptional range and ability who was yet unable to live by his pen, and because, as Bo Bennich-Björkman is almost alone in remarking, they 'may well...be related to central conflicts rooted in his life and writing.' 'All Strindberg's plans in this direction have still not been properly studied and seem to be regarded by a number of researchers as no more than passing fancies,'[45] Björkman observes. Seen in the context of the pressures imposed on him by his chosen mode of writing, however, they are illuminating. When, for example, he informs Bonnier that 'one fine day I will advertise for a position in a bookshop, as a correspondent, or for the tenancy of a market garden - I'm quite serious about this', his threat occurs in a letter where he once again describes writing as 'a raw and repulsive occupation' (V:121), and the stability of these alternative ways of earning a living also reflects that underlying concern over the apparently immoral ease and lack of constraint with which art and the artistic life were customarily associated in his mind. 'Everyone worked apart from him,' Johan reflects, in *The Son of a Servant*: 'When he now compared his dissolute, irregular life, without peace or quiet, to theirs, he considered them both happier and better. Their lives were serious and they carried out their tasks and fulfilled their duties without any hullabaloo or boasting' (18:397), and from the early comedy, *Anno '48*, and *The Red Room* (in which Olle Montanus's words from beyond the grave describe the artistic urge as 'resting upon a broad basis of a desire for freedom, freedom from useful work' (5:357)) to *To Damascus III*, where the choir of children intones 'Thou shalt feed thyself with the work of thine hands' (29:245), Strindberg is haunted by a sense of guilt at the artist's apparent immunity from 'the curse [incurred] in the Fall of Man' (5:357). And hence, against the remarkably constant anxiety which a 'life of poetic idling' (18:364) arouses in him throughout his career,

Strindberg also evokes a life of order, of clear moral precepts, firm parameters in a world that is secure, clean, harmonious, and, ultimately, patriarchal. On the one hand, there is the 'unnatural' isolation of 'the unclean bachelor life' (28:252) to which the practice of art seems periodically to reduce him; on the other, a 'natural' world of work and of the home, which promises him membership in a community whose lack has otherwise pained him from his first days at university in Uppsala, when the glimpse through a half-open door of 'a paterfamilias, a mother, and their children about a well-laid table' (I:30),[46] revealed a world from which he now felt excluded, and which continues to enchant him even as he attempts and fails to achieve it once again in his relationship with Harriet Bosse, to whom he writes: 'And I only see things in a good light when *we three* are together. We three, man, woman, child were a world, legitimate, whole, sufficient unto ourselves, and therefore beautiful' (XV:30).[47]

In one form or another, in *Master Olof, Getting Married, By the Open Sea, Inferno* or *To Damascus*, the conflict between isolation and community, the creative individual and the family, informs a large part of Strindberg's production, and throughout his work references to matrimony and the family are of course legion. 'The whole of my being rests upon my family' (IV:45), he maintains in 1884, and when he loses the first edition he laments: 'The worst of it is that work, life, business, cease to interest me when I do not have my family to struggle for, and in isolation I die' (VII:49). And yet, as a practising writer, his hold on family life is so demonstrably fragile. 'I was born for family life and a mate - and see what happened!', he exclaims on 6 September 1901 in *The Occult Diary*: the attempt to be both a writer and a family man repeatedly founders even as it becomes the object of insistent literary scrutiny, in the course of which he evolves the legend of himself as having been 'born out of grace, brought up as life's step child, harried, hunted, in a word, cursed' (29:241) to account for the failure of his 'youthful dream of a house, where peace and purity dwelt' (29:240). Thus, although he would certainly have distinguished himself from the standpoint of those writers (particularly Flaubert, the Goncourts, and Huysmans) who demonstrate their opposition to bourgeois society by rejecting the nineteenth-century cult of the family as inimical to art, Strindberg's predicament emerges, in practice if not in precept, as reminiscent of Flaubert, James, or Kierkegaard, for all of whom writing involves a sacrifice of life itself.[48]

Like Strindberg, too, these writers frequently stressed the complex interplay of forces by which, if art preyed upon other lives, it also fed upon the artist, however apparent his detachment from the text he produced. Flaubert, for example, often resorted to the same kind of violent physical image to describe his situation as Strindberg employed to encompass the enforced exposure of his inner life. Just as Strindberg was accustomed to see this as the painful and unsightly baring of his entrails (*inälvor*), so Flaubert protested: 'Un livre est une chose essentiellement organique, cela fait partie de nous-mêmes. Nous nous sommes arraché du ventre un peu de tripes, que nous servons aux bourgeois',[49] and wrote, once more to Feydeau, whose wife was dying: 'Tu as et tu vas avoir de *bons* tableaux et tu pourras faire de *bonnes* études! C'est chèrement les payer. Le bourgeois ne se doutent guère que nous leur servons notre cœur.'[50]   Moreover, the stress on method at the expense of experience in Flaubert's correspondence, and the theory of *impassibilité*, are in part a response to this situation. For if, as Lukács points out, the division of labour now excludes the writer from living a multifaceted life and isolates him 'as a subject, from all experiences not intended exclusively as the accomplishment of the work,'[51] the consequences are twofold. Firstly, as the experiential capital to hand diminishes, the writer is reduced to the role of observer. Secondly, when he is thus thrown back upon his private life and condemned to observe himself and those close to him, a condition arises (and not only for Flaubert at Croisset) in which it is the work that possesses life while its author, plundered by his creation, is emptied of vitality.

This situation has been conveyed in two striking images. In *Illusions perdues*, Claude Vigon observes:

> Le génie est une horrible maladie. Tout écrivain porte en son cœur un monstre qui, semblable au tænia dans l'estomac, y dévore les sentiments à mesure qu'ils y éclosent. Qui triomphera? la maladie de l'homme, ou l'homme de la maladie? Certes, il faut être un grand homme pour tenir la balance entre son génie et son caractère. Le talent grandit, le cœur se dessèche.[52]

In *The Will to Power*, meanwhile, Nietzsche, like Strindberg, prefers the vampire to the tapeworm:

> Artists are *not* men of great passion, whatever they may like to tell us and themselves. And this for two reasons: they lack any sense of shame before themselves (they observe themselves *while they live*; they spy on themselves, they are too inquisitive) and they also lack any sense of shame before great passion (they exploit it as artists). Secondly, however, their vampire, their talent, grudges them as a rule that squandering of force which one calls passion. - If one has a talent, one is also its victim: one lives under the vampirism of one's talent.[53]

But like Marx, who has his own vision of the vampire 'in the shade of capital, of dead labour, that dominates and pumps dry, living labour-power',[54] what both these passages emphasize is that the victories of art seem to be bought by a loss of character, and that this loss may be interpreted in two ways. Most palpably, it has to do with the moral dubiousness of the procedure already examined, in which the writer is obliged to turn his private life to account and encouraged to publicize himself. Irrespective of any autobiographical pact, therefore, the text and its author come to be regarded as commensurate with each other. As Basil Hayward remarks, in *The Portrait of Dorian Gray*, 'we live in an age when men treat art as if it were meant to be a form of autobiography',[55] and with the breakdown of that frank and familiar communication between writer and reader on which, for example, Dickens and Thackeray still congratulated themselves,[56] it is as if the reader comes to regard the story as something other than fiction, as if he learns to read it symptomatically as the more or less masked avowal of the writer's private life, a situation conceded even by many of Strindberg's more circumspect contemporaries such as Conrad, who admits: 'A writer of imaginative prose (even more than any other sort of artist) stands confessed in his works.'[57] But there is also a sense in which the seeming shamelessness of the writer, his self-exposure and lack of that moral singleness of character upon which Strindberg so often reflected, is turned back upon itself and the vampire becomes the prey. It is this that Victoria Benedictsson hints at when she observes: 'The people I invent batten upon me like vampires. They leave me hardly a drop of blood, for it is from me - from me they take their life.'[58]

These themes, and the conflicts which underlie them, are all revived in Strindberg's final major reckoning with the literary world, *Black Banners*, a book which is constructed to probe the permissable boundaries of his method and once again to attack the irresponsibility and immorality of his contemporaries in general, and of a way of life which permits a frivolous minority of artists 'to sit here in freedom like this, idle in the morning, while the whole of mankind was working' (41:78) in particular.

The society portrayed in *Black Banners* is populated by the descendants of his 'red' book, *The Red Room*, the inhabitants of 'humbug's perverse epoch' (41:32) in which, from values to reputations and from furnishings to opinions, everything is false, pilfered, and a lie: 'Lies in life and ways of living, lies in society, in friendship and love, in legislation, administration, government, politics and religion' (41:185). But what the book stresses is the economic basis by means of which (as he wrote to Schering, shortly after its completion), 'False values are put in circulation, stolen and begged-together reputations circulate, and the entire values of the time become fraudulent' (XV:44), and where it has become the norm 'to write about nothing, to fabricate art without content' (41:33). As Martin Lamm remarked, in response to this novel, 'exactly as in Balzac one observes in Strindberg how money is the mystical omnipotent power, which stands behind everything',[59] and the society depicted in the book is one of predatory animals in a vulgar Darwinist social jungle, creatures who evaluate every relationship in terms of profit and loss. The motif permeates the imagery. 'People were living in a practical age of political economy and did not squander on conversation', the Narrator explains, 'everything is bought nowadays, and merchants appoint professors' (41:5). Thus at the literary dinner with which the novel opens, Professor Stenkåhl's precocious daughter, who is learning fast, inquires of one of the guests 'Listen Kalkbrenner...have you bought pappa, or has he sold himself?' (41:18), while in Stenkåhl's ensuing embarrassment the listening Zachris 'perceived all the economic possibilities inherent in the painful situation' (41:25). Similarly, the Narrator remarks, of Zachris's wife, Jenny: 'Everyone who came to the house got to see her, but not for free. They had to pay with flowers, services, advertisements, feats of nature, and even with ready money' (41:44), while in organizing her funeral it is pointed out that 'Zachris, who for the moment was quoted at a low price on the [literary] market, did not want to risk a fiasco' (41:275).

This economic imagery is associated almost exclusively with Zachris and his circle. It is they, whose dark designs and shady practices are carried through under the black banners of the novel's title, who 'steal each other's thoughts, each other's addresses, each other's friends and one another's identities' (41:10). They live blindly behind their masks, ignorant of an alternative world which the novel also adumbrates, where values are solvent and true. In spite of the glasses which pointedly conceal his eyes rather than improve his sight, Zachris is unable to see this other order of existence which is visible to the group of intellectuals who have withdrawn to a spiritual retreat in the monastery on Siklaön, and which is eventually discerned, if dimly, even by Jenny. 'Eaters of men' and 'executioners' (41:17), these bohemians of the market place regard life 'as a battlefield, and existence as a struggle for bread, position, and woman' (41:288), a battlefield on which Zachris, the vampire, thrives as the most bitter and disturbing of Strindberg's studies of the Alrik Lundstedt-Peer Gynt motif, a merciless analysis of the characterless self, of the writer as 'a selfless jelly' (41:211) who has lost himself by impersonating others and playing every role except his own.

Because Zachris had 'an enormous empty space to fill' (41:48) within himself, he preys on others as 'the racketeer of literature, forming companies for mutual admiration, speculating in reputations...He undertook business trips to publicise himself, had agencies in every corner of the country, formed a company to export himself to Germany...was obliging, in order both to tie the hands of other people and bury his pound, which could be dug up again with interest when it suited him' (41:38-9). He places others in his debt in order to exploit them for his private profit, both as material for literary works and as the tools which literature manipulates. He is unable to 'live in and by himself, partly because his 'I' was weak from birth, partly because he had lost it in the course of life, or rather, sold it on fortune's market' (41:41) and hence 'he ate people, ate up their accomplishments, fed upon their private means, and possessed the ability to enter other lives, plough their furrow, so that he confused his person with other people's' (41:48).[60] Exactly as Strindberg testified to the confusion between fiction and reality in his own experience as a writer, so Zachris loses that firm consciousness of selfhood which is associated with the idea of 'character' that had been scrutinized in *The Son of a Servant*. 'To have a conscience one must know oneself and be a self,' the Narrator points out, and hence the immorality of the writer, Zachris, who 'had always lived other people's lives, never his own' (41:211). And hence, too, the veiled self-criticism in the novel, for if Zachris had 'given out roles, made types of himself' (41:211) all his life, he had done no more than Strindberg, who noted, at about this time: 'The poet sits and sees himself in certain scenes. Discovers he has distributed roles'.[61] The irony is, of course, that it is by means of a fiction that Strindberg, unwittingly or not, suggests the truth about his own failure to tell the truth about himself.

This lack of self is the basis of Zachris's vampirism, his ability to eat his way into other lives and steal other people's thoughts and emotions. But what commences as a long-meditated act of revenge directed by Strindberg against Gustaf af Geijerstam, the writer who he had long regarded as the pilferer of his [Strindberg's] experience, eventually develops more far-reaching similarities between the past and practice of its creator, and the methods attributed to his prey. There is of course the evident irony that in selecting a readily recognizable model for the character who is the main target of his satire, Strindberg has written a novel which solicits attention on precisely the interest-seeking grounds it criticizes in Zachris - as Erik Hedén remarked, it was such hardly concealed scandalous personal attacks which made the book 'a unique means of speculation'.[62] But what is more pertinent is that as always when he was committed to a subject, Strindberg's characters partake of his own flesh and blood (and the tired metaphor is particularly appropriate here), as well as the body and form which others, sometimes unwillingly, lend him, and Zachris is no exception. Indeed, at times his ability to evoke his creator is striking, notably in his compulsion to transform his experiences into literature and write himself free of a troublesome marriage, as Strindberg had done in *A Madman's Defence*, but also, as Hans Levander has pointed out,[63] in the often anachronistic reactivation of mnemonic traces which occur in the course of Strindberg's writing the novel, which endow Zachris with a substantial layer of experience in common with his creator. The return of a son from a former marriage affords one such episode (it is also recorded in *The Occult Diary* and *Alone*)[64] and material from the lonely winter Strindberg spent on Djursholm in 1891 after his parting from Siri von Essen, is woven into the melancholy Christmas Zachris spends when Jenny leaves him, as well as into the sufferings of the more apparent authorial surrogate, Falkenström. Although projected through the imagery of Strindberg's later point of view, as a potential Swedenborgian vastation on the way to Damascus, this recovery of previous experience provides yet another instance of that jealous reluctance to leave anything he had lived through unutilized, which was so characteristic of Strindberg.

Levander is no doubt correct in suggesting that such material recurs here because Strindberg's animosity towards Geijerstam and Ellen Key (on whom Hanna Paj is modelled) was partly prompted by their failure to respond as he wished to the relationship between his wife and children and the Danish painter (and according to Strindberg, lesbian) Marie David, in 1891. But it is more constructive to see the presence of such material here as a consequence of the conscious parallel which the novel establishes between the destinies of Falkenstöm and Zachris. Faithful to his normal practice, Strindberg distributes his own experience between more than one character, or constructs characters from material provided by several models. As he remarked, in the suppressed preface to the novel: 'That is what all of us do!...But we are not simply a camera show (*biografteater*)! We take a few features here and there, we work in mosaic; and when the hero (pardon the expression) is such a lump that he does not hold our interest, I have the right to knead in a little alien clay in order to pad out the match-stick man.'[65] If in most respects it is Falkenström who represents Strindberg in the scheme of the novel, then Zachris is his shadow, and the parallels between them are as essential as their divergencies. As Bertil Romberg observes:

There are several parallel patterns in the novel. Thus Zachris's marriage and its development is paralleled by what is related of Falkenström's marriage. The parallel is underlined by the somewhat complicated position that Zachris has once acquired in Falkenström's marriage, while Falkenström periodically lives as the third party in Zachris's household.[66]

More relevant than these facts, however, is the way in which the two writers react differently to two complementary experiences. This is stressed by the structural juxtaposition of Falkenström's suffering or passion, in Chapter Nine, and the agony of Zachris's Christmas, both of which represent a Swedenborgian vastation, wherein the individual is confronted by his past and provided with the evidence necessary for its correct interpretation, in much the same manner as similar experiences form the substance of the key scenes in Strindberg's post-Inferno drama. Falkenström thereby learns to see matters in a different light. He takes the commonplace, that the earth is hell, literally, and makes his way through the inferno to Siklaön, where he hesitantly undergoes initiation into a new and purer world view similar to the one that Strindberg glosses in the speculations of *A Blue Book*. That is to say, in the course of *Black Banners*, Falkenström moves beyond a Naturalist standpoint to accept the existence of another level of reality as it is expressed in one of Strindberg's favourite formulations - it is also inscribed near the head of *The Occult Diary*:

'If you want to learn to know the invisible, then observe the visible with the utmost care', the Talmud states. Everyday life is full of mysticism, but you see so badly; and you have to be a Naturalist in order to become mystic. But it is not only a question of being able to spell; you have to join it all together, otherwise you cannot read. (41:200)

Zachris, on the other hand, although offered one of the keys to correct interpretation in the work of Carl du Prel (41:172), from whose *Philosophie der Mystik*, Strindberg had drawn frequent enlightenment, remains an illiterate. Although it seems to him 'as if the devil himself had written the text today' (41:162) when he flees his isolation in a succession of unhappy encounters among those who might torment him into knowledge, he cannot decipher, in the minutiae of these experiences, a causal connection between events in which the meaning of his life would be spelled out. His life remains a textual enigma and he therefore persists in the blindness now associated with Naturalism, among those who live like the lascivious apes of Strindberg's post Darwinist ancestral nightmare: 'they walk in darkness and wound themselves, they root around in the earth like swine after truffles, they turn their backs upon the archetypes and see only the copies. Therefore they worship Maja, the earth spirit, woman, and when they do not wish to serve God in love they slave under Omphale in hate'(41:185-6).

However, it is their role as writers which forms the essential bond between Zachris and Falkenström. Both take their material directly from life, both are writing novels on living subjects (Zachris on Jenny and Falkenström on Zachris), and early on in the book Falkenström, too, is seen as a vampire 'gaping to swallow something as sweet as a woman's secret' (41:74) or literally biting Jenny's arm (41:65). But if Falkenström's literary exploitation of Zachris appears to be a replica of Zachris's treatment of his wife (and certainly it suggests too self-consciously the way in which the text recording this event is produced), Strindberg is concerned to represent it as something else. Where Zachris remains a Naturalist, Falkenström's entry into the retreat on Siklaön elevates his writing to another dimension. As a refuge from the economic forces controlling the production of literature, the monastery represents an ideal that had long fascinated Strindberg, in his letters to Littmansson during the 1890s, in *The Cloister*, and in *To Damascus*,[67] and now that the conception is realised (if only in imagination, and significantly even there, only on the poorly motivated basis of an inheritance which conveniently exempts the members of this fraternity from the importunate demands of earning a living in the market place), it enshrines an approach to experience for which he had long striven: 'This was the place where a few people had saved themselves from despair, turned their back on the world, lowered their demands, and preferred to suffer instead of being revenged' (41:256).

A similar view is advanced in *The Ghost Sonata* where the old vampire, Hummel, asserts his congenital right to punish and revenge. 'I was born like that - I can't forgive until I have punished. I took it as an imperative duty...and do so still, to clear away the weeds, expose the crimes, balance the books' (45:191). The terms he uses are those under which Strindberg has conducted many a literary campaign; they resemble those under which Zachris conceives the novel he is writing about his wife (41:213-4), and which might as well have been used by Strindberg to account for *A Madman's Defence* or *Black Banners*. But when, in *The Ghost Sonata* the Mummy intervenes at the climax of the second episode and unmasks the formidable Strindbergian unmasker, it is again with an appeal to suffering and repentance that she opposes Hummel's implacable desire for retribution: 'But I can halt time in its course. I can wipe out the past, undo what has been done. Not with bribes, nor with threats, however - but through suffering and contrition' (45:192).

From *Inferno* onwards these are the qualities on which Strindberg has placed particular stress in order to exonerate himself from the guilt attached to writing books like *A Madman's Defence* and *Black Banners*. As he maintains, via Falkenström: 'In order to write my collected works I have sacrificed my biography, my person' (41:196), and in an age when to write is to live precariously upon oneself and off others, suffering and sacrifice are the hostages to fortune by means of which the writer rejects his vampire's role and performs his 'duty as a citizen'.[68] But as *Black Banners* demonstrates, the past is not extinguished nor time stopped in its course by suffering or regret, and while the text demonstrates the effectiveness of writing as a means of revenge, it also conveys that it is, for Strindberg at least, an imperfect means of witting self-knowledge. Unwittingly, however, it provides the reader with a text in which to piece together the illusion of Strindberg's hopes and the anxieties as well as the probity of his practice, a practice described in an earlier narrative as one in which, for better or for worse:

> the writer takes, takes egotistically, what he comes across; takes an anecdote, which someone tells in his cups, takes a trait from other people's lives, which others have lived, takes his thoughts from the philosophers, his comments from the papers, his feelings from imagination, and then he puts his little name to it all and becomes great, and - that's all there is to it! The poet behaves like the boaconstrictor: he draws his slime over his prey and then it is his. He spins beautiful nets, out of himself so people say - but no one saw how many flies he sucked dry first. (15:168)

CHAPTER SIX

Conclusion

Bless me. . .whose greatest suffering was the pain of not being able to be
the one I wished to be.
- *The Great Highway*

With Strindberg the problem is always where and how to conclude. Protean not
only in the multitude of characters he animates and the guises he assumes, but also in
the variety of genres and fields of discourse in which he compiles the body of writing
that now represents him, the difficulty is that in this written universe, as in the
intractable world of fact and experience with which he, like Henry James, was
confronted, 'relations stop nowhere'.[1] But then Strindberg was rarely able to
reach a permanent conclusion himself. Having composed his own epigraph with
great solemnity in *The Great Highway*, he confounded expectation and violated
propriety yet again by instituting the political feud, known as 'Strindbergsfejden',
which he left to reverberate in his wake, and the successive segments of his
autobiographical project indicate not merely a voracious appetite for new experience,
but the insufficiency of the several strategies whereby he sought to recapture his life
and preserve the identity he valued so highly.

In its sheer extent, this writing represents what Strindberg's contemporary,
Walter Pater, described as 'that continual vanishing away, that strange perpetual
weaving and unweaving of ourselves,'[2] a process to which the committed
autobiographer is particularly condemned. For in contemplating the now distinct
image he has just produced in order to endow himself with the definition for which he
yearns, the baffling nature of this written other repeatedly prompts the query
directed by The Unknown to the Beggar at the end of the second part of *To
Damascus*: 'Are you you or are you me?' (29:225). 'I have seen a hundred portraits
of myself and have always asked: is this me?' (XI:152), Strindberg told Hedlund, at
the height of his Inferno crisis, and when the splitting or multiplying of identity
through which the self seeks to apprehend itself is compounded with the uncertainty
which a multiplicity of assumed roles may foster in the mind of their nourishing
author, recognition is placed in still further doubt. Either he feels himself slipping
towards the domain of fable or the words to which he delegates himself render an
incomplete, distorted, or misleading account that compels him to embark upon
another. And yet, although it is continually resumed and terminated only by the
event which necessarily lies outside the text approaching it, in that death which
Walter Benjamin sees as 'the sanction of everything the story-teller has to tell',[3] this

inconclusive autobiographical pursuit of the self entails its constant displacement into the vehicles through which it is filtered, screened, interpreted, and designed: into language, where the autobiographer is present not in person but as a figure of the text in words in which he transcribes or invents the past in order to represent himself as he believes he is or wishes to be seen; into literary genres and the plurality of codes in which, to the extent that they are conventional, the individual experience they recuperate is depersonalized and stereotyped; into roles, which dramatize the tension between writing as a surrogate life and its tendency to come to life independently of its nominal creator by conferring on the discrete particles of experience in their narrative enchainment not the unity of a life through time but the unity of the text; and into a network of witting or unwitting literary and mythical identifications in which, as Job, Faust, or Oedipus, a unique story becomes a tale, and hence a destiny, which its teller shares with others, as indeed Northrop Frye's plural reference to the *pharmakos* figures encountered 'in stories of artists whose genius makes them Ishmaels of a bourgeois society'[4] nicely implies.

In retrospect, too, it is easy to discern how Strindberg's autobiographical enterprise, which puts in doubt both the notion of autonomous identity and the ideology of a unique existence which autobiography is ordinarily assumed to predicate,[5] is related to what is currently termed the 'deconstruction' of the idea of a fixed and substantial selfhood undertaken by Nietzsche and Freud, as well as to a modernism in which (for example, in Musil, Proust, or Joyce) the persona of the author outside the work carries almost as much dramatic weight as the supernumaries within it, and which explores other forms of plausibility and order beyond the principle of continuity applied almost universally in the nineteenth century, in the belief that in every sphere continuous sequence, inflexible order, and eternal law prevailed. And yet, unlike for example Yeats, with whom he had at one time much in common, Strindberg belittled neither Naturalism nor the nineteenth century even when he had moved beyond them. 'The nineteenth century is doubtless the greatest of all centuries. It is the age of great discoveries and inventions, constitutions, parliamentarism, and social revolution' (54:378), he declared, in 'The Mysticism of World History', and it was by insisting upon the notions of growth and development which permeated organicist, determinist, and evolutionary thinking that he probed the limits of what could be said and thought within the discourse in which he first sought to inscribe himself, and so pressed Naturalism until it yielded the material of its own undoing. As he enquired: 'Why scoff at Naturalism when it has shown itself capable of inaugurating a new stage in art, and has been accorded the possibility of growing and developing?' (28:59). For it was by applying the Naturalist model, with its emphasis on physiological and psychological cause and effect, on heredity, environmental forces, and the unconscious as well as conscious systems of meaning which the individual inherits as the field of his development, that Strindberg derived a conception of the self in which discontinuity, the unconscious, the irrational, and the indeterminate predominate, where discourse is lacunary and character the unstable mosaic of 'conglomerations', 'fragments', and 'torn shreds of once fine clothing' that he defines in the foreword to *Miss Julie*, where the individual is depicted as the product of impersonal forces and the discourses that flow through him.

Thus, like J.P. Jacobsen, Strindberg discovers that in 'The real history of a human being's development...the characters will seem to lack coherence', that 'in reality there are individual sides in people which do not hang together',[6] and that even if the laws of nature should prove consequential and rational, they nevertheless manifest themselves in the individual by unconscious and irrational drives, as 'an unconstrained break out of repressed instinct' (23:105) which overwhelms both the individual and the social and moral categories designed to buttress his world. Like Dreiser's Carrie Meeber, the Naturalist protagonist is very much 'a waif amid forces' and hence, as Richard Chase remarks, 'at the mercy of circumstances rather than of himself, indeed he often seems to *have* no self',[7] for what he does is at once himself and yet, on the unconscious level at which his fate is already decided, not himself. Determined, his determinations are not necessarily his own, and Johan can never 'be who I wanted to be' because from the outset 'his way was necessarily determined by his blood inheritance, temperament, [and] position in society' (19:189), and as the choiceless subject of 'inherited instinct' (19:41), he is always prevented by the encrustations of his family, period, religion, and culture from attaining what Strindberg sometimes refers to as 'his right, his better self' (19:42) because what he regards as his genuine self is repressed, proliferates, and vanishes in the multiple forms he gives himself or has imposed on him.

As time passes, moreover, his life mounts up not as a chain of events but a network of relationships, a densely textured web of meaning, and to interpret it he requires (but again, it is Naturalism, with its focus on the quotidian and superficial which opens a way to the mysterious in the mundane)[8] a more refined instrument for the collection and analysis of the trivia of which it is composed, and he seeks by means of analogy and the collage-like appropriation of the real world in the fabric of *The Occult Diary*, to disengage the significance of events from the superficiality of their notation, to interrogate and decipher the often enigmatic graphism of the world in which the cryptic text of his life seems to him also to be written. This is of course the context in which Strindberg's kinship with Freud is most apparent, but it would be equally appropriate to quote Nietzsche's contemporary comment, 'Against positivism, which halts at phenomena - "There is only *facts*" - I would say, No, facts is precisely what there is not, only interpretations',[9] or to anticipate Proust who, in claiming that 'ce livre, le plus pénible de tous à déchiffrer, est aussi le seul que nous ait dicté la réalité',[10] stressed the task of the interpreter in penetrating the surface at which a literature content with merely describing the world is arrested. It is not the life as a succession of natural events that possesses meaning but the interpreted series into which it is transformed, and whether in fiction, autobiography, or science all perception is, Strindberg tirelessly maintains, a subjective projection. 'The only thing that exists is the self (le culte du moi), and of the world and 'the others' I know nothing except through the self' (X:150). Every organ or instrument of perception frames the world it perceives and dictates what and how it is apprehended. They extend the self into the world and reduce the world to an extension of the self. And if, as Strindberg senses, with a customary nod in the direction of Schopenhauer, that 'what we imagine possesses a higher reality', it is because 'Reality cannot penetrate within me and be expressed again without having taken form as idea or imagination. Thus we know reality only through our idea of it, and therefore our representations of an apprehended reality vary so enormously' (40:288-9). But hence, too, Strindberg's delighted recognition in a world so insistently shaped and designed by his own needs and desires, of plots and scenarios already imprinted upon the otherwise inchoate multiplicity of events in which he was both actor and spectator.

But however they are apprehended, both the text of the self and the text of the world whose imprint it bears, are arranged, schematized, framed, and translated into a language which facilitates their temporary identification, and it is there, where he attempts to represent himself to himself in the essentially auto-generative act of self-interpretation, that Strindberg at once writes and then reads his life, before he again relinquishes his identity and the life he has lived to the reader or spectator who will, on occasion, attempt to reconstitute an image of this 'rival to Orpheus' (28:81) as it is dispersed throughout the series of texts in which, like Beckett's Unnamable, he implicitly entreats this other to 'equate me...with him whose story this story had the brief ambition to be.'[11] Brief, however, it is not, and as the author of an unsigned review of Strindberg's letters has so finely observed, when seeking to convert the raw material of his life into literature, Strindberg repeatedly comes upon his life already arranged and written by 'Life's designing purposes much as a fictive character is subject to the author's will; and one realizes, with a sense of awe that of course this is what happens when Niels Lyhne's prayer is answered':

> Life, a poem! But not in the sense that one 'wrote' one's life instead of living it. How meaningless that would be, empty, empty, empty. This hunting for oneself, sharply observing one's own trail - in a circle of course; this pretense of throwing oneself into the stream of life, while at the same time sitting down and angling for yourself, and fishing oneself out in some curious disguise or another! If only something would take one in its grip - life, love, passion - so that one no longer 'wrote' but 'was written'.[12]

In short, as Strindberg writes his life, Life writes Strindberg.

NOTES

1. Unless otherwise stated, all references to Strindberg's works and letters are, for the works, to John Landquist's edition of *Samlade skrifter*, 55 vols (Stockholm, 1912-20), and, for the letters, Torsten Eklund's edition of *August Strindbergs brev*, 15 volumes to date (Stockholm, 1948-). Volume number and page reference are identified in the text in parenthesis after a quotation, and to distinguish between the two series, the volume number of the *Brev* is denoted by Roman numerals. References to three other books are also carried in the text: *A Madman's Defence* in the edition published in Lund, 1976 (hereafter 'MD'), *Vivisektioner* (Vivisections), Stockholm, 1958 (hereafter 'VR'), and *Klostret* (The Cloister), Stockholm, 1966 (hereafter 'C'). Quotations from *Ockulta dagboken* (The Occult Diary) are drawn from the facsimile edition (Stockholm, 1977) and where possible identified by their date. Unless otherwise stated, all translations from the Swedish are my own.
2. *Oeuvres complètes*, édition publiée sous la direction de Bernard Gagnebin et Marcel Raymond, 4 vols (Paris, 1959-69), I, 20.
3. *Heaven and Its Wonders and Hell* (London: Swedenborg Society, 1966), p.342.
4. *Samlade otryckta skrifter*, 2 vols (Stockholm, 1918), I, 302.
5. *Oeuvres complètes*, I, 1149. The claim to be the only true or appropriate witness of one's life is a not uncommon justification for writing an autobiography. Gibbon, for example, observes that 'the public are always curious to know the men who have left behind them any image of their minds...and I must be conscious that no one is so well qualified as myself to describe the series of my thoughts and actions', *Memoirs of My Life and Writings* (London, 1970), p.3.
6. Quoted in Walter A. Berendsohn, *Strindbergs sista levnadsår* (Stockholm, 1948), p.119.
7. In their emphasis on the advantages of literacy, this argument, like those in the long letter on writing to Siri von Essen (I:186f.), recall Taine's remark 'que tout homme cultivé et intelligent en ramassant son expérience, peut faire un ou deux bons romans, parce qu'en somme un roman n'est qu'un amas d'expériences.' Quoted in Pierre Martino, *Le Naturalisme français*, 2nd edition (Paris, 1930), p.22.
8. Birger Mörner, *Den Strindberg jag känt* (Stockholm, 1924), p.168. See also *The Son of a Servant* (18:457) and the possibly apocryphal but characteristic idea which Frida Uhl, his second wife, attributes to Strindberg, of a secret depository to be provided by the British Museum where 'concealed by the night, unseen and unknown', people could leave a true and anonymous account of their lives. *Strindberg och hans andra hustru*, 2 vols (Stockholm, 1934), II, 29.
9. *The Gay Science*, translated Walter Kaufmann (New York, 1974), p.133.
10. See *Jonas Lie og hans Samtidige* (Kra, 1915), p.186 and Bjørnson's contribution to *En bok om Strindberg* (Karlstad, 1894), p.52.

11. *Den unge Strindberg och väckelserörelsen* (Malmö, 1953), p. 144.
12. 'De l'autobiographie initiatique à l'autobiographie genre littéraire', *Revue d'histoire littéraire de la France*, 75:6 (1975), 957-994 (p.990). Among many studies of the Puritan or Pietist phase of autobiographical writing, see Margaret Bottrall, *Every Man a Phoenix* (London, 1958), Paul Delaney, *British Autobiography in the Seventeenth Century* (London, 1969), Joan Webber, *The Eloquent 'I'* (Madison, 1968).
13. Carl Reinhold Smedmark, *Mäster Olof och Röda Rummet* (Stockholm, 1952), p.23.
14. *Repetition*, translated by Walter Lowrie (Princeton 1946), p.94.
15. *Repetition*, p.58.
16. *The Will to Power*, translated by Walter Kaufmann and R.J. Hollingdale (London, 1968), p.50.
17. *Monsieur Nicolas*, 6 vols (Paris, 1959), IV, 152. See also I, xvi: 'L'exactitude et la sincérité sont absolument nécessaires dans mon plan, puisque je dois anatomiser le coeur humain sur mon sens intime et sonder les profondeurs du *moi*.' Whether he is to be believed or not, Restif's declarations of intent respecting his 'anatomie de moi-même' (II, 149) frequently suggest Strindberg, as does what David Bryant calls his 'imperative need...to see life in terms of the projection and recording of his own history','Fiction and Truth in Restif's *M. Nicolas*', *Trivium*, 14 (1979), 127-34 (p.127).
18. *Correspondance*, nouvelle édition augmentée, 9 vols (Paris, 1926-33), III, 368. See also pp.158, 285-6.
19. 'Livres d'aujourd'hui et de demain', quoted in L.A. Carter, *Zola and the Theatre* (New Haven, 1963), p.21.
20. *Chérie* (Paris, 1884), p.iii.
21. *Sur l'eau* (Paris, n.d.), 115-6.
22. This is common practice even in texts that are not immediately autobiographical. In *Storm* (Oväder), *The Father*, *Playing with Fire*, and *Debit and Credit*, for example, he uses literature to explore the possibilities inherent in his immediate situation.
23. Chekhov's comment, 'A writer must be as objective as a chemist', has a special resonance when applied to Strindberg. *Letters*, edited by Louis S. Friedland (New York, 1924), p.275.
24. Claude Bernard, *Introduction à l'étude de la médecine expérimentale* (Paris: Classiques Garnier, 1966), p.303.
25. Bernard, p.52.
26. Zola, *Le Roman expérimentale*, edited Aimé Guedj (Paris: Garnier-Flammarion, 1971), p.41.
27. See George Misch, *History of Autobiography in Antiquity*, translated by E.W. Dickes, 2 vols (London, 1950), I, 2. Strindberg's allusion in the Foreword to *The Son of a Servant* to Pitaval and Feuerbach's lives of the criminals and his advocacy of an archive of anonymous autobiographies (18:457) echo these ideas.
28. For a survey of these events, see Harry Jacobsen, *Digteren og Fantasten.*

Strindberg paa Skovlyst (København, 1945).

29. *Strindberg: en ledtråd vid studiet av hans verk* (Stockholm, 1921), p.186; *Tjänstekvinnans son: en psykologisk Strindbergsstudie* (Stockholm, 1948), p.195. For a survey of Strindberg scholarship, see Göran Lindström, 'Strindberg Studies 1915-1962', *Scandinavica*, 2:1 (1963), 27-50.

30. For a reading of *The Roofing Feast* which distinguishes itself from such a reductionist approach, see Per Arne Tjäder, 'Strukturen i Strindbergs *Taklagsöl*', *Tidskrift för litteraturvetenskap* (Umeå), 7:1 (1978), 30-43.

31. 'A First and Last Declaration', *Concluding Unscientific Postscript*, translated by David F. Swenson and Walter Lowrie (Princeton, 1941), p.552.

32. See *Inferno*, 28:191 and *The Occult Diary*, 1 March 1903.

33. Berkeley, 1968.

34. 'What is an Author', *Language, Counter-Memory, Practice*, edited by Donald F. Bouchard (Oxford, 1977), p.123.

35. Strindberg's fusion of contemporary notions of scientific experiment with the underlying influence of Kierkegaard is particularly evident in the passage immediately preceding this quotation from the late novel, *Gothic Rooms*. Speaking of Arvid Falk, one of Strindberg's earliest representatives in his first published success, *The Red Room*, and specifically identified with his author both here and in his next novel, *Black Banners*, where he is described as having 'steeled himself in the Bessemer ovens of Inferno' (41:33), Dr Borg (another survivor from *The Red Room*) explains how 'He experimented with points of view, and like a conscientious laboratory worker, made control experiments, placed himself experimentally on his opponent's side, checked the proofs against the original, tested the result in reverse, and when the control experiment had a negative outcome, he returned to the proven point of departure...Falk would have clarified his position, if he had used Kierkegaard's method. The latter invented authorial personages and gave himself a new pseudonym every time. Victor Eremita is not Johannes Climacus; Constantin Constantius is not Johannes de Silentio; but all of them together are Sören Kierkegaard. Falk was a vivisector who experimented with his own soul, always went about with open wounds, until he gave his life for knowledge, I don't want to use the abused word truth' (40:45-6).

36. *Beyond Good and Evil*, translated by R.J. Hollingdale (Harmondsworth, 1973), p.19.

37. 'Coming into One's Own', in *Psychoanalysis and the Question of the Text*, edited by Geoffrey Hartman (Baltimore, 1978), pp.114-148.

38. *Tourguenief* (Paris, 1931), p.196.

39. 'The Text, the World, the Critic', in *Textual Strategies: Perspectives in Post-Structuralist Criticism*, edited by Josué V. Harari (London, 1979), p.163.

40. *Roland Barthes by Roland Barthes*, translated by Richard Howard (London, 1977), p.137.

41. See especially 'The Rhetoric of Blindness' in *Blindness and Insight* (Oxford, 1971), pp.102-41.

42. 'Imaginary and Symbolic in Lacan', *Yale French Studies*, 55/6 (1977), 338-

395 (p.340).
43. Preface to *Pierre et Jean*, in *Romans*, texte définitif établi par Albert-Marie Schmidt (Paris: Albin Michel, 1959), p.838.
44. *Journal*, 4 vols (Paris, 1956), III, 1159.
45. *Soliloquy, or Advice to an Author* (1710), *Standard Edition* (Stuttgart: frommann-holzboog, 1981), I, 100.
46. *A Personal Record* (London, 1923), pp.xviii, 95.
47. Nordiska Museets Strindbergsarkivalia in Kungliga Biblioteket, Stockholm, File 1, folder 1. Hereafter reference to this material will be identified by the abbreviation 'NMS', the file number, and where possible (that is, in files 1 - 10) a number indicating the folder, e.g. NMS 1 (1).
48. 'Le Pacte autobiographique', *Poétique* 14 (1973), 137-162 (p.149). Also in *Le Pacte autobiographique* (Paris, 1975). Strindberg makes his most explicit autobiographical pact, that is, identifies himself with the destiny of the character of whom he is narrating on the final page of *Inferno*, where the reader is invited to verify his current text with the diary he claims it reproduces and also declares: 'If the reader doubts the truth of my assertions, and considers this all too pessimistic, he may read my autobiography *The Son of a Servant* and *Le Plaidoyer d'un Fou* (Paris, 1895)' (28:205).
49. *Journals of Anaïs Nin* (London, 1973), I, 6.
50. NMS 77. It is precisely the absence of an obvious signified for 1857 which makes this date so tantalizing. What event (memory) does it evoke (screen)? One of the numerous scenes of crime and punishment which reverberate down from his childhood throughout his work would seem most likely, and in *The Burned House* 1857 is given as the date of one such event, recalled with Rousseau and the famous episode of the purloined ribbon in the *Confessions* in mind, when The Stranger finds a book in the ashes of his childhood home: 'This was my book! which I got for Christmas in 1857. My name has been rubbed out. So, it was stolen from me and I accused one of the maids, who was dismissed!' (45:113-4).
51. NMS 9 (2). Even so drastic a summary is not discontinuous with previous accounts. *The Son of a Servant* mentions 'woodsheds and toilets' (18:19-20) and 'the dustbin' (30), and *A Madman's Defence* records how the Baroness's elderly relations interrupted a scene between her and Axel by passing through the room to the toilet (p.107).
52. *L'Autobiographie en France* (Paris, 1971), p.36.
53. This is also conveyed by Roy Pascal's definition in his influential *Design and Truth in Autobiography* (London, 1960): 'Autobiography...involves the reconstruction of the movement of a life, or part of a life, in the actual circumstances in which it was lived. Its centre of interest is the self, not the outside world...autobiography is a shaping of the past. It imposes a pattern on a life, constructs out of it a coherent story' (p.9).
54. *Stendhal et les problèmes de l'autobiographie*, edited by Victor Del Litto (Grenoble, 1976), p.26.
55. The name (Strindberg's first) given to the protagonist of *The Son of a Servant*

also incorporates the third person masculine pronoun in Swedish, 'han'. Unfortunately, neither in 'Le Pacte autobiographique' nor in his later essay devoted to the topic ('Autobiography in the Third Person', *New Literary History*, 9:1 (1977), 27-50), does Lejeune notice Strindberg's contribution to the genre.

56. *L'Autobiographie en France*, p.36.

57. 'Notes for an Anatomy of Modern Autobiography', *New Literary History*, 1:3 (1970), 485-511 (p.500).

58. *The Examined Self*, (Princeton, 1964), p.127.

59. *Surface and Symbol: The Consistency of James Joyce's Ulysses*, (New York, 1962), p.249.

60. 'Strindberg écrivain francais', *Revue d'histoire du théâtre*, 30:3 (1978), 243-265 (p.253).

Chapter Two: Writing Out and Repetition

1. *The Mirror and the Lamp* (Oxford, 1953), pp.48, 138.

2. Abrams quotes from Byron and Keble on pp.139, 145, 147.

3. For example by Walter Berendsohn, *Strindbergsproblem* (Stockholm, 1946), p.54.

4. *Standard Edition of the Complete Psychological Works of Sigmund Freud*, 24 vols (London, 1953-73), IX, p.148.

5. Compare II:164, IV:37, 85, 270, IX:29.

6. *Standard Edition*, II, 305.

7. 'Sin egen psykiater', *Bonniers Litterära Magasin*, 32:7 (July 1963), 556-8 (p.557).

8. *Freud och hans tid* (Stockholm: Aldus edition, 1970), p.96. An English edition of the German translation of Brandell's book has been published in England by Harvester in 1979.

9. 'Attente et intuition de la psychanalyse dans le théâtre de Strindberg', *Scandinavica*, 12:1 (1973), 1-16 (p.1).

10. *The Discovery of the Unconscious* (New York, 1979), p.537.

11. For Freud and Taine, see Joan Wynn Reeves, *Thinking About Thinking* (London, 1965), pp.109-14, and *Freud och hans tid*, pp.67-74; for Taine and Strindberg, see Hans Lindström, *Hjärnornas kamp. Psykologiska idéer och motiv i Strindbergs åttiotalsdiktning* (Uppsala, 1952), p.59, also the standard source of information about Strindberg's familiarity with contemporary psychology. Although Freud denied reading Schopenhauer before 1900 (*Standard Edition*, XX, 59), he moved in a culture (whether briefly in Paris in 1885 or in Vienna) where his ideas circulated, and he eventually concedes that Schopenhauer's 'unconscious Will is the equivalent to the mental instincts of psycho-analysis' (*Standard Edition*, XVIII, 143-4). Strindberg frequently acknowledges his respect for Schopenhauer, 'the most profound thinker I know' (VII:247). All accounts of the early Strindberg

repeat his own acknowledgement of Hartmann's impact (19:60f.), and Freud, too, in the notes to *The Interpretation of Dreams*, recognizes his presence in any late nineteenth-century discussion of the unconscious. Nietzsche's influence, either direct or mediated by Georg Brandes's 1888 lecture, published in *Tilskueren* (August 1889, pp.565-613), is too well-known to require comment (but see Eklund, *Tjänstekvinnans son*, pp.394-418). The relevance of Ibsen for Freud is explored in *Freud och hans tid*, pp.40-58; Sten Linder's 'Ibsen och Strindberg', *Samlaren*, 13 (1932), 52-105, offers an early comparison of the two dramatists which has had many successors.

12. *Pathology of Mind* (London, 1895 edition), pp.46-7. Maudsley's importance for Strindberg is discussed by Eklund, pp.362-66, 379-382.

13. *Freud och hans tid*, p.22.

14. *Freud och hans tid*, pp.96, 16.

15. See *Standard Edition*, II, 160, VII, 59-60. From his first critics, such as Alfred von Berger, who reviewed *Studies on Hysteria* as 'nothing but the kind of psychology used by poets' (Ernest Jones, *Sigmund Freud*, 3 vols (London, 1953), I, 253), to late admirers such as Arnold Zweig, who regarded Freud as 'the culmination of Austrian literature' (*The Letters of Sigmund Freud and Arnold Zweig* (New York, 1970), p.61), Freud had to contend with both critical and laudatory indiscriminations.

16. Quoted in *Thinking About Thinking*, p.219.

17. *Freud: The Mind of a Moralist* (London, 1960), p.90.

18. *Standard Edition*, IV, 102-3, *Samlade Skrifter*, 18, 277,

19. *Inferno,* edited by C.G. Bjurström (Paris, 1966), pp.12-13.

20. 'Tankens genvägar', *Bonniers Litterära Magasin*, 38:8 (October, 1969), p.601.

21. 'On the Universal Tendency to Debasement in the Sphere of Love', *Standard Edition*, XI, 187.

22. *Standard Edition*, XIII *(Moses and Monotheism)*, p.222.

23. He quotes from *Gothic Rooms* (40:241-2) on page 212 of the *Standard Edition*, Vol. VI.

24. Compare Freud's discussion of the 'category of what is accidental', in *The Psychopathology of Everyday Life*, p.255f.

25. *Standard Edition*, XVI (*Introductory Lectures*), p.368.

26. *Standard Edition*, V, 454.

27. 'The New Model Autobiographer', *New Literary History*, 9:1 (1977), 51-64 (p.59).

28. This is substantially Evert Sprinchorn's argument in 'The Zola of the Occult: Strindberg's Experimental Method', in *Modern Drama*, 17:3 (1974), pp.251-266. Just as he sought to go beyond Zola's fiction in *The Son of a Servant*, so he then attempted to exceed in rigour the authorities on whom he had once relied, for they had not experienced the insanity of which they wrote any more than Zola had direct access to another's inner life as the basis of his fiction.

29. See e.g. his comment on 'a modesty, which stands guard at the threshold to the

unconscious'. Freud introduces the image as early as *Studies on Hysteria*: 'The situation may be compared with the unlocking of a locked door'. *Standard Edition*, II, 383.

30. *Standard Edition*, II, 8. Intriguingly, Strindberg also recognizes the cathartic role of revenge. 'Artistic production can nowadays only be occasioned by one or other of the stronger sensations such as the desire for revenge' (VI:80), he tells Bonnier, and where no cause for redress exists he can often be discovered stimulating its effect since 'he who is angry speaks excellently, but writes even better' (I:190).

31. *Standard Edition*, XX (*An Autobiographical Study*), p.30. See also *Inhibitions, Symptoms and Anxiety*, where he repudiates the notion that the intense and frequent reproduction of a trauma can effect its removal (*Standard Edition*, XX, 151), and 'Remembering, Repeating and Working-Through', where he discusses the necessary 'expenditure of work' by which the patient becomes conscious of the resistances in the material produced by free association (*Standard Edition*, XII, 147).

32. *Standard Edition*, III, 315.

33. *L'Autobiographie en France*, p.99.

34. *Tjänstekvinnans son*, p.33.

35. *The Origins of Psychoanalysis* (London, 1954), p.275.

36. *Freud and His Followers* (Harmondsworth, 1979), p.107. Hedlund was so insubstantial to Strindberg, that the latter was surprised to find him twenty years older than he had imagined (XI:247).

37. See *Standard Edition*, II, pp.138, 281.

38. *Nouvelle Revue Française*, 18, No.10 (Octobre, 1970), 144-163 (p.154).

39. Pingaud, p.157.

40. Pingaud, p.159-60.

41. *The Cloister*, pp.28-9.

42. 'The Uncanny', *Standard Edition*, XVII, 237.

43. *Standard Edition*, XVII, 250.

44. See Carl Fehrman, 'Slutscenen i *Ett Drömspel*', in *Poesi och parodi* (Stockholm, 1957), pp.84-95. Fehrman makes the point that the idea of the dying man's review of his life was taken seriously by contemporary psychologists in books and journals with which Strindberg was familiar, e.g. Ribot's *Les Maladies de la mémoire*, and *Revue philosophique*, which printed two essays by Victor Egger, 'La durée apparente des rêves' (1895) and 'Le moi des mourants' (1896). Also well known to Strindberg was Carl du Prel's *Philosophy of Mysticism* : see Volume II, pp.42-50 (London, 1889) on 'Memory in the Dying'.

45. *Samlade otryckta skrifter*, I, 299. The theme is explored by Richard Vowles in 'Strindberg and the Symbolic Mill', *Scandinavian Studies*, 34:3 (1962), 111-119.

46. *Strindbergs infernokris* (Stockholm, 1950), p.247.

47. See also *The Occult Diary*, 1 March 1903, and NMS 3 (8) and NMS 4 (3) for repetitions of this formula regarding *Master Olof*.

48. The Hagar and Ishmael passage is in NMS 9 (3) as is the wine bottle episode.

Klara School appears in NMS 9 (1) under the heading 'Offerkistan', alongside the wish (Cf. *The Nightingale of Wittenberg* (39:10) and *The Burned House* (45:132)): 'If only there was a conflagration we would be made free' (Om det ville bli eldsvåda så fick vi lof). See also NMS 3 (12): 'Born again and gets the same father he has hated. Gets the same school and teachers'.

49. 'Det ohjelpliga', which runs from his return to Norrtullsgatan to the evening before the Baroness's departure for Copenhagen, is in NMS 3 (22), 'Affaire W - - - - -l' in 9 (3).

50. See e.g. VII:142, IX:223, 28:137, 363, 41:71, 45:137.

51. See *A Madman's Defence*, p.33. Without Gustav, Maria ceases to be a 'virgin mother' and becomes Axel's wife or mistress.

52. NMS 9 (3).

53. *Occult Diary*, facing p.124, and 14 February 1901.

54. See NMS 9 (3).

55. An earlier title for *The Dance of Death*, where the relationship between the Captain, Alice, and Kurt continues to evoke 'Affaire W - - - - -l', was 'Everything Repeats Itself' (*Allt går igen*), NMS 4 (23).

56. NMS 5 (10).

57. For Strindberg's fire imagery in general, see Sven-Gustaf Edqvist, 'Elden och pånyttfödelsen', *Ord och bild*, 67, No.5 (1958), 333-344, and Gunnar Axberger, *Diktarfantasi och eld* (Stockholm, 1967), pp. 257-367. In the present context, note the suggestion that a pile of wood is 'a pyre erected for me' (*Occult Diary*, 30 May 1907). Related to his view of the sacrifice which writing demands of the writer, this is developed in the conception of 'a monument to Shakespeare, representing Hercules lighting his own pyre on Mount Oeta, giving his rich life as a self-sacrifice for mankind!' (46:72). Note, too, Hans Brevmålare's fate in *Swedish Destinies* (11:192) and Starkodd, who is linked with Hercules in NMS 5 (10) and dies by fire with an autobiographical lament on his lips in 'The Saga of Stig Storverk's Son' (43:52). The pyre of sexuality is described in *Jacob Wrestles* (28:362).

58. *Strindbergs bildspråk*, p.243.

59. 'Tankens genvägar', p.600. Compare *The Roofing Feast*, where the Narrator sees that the house being built outside his window will obscure the green light shining in his old rival's window: 'Then I understood that it had to be built, and I was heartened...that a cairn of stones would be laid upon the corpse, the past concealed and forgotten' (44:20). Once again it is Strindberg's relationship with Carl Gustaf Wrangel, whose window he could see from the room where he was sitting, that prompted this motif in a late work.

60. 'Ambiguities and Archetypes in Strindberg's Romantic Organist', *Scandinavian Studies*, 48:3 (1976), 256-271 (p.263).

61. *Beginnings* (New York, 1975), p.33.

62. *Samlade otryckta skrifter*, II, 205. See also XI:176 on the 'snedhet' (crookedness) he falsely associates with his conception and from which he concludes that 'everything in my life has been somewhat awry (*på sned*).'

63. In *The Roofing Feast*, for example, he refers (44:14) to L.B. Hellenbach, who

treats 'Die Periodicität im menschlichen Lebenslaufe' in *Magie der Zahlen* (Vienna, 1882), pp.99-120.
64. *Standard Edition*, XXII, 72.
65. In indicating the universal nature of his guilt feelings to Lundstedt, the Pastor (like the Father in *To Damascus I*) performs something resembling a psychoanalysis: at least, Lundstedt is henceforth able to express himself in words as well as in music, even if the profit he draws from it is only to repeat his story to anyone who bought him 'a couple of drinks' (21:258).
66. *Unto This Last* (London, People's Library, 1908), p.181.
67. Compare the exchange in *The Pelican*: '(The Son):...Let's live to rehabilitate ourselves, and our father's memory! (Gerda): And seek justice. (The Son): Say revenge!' (45:254) with the note: 'It is not revenge, it is justice, for people must see that such a thing exists' (NMS 4 (13)).
68. For the way in which the act of punishment was woven into his literary intentions, see Karl-Ivar Hildeman, 'Strindberg, *The Dance of Death*, and Revenge', *Scandinavian Studies*, 35:4 (1963), 267-294. Note, too, the sections 'Paid Debts', 'Hard to Unravel' and 'The Art of Settling Scores' in *A Blue Book*, 46:182, 124ff.
69. *Repetition*, pp.52-3.
70. *Standard Edition*, XVIII, 36.
71. *Standard Edition*, XVIII, 17.
72. *Standard Edition*, XII, 150.
73. *Standard Edition*, XII, 149.
74. *Problèmes de la linguistique générale* (Paris, 1966), p.25.

Chapter Three: Writing, not Speaking

1. Axel made the revelation in *Dagens Nyheter* (3 March 1924): 'I have just been reminded of it |his shyness| because he has recently been portrayed naked |in a sculpture by Carl Eldh|. He was so shy even of us brothers, that when he changed his underclothes, he got into a wardrobe!' Cf 18:173: 'But Johan was naturally shy. He did not want to show himself naked.'
2. See Fanny Falkner, *August Strindberg i Blå Tornet* (Stockholm, 1921), pp.31, 74, and Maria Schildknecht, quoted in Sven Hedenberg, *Strindberg i skärselden* (Göteborg, 1961), p.167.
3. *Tjänstekvinnans son*, p.94.
4. Compare Nietzsche's query from the same year: 'Does not one write books precisely to conceal what lies within us?' *Beyond Good and Evil*, translated by R.J. Hollingdale (Harmondsworth, 1973), p.197.
5. But see Göran Printz-Påhlson, 'Strindbergs totemism', *Konstrevy*, 45:4 (1969), 154-160.
6. *Problèmes de la linguistique générale*, p.52.

7. The 'teacher' here is undoubtedly Kierkegaard, who quotes Talleyrand's remark in *The Concept of Dread* and again in Quidam's Diary (19 May) in *Stages on Life's Way*.

8. *The Philosophy of Karl Popper*, edited P.A. Schilpp (Illinois, 1974), p.1113. See George Steiner, *After Babel* (Oxford, 1975) where the passage is quoted (p.224) for a discussion of the role of lying in the development of language.

9. *Oeuvres complètes*, IV, 285.

10. Jean Starobinski, *La transparence et l'obstacle* (Paris, 1971), p.365.

11. 'On Truth and Lie in an Extra-Moral Sense', *The Portable Nietzsche*, translated by Walter Kaufmann (New York, 1954), p.45. Much of what Nietzsche writes in this fragment on how in man 'deception, flattery, lying and cheating, talking behind the back, posing, living in borrowed splendour, being masked, the disguise of convention, acting a role before others and before oneself - in short, the constant fluttering around the single flame of vanity is so much the rule and the law that almost nothing is more incomprehensible than how an honest and pure urge for truth could make its appearance among men' (p.43), is related to Strindberg's diagnosis of 'The public lie' and the mendacity to which even the truthfully inclined are driven, and possesses far greater relevance for a comparison of the two authors than the superficial application by Strindberg of a borrowed Nietzschean rhetoric in, for example, the novella, *Tschandala*.

12. See also *A Blue Book* (46:29, 47:552), *Armageddon* (54:155), and *The Roofing Feast* (44:56).

13. *Sprak och lögn: En essä om språkfilosofisk extremism* (Stockholm, 1978), pp.14, 147.

14. London, 2nd edition, 1895, pp.330-1.

15. *Samlade otryckta skrifter*, II, 199. Compare NMS 3 (1): 'Why does life make people false. Deference: politeness; conflicting interests', and the account of a similar scene in *The Pelican* (45:358).

16. *Samlade otryckta skrifter*, I, 303.

17. *Oeuvres complètes*, I, 199.

18. *Strindbergs brev till Harriet Bosse* (Stockholm, 1932), p.309.

19. *Oeuvres complètes*, III, 193.

20. *Samhällets fiende*, passim.

21. *Oeuvres complètes*, III, 174.

22. *La transparence*, p.9.

23. Besides Edqvist, Alfred Jollivet, 'Le Rousseauisme d'August Strindberg', *Revue de littérature comparée*, 13:4 (1933), 606-22, and Elie Poulenard, *Strindberg et Rousseau* (Paris, 1959) discuss the influence of his social and political thought. On the debt *The Son of a Servant* owes the *Confessions*, see Martin Lamm, 'Quelques influences françaises sur l'autobiographie d'August Strindberg', in *Mélanges d'histoire littéraire générale et comparée offerts à F. Baldensperger*, II, (Paris, 1930), pp.22-27, and Elie Poulenard, 'Les Influences françaises dans l'autobiographie d'August Strindberg', *Scandinavica*, 1:1 (1962), 29-50. For some general observations on the affinity between Rousseau and

Strindberg, see Eklund, *Tjanstekvinnans son*, p.26 and John Landquist, 'Strindbergs filosofi', *Filosofiska essayer* (Stockholm, 1906), pp.292-3. Strindberg is sparing in his specific allusions to the *Confessions*, but Rousseau's 'horrible confessions' are given passing acknowledgement in the letter on writing (I:188) and in 'Soul Murder' he recalls that Rousseau 'had stolen a bit of ribbon in his youth' (22:198). Note, too, the curious appropriation of the purloined ribbon episode that ends Book 2 of the *Confessions* to point the account of a stolen book in *The Burned House* (45:114), and the remark: 'Yes, if we were to express all our thoughts...Rousseau was unwise enough to do so' (40:294).

24. The most important contexts in which one or other of the several incidents of accusation, both just and unjust, of theft, or of wrongful punishment, to do with stolen wine, fruit, books or speaking out of turn, occur in *The Red Room* (5:320), 'An Unwelcome Addition' (11:73), 'A Child's Story' (37:47), *To Damascus* (29:347), *The Nightingale of Wittenberg* (39:30), 'Hund's Foot' (48:1024), *The Burned House* (45:99, 114), *The Pelican* (45:265), and 'August Strindberg About Himself' (54:465-6). The motif appears frequently in the surviving papers. A page headed 'Mea Culpa' (NMS 6 (16)) lists 'Robinson. Injustices. The Screws (*Muttrarna*): ABC Book: school. The Plum Tree', and the latter appears on several pages in NMS 9 (3) among lists of events and encounters via which Strindberg appears to be sketching possible literary projects and attempting to perceive the patterns of recurrence and meaning in the life that has witnessed these events. Perhaps the most pathetic of all these incidents, however, occurs in *Gothic Rooms*, when Borg reflects on how to dispose of the piece of paraffin-scented bread and mustard he has taken to quell his hunger: 'If I put it in the stove it might be found in the morning by the maid; she will take it straight to her mistress and of course accuse the children, or the child she likes least, and then there is a beating, first for the crime, and then for denying it. I've been through that myself' (40:151).

25. There is an important distinction, however. Whereas the scene in which Jean-Jacques is punished for something which he did not do is set against one in which he is taken at his false word, *both* scenes in *The Son of a Servant* argue Johan's innocence.

26. *Le Pacte autobiographique*, p.94.

27. *Stendhal et les problèmes de l'autobiographie*, p.88.

28. *Strindberg och makterna* (Uppsala, 1936), p.22.

29. *Strindbergsproblem*, p.106.

30. Compare the Stranger's outburst in *The Burned House* (45:114), *The Ghost Sonata* (45:209), or 'Where Are We At Home?' (47:619).

31. For intimations that 'we are not at home here, and we are too good for this wretched existence' (*Occult Diary*, 6 September 1901), see the Vivisection 'Where Have We Come From?' and XI:270-1. Berendsohn's early discussion of Strindberg's use of Swedenborg in *Armageddon* (*Strindbergsproblem*, pp.98-106) has been expanded upon by Göran Stockenström in *Ishmael i öknen* (Uppsala, 1972) and 'The Journey from the Isle of Life to the Isle of Death', *Scandinavian Studies*, 50:2 (1978), 113-149.

32. *De Telluribus* (London, 1894), para 52-5, 87-8.

33. *De Telluribus*, pp.26, 28.

34. *De Telluribus*, p.27. The germ of *Armageddon* is in fact contained in Swedenborg's general remarks on 'the other life: there, no one is allowed to speak one way and think another. There, also, the variance is clearly perceived in each single expression, and when it is perceived, the spirit in whom there is such variance is expelled from society, and punished.' (p.27).

35. *The Portable Swift* (New York, 1948), p.462.

36. *Strindbergs brev till Harriet Bosse*, p.30.

37. *Samlade otryckta skrifter*, I, 298.

38. NMS 4 (4).

39. *Aftonbladet*, 30 December 1879.

40. *Strindbergs dramer*, I, 23. *Tjänstekvinnans son*, pp.95-111.

41. *Course in General Linguistics* (London, 1974), p.25.

42. See Derrida's discussion of phonocentrism and the meaning of being in *Of Grammatology*, translated Gayatri Chakravorty Spivak (Baltimore, 1974), p.12.

43. *Thought and Language*, translated Eugenia Hanfmann and Gertrude Vakar (Cambridge, Massachusetts, 1962), p.99.

44. 'What is a Text', In David M. Rasmussen, *Mythic-Symbolic Language and Philosophical Anthropology* (The Hague, 1971), p.137.

45. *Interpretation Theory* (Fort Worth, 1976), p.36.

46. *Interpretation Theory*, p.31.

47. *Obliques: Littérature-Théâtre*, 1:1 (1972), 63-68. Also in *Ystads Allehanda* ('Vem förföljde Strindberg?'), 19 September 1970.

48. *Oeuvres complètes*, I, 116. But for Rousseau's sense of loss of himself in speech, see pp.114, 181, 1034.

49. *The Expression of the Emotions in Man and Animals* (London, 1872), pp.326-7.

50. *Keats and Embarrassment* (Oxford, 1976), p.51.

51. *Oeuvres complètes*, I, 1123.

52. *Pubertet* (Stockholm, 1978), p.319.

53. *Extraterritorial* (Harmondsworth, 1975), p.67.

54. *Extraterritorial*, p.67.

55. *Interpersonal Perception* (London, 1966), p.5-6.

56. *L'Oeil vivant* (Paris, 1961), pp.94, 100.

57. For Strindberg's conviction that he stood model for Hjalmar Ekdal, see MD:218. His view of the genesis of *Hedda Gabler* is given in two letters, 4 and 8 March 1891.

58. *Oeuvres complètes*, I, 985.

59. NMS 9 (7).

60. *Oeuvres complètes*, III, 7.

61. *Oeuvres complètes*, I, 116, 175.

62. *Oeuvres complètes*, I, 19.

63. *Oeuvres complètes*, I, 20.

64. Strindberg evokes the Fall, or at least the fallen nature of this world, on numerous occasions, at times in relation to the image of the lost paradise whose image he discerned in the Stockholm archipelago, his blessed isles. Elsewhere the Fall appears in more conventional contexts, in relation to sexuality (e.g. 23:390, 30:202, 37:107, 45:265) or the descent from nature to art (or authenticity to the corruption of illusion by eating from the tree of knowledge), see 29:87, 277, 340, 44:56, 54:199. Both Strindberg and Rousseau attempt to restore the original pristine clarity and truth they presume was lost with their entry into this world. For an account of autobiography in these terms, see Martha Rank Lifson, 'The Myth of the Fall: A Description of Autobiography', *Genre*, 12:1 (1979), 45-67.
65. NMS 12.
66. *The Oxford Ibsen*, III, Edited J.W. McFarlane (Oxford, 1972), p.89. For the authority of *Brand* in Sweden in the 1880s, see Fredrik Böök, *Från åttiotalet* (Stockholm, 1926), p.278, and Axel Lundegård, *Röda prinsen* (Stockholm, 1889), p.218.
67. 'Strindberg under mask', *Dagens Nyheter*, 29 July 1928. Strindberg was inclined to extend the list: 'Fru Vahlenberg is writing a novel about me! Thor Hedberg a play! Staaff and Geijerstam a theatrical lampoon. Ola Hansson-Marholm a novel, Albert Bonnier is publishing my letters, *Aftonbladet* and the whole nation are on tenterhooks' (IX:327).
68. *Samlade otryckta skrifter*, I, 307. Cf. The Hunter's sense, in *The Great Highway*, of having lost his soul through having lived too long among men (51:7).
69. *The Divided Self* (Harmondsworth, 1965), p.44.
70. Writing, which permits the writer to 'make homunculi ...reproduce himself ...multiply (*polymerisera*) himself' (46:112) offers the most effective method of excluding woman from the business of [pro-]creation, but Strindberg was ready to consider other possibilities. The Faustian notion of a homunculus was one on which he speculated elsewhere than *By the Open Sea*, drawing encouragement from an idea he claimed to have discovered in Buffon, namely that 'fertilized eggs have been discovered in male sperm tubes' (IX:357). This idea, too, became one of his seeds: 'Give Schleich this idea and we'll see if my egg grows, as before, in his brainpan.' Autobiography also promised his own self-engendering.
71. 'Strindberg, kvinnan och alstringen', *Meddelanden från Strindbergssällskapet*, 16 (1960), 11-16 (p.11).
72. *Will to Power*, p.429.
73. Ekenvall, p.12.
74. *Strindbergs bildspråk*, p.182. The sexual imagery is most prevalent in the period of marital crisis preceding and during the writing of *A Madman's Defence* when he feels compelled to 'exonerate himself thoroughly even for the accusation of not being a man' (VI:251). The *locus classicus* is, of course, the account of his journey to a Genevan brothel where he 'passed the test' (VI:252) in the presence of a doctor.
75. *Philosophy of the Unconscious* (London, 1931 edition), p.117.
76. *L'Amour* (Paris, 1859), pp.325-6. See also pp.449-52.

77. *Madeleine Férat* (*Oeuvres complètes*, Paris, 1927), pp.39, 179.

78. *Samlade otryckta skrifter*, I, 302.

79. For Strindberg and Charles XII, see Göran Stockenström, 'Strindberg och historiens Karl XII', *Meddelanden från Strindbergssällskapet*, 47-8 (1971), 15-37, and 'Kring tillkomsten av Karl XII', *Meddelanden*, 45 (1970) 20-43. For his ambivalent attitude to uniforms and the army, see Arne Häggqvist, 'Strindbergs Samvetskval', *Edda*, 39 (1939), 257-307 (p.271), 10: 40-53, 18: 146-8, 19: 76-7, and MD:38, 97.

80. On the Peer Gynt theme in Strindberg, see Eklund, *Tjänstekvinnans son*, p.320, and Johannesson, *The Novels of August Strindberg*, p.292.

81. *The Letters of John Keats 1814-1821*, 2 vols (Cambridge, Mass., 1958), I, 386-7.

82. NMS 3 (9), NMS 4 (21).

83. *Oeuvres complètes*, I, 1153.

84. *Pubertet*, p.448.

85. Joseph Conrad, *Lord Jim* (London, 1923), p.225.

86. Roman Jakobson, *Essais de linguistique générale* (Paris, 1963), p.33.

87. *Problems of Dostoyevsky's Poetics* (Ardis, 1973), p.163.

88. *Standard Edition*, III, 321.

89. *Pubertet*, p.137. Lo-Johansson sets this moment at his seventh year. In 'Screen Memories', Freud states: 'It is only from the sixth or seventh years onwards - in many cases only after the tenth year - that our lives can be reproduced in memory as a connected chain of events'. *Standard Edition*, III, 303.

90. *Ecrits*, translated Alan Sheridan (London, 1977), pp.46-7.

91. See 'Notes for an Anatomy of Modern Autobiography', p.492, for some of the criteria governing the selection of the first person persona.

92. 'Autobiography in the Third Person', p.30.

93. *The Unnamable* (London, 1959), p.296.

94. 'The Forms of Time and the Chronotopas in the Novel', *PTL*, 3:3 (1978), 493-528 (p.526).

95. See Anika Lemaire, *Jacques Lacan* (London, 1977), p.68.

96. *The Confessions*, translated Rex Warner (New York, 1963), p.118.

97. *Les Maladies de la personnalité* (Paris, 5th edition, 1894), p.94.

Chapter 4: Plot and Counter Plot

1. *Semiotikè* (Paris, 1969), p.146.

2. *S/Z* (Paris, 1970), p.16.

3. Compare 24:44 where Borg's father is described as an 'unfinished' type, 'a compound like a conglomeration and cemented together from splinters, the refuse of earlier periods, assembled by chance after the great eruption at the end of the

previous century', the description of Maria and her 'ragged scraps (*traslappar*) of a soul' (24:114), and the Vivisection, 'Moi', where Strindberg recognizes a need to reassemble 'les haillons de mon âme' (VR:12).

4. 'Fictions of the Self: The End of Autobiography', in James Olney, editor, *Autobiography: Essays Theoretical and Critical* (Princeton, 1980), p.325.

5. NMS 6 (15).

6. Strindberg's use of the Tarot pack as a means of placing his friends and enemies, implemented in a pocket notebook dating from the early 1890s (NMS 74), represents the application in another sphere of the scientific project for a study of man which Borg undertakes in *By The Open Sea*: 'He subsequently drew up an account of all the individuals he had met in the course of his life, from relations, nurses, servants, to school friends, fellow-students, acquaintances and friends, superiors, in short all those who had entered his circle of observation' (24:63). However, whereas the latter undertaking aimed at augmenting personal observation with documentary evidence, the former relied heavily upon the taxonomist's subjective response for the allocation of individuals to the appropriate category.

7. Compare XI:168, 270, 322, 392.

8. *La Nausée* (Paris, 1938), p.57.

9. *La Nausée*, p.57.

10. *Loqiques* (Paris, 1968), p.228.

11. *Strindberg i offentligheten, 1887-1892*, edited Björn Meidal (Uppsala, 1980), p.162.

12. *Strindberg och hans andra hustru*, vol.II, p.182. Compare 29:155: 'Try and say something wicked which "the other" hasn't said before'. Note, too, Strindberg's attempts to use the plot of *Swanwhite*, written early on in his relationship with Harriet, to influence her later association with Gunnar Wingård, her next husband. Were she and Wingård to act in the play, Strindberg hoped the chaste prescriptions regarding sexual behaviour in the text might stem the impulse of their sexual desire. Hence, too, his frustrated question to Harriet in 1908: 'Why wouldn't you be the person I turned you into (*diktade dig till*)?' *Brev till Harriet Bosse*, p.287.

13. *Le Psychothéâtre de Strindberg* p.224.

14. NMS 3 (21).

15. Inconsistencies in the order of the letters are discussed by C.G. Bjurström in his excellent French edition, Paris, 1965, where the sequence is reconstructed and the omitted letters included in an appendix. However, Bjurström does not perform the same service for Siri von Essen's side of the correspondence. In NMS 68 there are letters and drafts not included in the book. Several of the most important are printed in Karin Tarschys, 'Några brev från Siri von Essen till August Strindberg som uteslutits in Han och hon', *Meddelanden från Strindbergssällskapet*, 45 (1970), 11-19. As Tarschys suggests, these reveal a more mature 'She' than the novel, and raise questions regarding a woman's role in marriage and society which would have been uncomfortable for Strindberg given his standpoint in the mid 1880s.

16. Many of the letters have pencilled inscriptions placing them in relation to Strindberg's recollection of events, e.g. 'When Siri W fled to Mariefred in fear of her

inclination which was not yet clear to her'. Letters not for publication in the novel are crossed through in red crayon. Occasionally, however, documentary rigour is coloured by later emotion, as when he appends to a letter beginning 'My dear Ina', 'Ina Forsten later Algot Lange's wife and after 25 years of horrible married life, separated wife!'

17. This accounts for other omissions, e.g. the reference to his sister, Elisabeth, in I:278 (55:75-6) and I:280 (55:79).

18. Other letters mentioned in the text, for example those passing between Stockholm and Copenhagen, and which are mentioned as being held back or lost when the lovers were parted, would have formed the basis for the type of intrigue the genre is peculiarly fitted to convey, and had this been a genuine epistolary novel much might have been made of them.

19. E.g. in Strindberg's letters to the Wrangels, 3 and 8 August 1878, where he quotes from Heine's *Die Heimkehr* three times. These are omitted from Johan's letters although the wording of one ('Sie liebten sich beide, doch keiner / Wollt es dem Andern gestehn', I:214) would have fitted the novel well at this point. He had already used the same passage in another highly crafted letter, his proposal to the young woman named 'Elisabeth' (I:175).

20. Bo Bennich-Björkman's acute analysis of Strindberg's imagery of flight, birds, heights, and depths demonstrates the similarity in theme and language between Strindberg's correspondence and *Herr Bengt's Wife*. See 'Fåglar och författarroller hos Strindberg', *Samlaren*, 83 (1962), p.10. When convenient, however, Strindberg employed identical imagery to support a contrary thesis, e.g. in *Swanwhite*, where he argues in favour of chastity: 'Little bird, fly, hold yourself high above the gravel and always keep the air under your wings!' (36:131).

21. *Strindbergs systrar berättar* (Stockholm, 1926), p.64.

22. See also 55:183 and 55:94 where the letter in which Maria finally expresses her true feelings becomes a model of the type of verbal unburdening advocated by Strindberg in 'The Art of Becoming a Writer'.

23. According to the preface to *A Madman's Defence*, Maria's mother also recognized the literary possibilities inherent in the situation: 'There's undoubtedly material for a novel here for you, isn't there?' (ED:5).

24. See 55:212 and Maria's somewhat testy suggestion that neither Johan or Gustav have cause for complaint since both come out of the affair with the partner of their choice.

25. NMS 68. A literal translation yields 'I stood alone at the window, so alone I stood there / Although *he* was out in the room, although my child was near. / Upon my head there hung a ceiling of melancholy - so heavy. / And my thoughts were exhausted, but still were...'

26. *Strindbergs första hustru* (Stockholm, 1925), pp.130-135.

27. *Strindbergs första hustru*, pp.134, 135, 131.

28. 'Cain', *Poetical Works* (Oxford, 1970), p.544.

29. *Strindberg och kvinnofrågan* (Stockholm, 1969), p.151. For Strindberg's reading of Sand, see pp.109, 138, 452.

30. According to Boëthius (p.455), Strindberg borrowed the book from the Royal Library from 25 February to 26 September. From 5 July to 27 September, when it is likely the project for a novella was under discussion, he also borrowed parts 7 to 10 of Sand's *Histoire de ma vie*.

31. Strindberg gave Siri von Essen *Madame Bovary* to read early in their acquaintance, hoping she might translate it. In the course of the letter in which she first declares her feelings for him, she breaks off to criticise the book on moral grounds. However, she adds, 'nevertheless I am terribly fond of the book - it is marvellously well written' (55:69). At one point, when Johan writes as 'Léon' to 'Thérèse' the protagonists of the Flaubertian and Sandian texts intersect ominously in Strindberg's mind. When the period reoccupies his attention, shortly before writing *A Madman's Defence*, it is noteworthy that *Madame Bovary*, with Emma as the model of the faithless wife, and Charles as the betrayed husband, again attracts his attention: 'Never marry', he advises Pehr Staaff, 'for like Herr Bovary you can live all your life, without knowing to whom you are married' (VI:241).

32. Had he read more carefully or heeded her warning he might not have come to write: 'I have been married for 13 years - and don't know who I have been married to!' (VIII:177).

33. Responding to *La Confession d'un enfant du siècle*, Sand's text was in turn answered by Paul de Musset in *Lui et elle*, and another of Musset's mistresses - and Flaubert's, too - Louise Collet, joined in with the at least briefly titled *Lui*, based ostensibly on conversations with Alfred de Musset.

34. H. Guillemin, editor, *Elle et lui* (Neuchâtel, 1963), p.120.

35. See especially *Elle et lui*, p.180.

36. *Elle et lui*, p.194. See also pp.147, 150, 176, 181, 237, 241, 261, 282.

37. *Elle et lui*, p.158, 209.

38. *Elle et lui*, p.182.

39. See also 55:73, 86, 93, 119, 125, 126, 163.

40. A similar idea lurks even in the innocence of *Swanwhite*, where Swanwhite and the Prince are described as 'brother and sister' (36:150 -två syskon), but only after the King, her father, has departed with the words, 'If I return, well and good, I shall return, if not my eye will watch over you from the starry vault and then I shall never cease to see you, for there above one becomes all-seeing like God the creator!' (36:132).

41. *Elle et lui*, p.283.

42. Siri von Essen often catches the genuine Strindbergian note, as when she reminds Gustav: 'I have said to you once that I must be a proscribed spirit who is now condemned to continual unrest for a crime committed in a previous existence' (55:26).

43. *Poetical Works*, p.390.

44. *Repetition*, translated Walter Lowrie (Princeton, 1946), p.102.

45. Not that The Unknown is free from the coquettish attitude to death in which Johan indulges. See his exchanges with The Lady, 29:9. But what *To Damascus* offers is another reading of this primary identification. In place of the enlightened

Lucifer of *Master Olof*, who owes much to Georg Brandes's portrait of Byron's Cain in *Naturalismen i England* (see *Hovedstrømninger*, IV (Kjøbenhavn, Jespersen og Pios, 1967), p.308), and against the image of the light-bringing liberator represented in his suggestion for an inscription on a medal to commemorate the *Giftas* trial ('I am called the liberator, who came too early, I am called Satan, I am called Johan August Strindberg' (IV:383)), *To Damascus* is, like *Legends* and *Jacob Wrestles*, an attempt to amend and rewrite the past, to make recompense for precisely the act of liberation he had striven to accomplish by his writing in the 1880s.

46. See *Strindbergs infernokris*, pp.33-40.

47. *Von Reimarus zu Wrede. Geschichte der Leben-Jesu Forschung* (Tübingen, 1913), p.193. Quoted in Norman, *Strindberg och väckelserörelsen*, p.273. No doubt this is what Strindberg intended in the abandoned play, 'Jesus av Nazareth', begun in 1869.

48. Norman, p.276.

49. That Strindberg mislead his readers in *The Cloister* when he maintained that it was only long after writing a book entitled *The Son of a Servant* that he realized the Biblical connotation of the title, has been conclusively demonstrated by Teddy Brunius in 'Studier i August Strindbergs ungdomslyrik', *Samlaren*, 31 (1950), 102-109. See also Gunnar Ollén's remarks in a review, *Samlaren*, 29 (1948), p.124.

50. *Strindberg and the Poetry of Myth* (Berkeley: University of California Press, 1982), p.9.

51. NMS 4 (11).

52. Carlson, p.14.

53. *The Novels of August Strindberg*, p.174.

54. *Svensk litteraturtidskrift*, 22:4 (1959), 151-170 (p.162).

55. Note, however, that in his next letter Strindberg admits his calculations are based on the date of his conception since in the sign of his birth (Aquarius) 'there is nothing that fits, not even in the material points' (XI:284).

56. 'Restitutional Functions of Symbol and Myth in Strindberg's *Inferno*', *Psychiatry*, 36:3 (1973), 229-243 (p.231).

57. *Strindbergs infernokris*, p.89.

58. Quoted in Anika Lemaire, *Jacques Lacan* (London, 1977), p.72.

59. *The Philosophy of Symbolic Forms*, translated Ralph Manheim, 3 vols (London, 1953), I, 113.

Chapter Five: Publishing the Private

1. *August Strindberg: Ungdom och mannaår*, edited by Stellan Ahlström (Stockholm, 1959), p.144.

2. See *Kronbruden* (The Virgin Bride) *passim*, 28:193, 29:100.

3. See VII:77, 79, 81.

4. Even so the new work was not inopportune. Strindberg's remarks may well conceal a practical response to Bonnier's wish that the collection be enlarged, preferably with 'a longer narrative' (VII:87).

5. 'The Distresses of a Hired Writer', *New Essays*, edited by R.S. Crane (Chicago, 1927), p.135.

6. See 'Narrate or Describe?' *Writer and Critic* (London, 1970), pp.110-148, especially pp.118-9. Both the variousness of Strindberg's production and his many attempts to diversify his activities indicate the reluctance with which he accepted a life devoted solely to literature.

7. *Correspondance de Balzac*, textes réunis classés et annotés par Roger Pierrot, 5 vols (Paris, 1960-69), II, 141.

8. Other distinguishing features between these and Strindberg's ordinary letters to Hedlund are pointed out by Göran Stockenström, *Ishmael i öknen*, p.45. That Strindberg never entirely neglected imaginative literature at this time as completely as he has led critics to believe is evident from the draft for an autobiographical volume entitled 'P-aris' (NMS 15). See Michael Robinson, 'P-aris: Notes for an Unwritten Volume of Strindberg's Autobiography', *Scandinavica*, 19:1 (1980), 63-7.

9. If this passage appears to be only a colourful turn of casual phrase, it is worth pondering that the next day Strindberg remarked (and not for the last time) 'a coincidence which cannot be chance' (X:153). Such coincidences confirm Sven Delblanc's reading of 'the Inferno crisis as an active rather than a passive process', *BLM*, 38:6 (July, 1969), p.406.

10. *Studies in European Literature* (New York, 1964). p.49.

11. *Den litterära institutionen* (Stockholm, 1975), pp.21-24.

12. *Le Degré zéro de l'écriture* (Paris, 1968), pp.55-6.

13. *Correspondance*, VII, 280 (20 December 1875).

14. *Early Writings* (Harmondsworth, 1975), pp.324-5. Compare Anthony Wilden in his presentation of Lacan: 'Know thyself means on the one hand seek to isolate and examine the alienated, mediated and inauthentic construct we call our self; on the other, it means that we cannot know ourselves 'authentically' unless we are in the world, unless we know others, for our self has no meaning and no existence except in its relationship to Otherness. But in our mediation by the Imaginary Other, we lose ourselves in the objectifications of the socio-economic discourse. Our cherished self turns out to be a thing, a piece of property, a commodity'. *The Language of the Self* (Baltimore, 1968), p.108.

15. 'Akademikultur och litterär institutionen på 1880-talet' in *Den litterära institutionen*, p.188.

16. *Edvard Bäckström och hans dramatiska diktning* (Göteborg, 1947), p.63.

17. See Allan Hagsten, *Den unge Strindberg* (Stockholm, 1952), p.356.

18. Quoted in Hagsten, pp.474-5.

19. *Före Röda rummet*, p.240.

20. He quotes the same remark in a letter to Lie (IV:193). See also to Fahlstedt (I:168): 'I have decided to make a stir in the world whatever the cost; however,

preferably without any physical discomfort'.

21. To monitor his status as a public figure, Strindberg once kept a check on his standing in the eyes of the world with the aid of Courrier de la Presse, a cuttings agency. See Göran Söderström, *Strindberg och bildkonsten*, p.296.

22. As in Balzac, the process is given additional force by the fact that the capitalization of literature was taking place as a contemporary event and not as something securely accomplished. In this respect *The Red Room* is the historical and thematic counterpart to *Illusions perdues*, and as Stellan Ahlström has indicated ('Balzac och *Röda Rummet*', *Svensk litteraturtidskrift*, 17:4 (1954), 175-9), the book in which Arvid Falk repeats Lucien de Rubempré's discovery that ideas are for sale and every product has its price, deploys many of the earlier novel's major motifs. But Strindberg's experience of the *Gründer* period's speculation in literature, as in the railways and timber on which its production and mass-dissemination depended, was also gained at first hand. He was familiar both with the tribulations and the subterfuges of the *declassé* intellectual, and on one occasion he wrote, naively or cynically, to Rudolf Wall: '...I wanted to propose to Herr Wall, who seems to be alone in considering me worth anything as a writer, a piece of business! Buy me - living; I am very cheap' (I:277). For the major shift in literary style and matter, and in the writer's status and role, which *The Red Room* both represents and describes, see Gunnar Ahlström's general background to *Det moderna genombrott i Nordens litteratur* (Stockholm, 1947), Lennart Thorsell's meticulous investigation of the democratisation of Swedish writing, 'Den svenska parnassens demokratisering och de folkliga bildningsvägarna', *Samlaren*, 38 (1957), 53-135, and for the difficulties inherent in Strindberg's own attempt to become 'our first modern professional writer', see Allan Hagsten's account of what he concludes was a slightly premature venture, *Den unge Strindberg*, p.470f. Strindberg's own account in *In the Red Room* is of course shorter and more entertaining, and many of his early articles, now collected in *Före Röda Rummet*, exhibit a contemporary awareness of the upsurge in literary activity, in which new markets, new writers, and new genres were rapidly discovered and as rapidly exploited, e.g. p.204 on calender poetry and short story competitions.

23. *Brev till min dotter Kerstin* (Stockholm, 1961), p.164.

24. *Dagboksblad och brev*, 2 vols (Stockholm, 1928), I, 330.

25. *Le Journal intime* (Paris, 1976), p.54. When Didier observes how prevailing ideas encourage the writer 'de garder jalousement la trace de tous les événements de sa vie' (p.52) and considers 'le journal intime est à la fois une bonne affaire et une bonne action. Le diariste augmente chaque jour son capital-écriture, tout en ayant le sentiment d'accomplir un exercise spirituel qui lui permet un progrès intérieur' (p.56), her discusson of a single autobiographical genre suggests a context relevant to Strindberg's project as a whole.

26. Compare 54:332: 'My experiences are mine and no one else's, and anyone who wants to deprive me of my property, is a thief'.

27. *Strindbergsproblem*, p.50.

28. 'Le Voyage', *Les Fleurs du mal* (Paris: Classiques Garnier, 1961), p.160.

29. Note his response to Sudermann's often quoted remark, 'Vom Norden her kommt uns das Licht!': 'That was a decisive moment in literary history' (IX:123), and the observation in *Inferno*: 'The great event of the season in Paris was the critic Brunetière's outcry on the bankruptcy of science' (28:34). Both moments are normally given prominence in later surveys of the period.

30. For Strindberg's reaction to Heidenstam's *Renässans*, see *Strindbergs infernokris*, p.154; Karl-Erik Lundevall, *Från åttital till nittital* (Stockholm, 1953), pp.227, 295; Børge Gedsø Madsen, *Strindberg's Naturalistic Theatre* (Copenhagen, 1962), p.127.

31. Baudelaire, 'L'Art romantique', *Oeuvres complètes* (Paris: Editions de la Pléiade, 1951), p.1078.

32. *Strindberg och bildkonsten*, p.282.

33. 'On Tolstoy's Crises', in Victor Erlich, editor, *Twentieth Century Russian Literary Criticism* (New Haven, 1975), p.99.

34. *The Symbolist Aesthetic in France 1885-1895*, 2nd edition (Oxford, 1968), p.52.

35. *Före Röda Rummet*, p.242.

36. Compare IV:66, V:62, 121, 122, VI:223, and his description of writing as 'an unnatural and revolting occupation. It sometimes seems to me to be like the work of those women who display themselves naked in brothels for money', *Meddelanden*, 34 (1964), p.18.

37. In *L'Avenir national*, 25th February 1873.

38. *An Autobiography* (Oxford: World's Classics, 1980), p.71.

39. See VI:317, 389, and for Zola's *L'Oeuvre* as autobiography, 18:457-7.

40. For Strindberg's admiration of Hans Jæger's novel, with its intimate scenes documenting contemporary life, see V:317, 328.

41. *Svensk litteraturtidskrift*, 28:2 (1965), 63-75 (p.63).

42. In fact his discourse may well be transformed from the private and the naked to the public and the veiled, from fact to fiction, or autobiography into novel, by switching from one language to another, as he knows: 'What they turn into a scandal in Sweden, I make into literature in France' (IV:127).

43. See *Strindberg och bildkonsten*, p.298.

44. NMS 6 (14).

45. 'Heidenstam, Strindberg och diktargagen', *Litteratur och samhälle*, 3:39 (1967), 1907-1918 (p.1908).

46. Compare this with those glimpses into an integrated and unselfconscious family life which Kafka affords many of his protagonists. Moreover, in both Strindberg and Kafka the continually felt tension between writing and a family life is often allied with considerations of appropriate nourishment. As Sven Delblanc has indicated in his splendid article, 'Kärlekens föda, ett motif i Strindbergs Kammarspel' (in Egil Törnqvist, editor, *Drama och Teater*, Stockholm, 1968, 93-112), Strindberg's querulousness about food in his later years was no mere personal idiosyncracy but integral to the system of social values to which he subscribed, and which were centred on the idea of the patriarchal family. In Kafka, meanwhile, a healthy

appetite is an attribute of ordinary, unselfconscious, non-literary life. It is one of the qualities with which he endows his father; in *Metamorphosis*, the family's revitalization after Gregor's death is signalled by the butcher's boy who climbs the stairs with a tray of meat; and a lack of appetite represents the innate deficiency at the root of the Hunger Artist's art. For discussion of Strindberg and Kafka, see 'Strindberg et Kafka', *Etudes Germaniques*, 8:2-3 (1953), 118-140, and Walter Baumgartner, 'Kafkas Strindberglektüre', *Scandinavica*, 6:2 (1967), 95-107.

47. Compare the descriptions of the family as a trinity and an indivisible organism in *Black Banners* (41:189) and *A Madman's Defence*, p.198. Marriage and celibacy are contrasted in *A Blue Book*, 48:983.

48. To Flaubert marriage was an apostacy from the call of art and he considered each friend who married as lost to him and a gain for the bourgeoisie. For James's choice of celibacy, see Leon Edel, *The Life of Henry James*, definitive edition, 2 vols (Harmondsworth, 1977), pp.48-9, and for one among the many discussions of the motif as it appears in his stories of art and artists, Susanne Kappeler, *Writing and Reading in Henry James* (London, 1981), pp.75-82. Victor Eremita's comment in 'In Vino Veritas' may stand for many another in Kierkegaard: 'Many a man became a genius through a girl, many a man became a hero through a girl, many a man became a poet through a girl, many a man became a saint through a girl, but he didn't become a genius through the girl he got, for through her he only became a Privy Councillor', *Stages on Life's Way*, translated by Walter Lowrie, (New York, 1967 ed.), p.70. Indeed there is a definite tradition in which the quality of the work of art is considered commensurate with the degree to which its maker is estranged from customary human relationships. The theme is explored at length by Balzac in the career of Wenceslas Steinbock in *La Cousine Bette*, but Yeats is more succinct not only in observing that man must choose perfection of the life or of the work, but also that he had seen more artists ruined by their wives and children than by harlots. For, as numerous nineteenth-century texts abundantly testify, the artist's kinship was felt to lie not with a wife but with the whore, who was likewise seller and commodity in one. This applies both to the predatory warm-blooded courtesans of the *Comédie humaine*, and to the frigid, enigmatic creature of Baudelaire and Mallarmé, 'subtly of herself contemplative' in Rossetti's phrase, flowering for herself alone in Mallarmé's, where she becomes an emblem of the finished work of art divested of its producer. However, where these writers frequently appear to exult in their difference, Strindberg does not: compare Nietzsche's astringent comment in *The Case Wagner*: 'What becomes of the eternal "Wandering Jew" whom a wife adores and settles? He merely ceases to be eternal; he gets married and does not concern us any more' (*Portable Nietzsche*, p.461), with Strindberg's contrary concern for a creative married life from *Getting Married* to *The Flying Dutchman*.

49. *Correspondance*, IV, 305 (11 January 1859).

50. *Correspondance*, IV, 340 (October 1859).

51. 'Die Subjekt-Objekt Beziehung in der Ästhetik', quoted in Paul de Man, *Blindness and Insight*, p.43. Lukác's remarks here on the author's 'isolation from all kinds of objective entities, from all forms...of human and collective relationships

as well as...from the entirety of his own personality' foreshadow the argument of 'Narrate or Describe?'

52. *Illusions perdues* (Paris: Classiques Garnier, 1956), p.530.

53. *The Will to Power*, p.431.

54. *Capital*, translated from the third German edition by Samuel Moore and Edward Aveling (London, 1970), p.423.

55. *Complete Works* (London: Collins, 1948), p.25.

56. In e.g. the prefatory note to the concluding number of *Dombey and Son* and the preface to *Pendennis*, where Thackeray refers to the 'constant communication' between writer and reader which forces the former into 'frankness of expression'. It is, he concludes, 'a sort of confidential talk between writer and reader'. (Penguin English Library edition, 1972, p.33).

57. *A Personal Record* (London, 1923), p.95.

58. Quoted in Sten Linder, *Ernst Ahlgren i hennes romaner* (Stockholm, 1930), p.311.

59. *August Strindberg* (Aldus edition, 1961), p.370. Money, its brute presence and power to misrepresent, falsify, and govern lives remains a dominant factor in Strindberg's major late works where the social critique of the 1880s is in fact intensified. There is no fissure between these works (*Black Banners*, the Chamber Plays, *The Scapegoat*) and the direct criticism of the polemical *Speeches to the Swedish Nation*, and it is worth remarking that it is his deepening insight into the way in which people withdraw behind their masks and live a social lie which encourages him to depart from the psychological naturalism he defends in the preface to *Miss Julie*. Since everything is pretext and disguise even what can be observed is no longer wholly pertinent; what must be conveyed instead are the supple and fluid movements of these unstable compounds in their continual precipitation and dissolution.

60. Compare Alf Ahlberg's comment in 'Det ondas problem i Strindberg's diktning', *Filosofi och dikt* (Stockholm, 1924), where he argues that in Strindberg evil is that which is 'in itself without power or being, the *non-existent*, whose only reality is that it can suck from the good' (p.153).

61. NMS 3 (21).

62. *Eros och Polemos* (Stockholm, 1916), p.39.

63. See 'Kring en "nyckelroman"', *Meddelanden från Strindbergssällskapet*, 17 (1955), 3-5; Margit Pohl, 'Några bärande motiv i *Svarta fanor*', *Meddelanden*, 29 (1961) and 30-31 (1962), pp.12-19, 20-29; Bertil Romberg, 'Strindbergs *Svarta fanor*', *Svensk litteraturtidskrift*, 32:1 (1969), 30-45.

64. See 3 December 1900 and 38:183.

65. Compare Strindberg's letter to Schering on *The Ghost Sonata*: 'it is mosaic work as usual, from other lives and from my own, but please don't take it as autobiography or confessions' (XV:356).

66. 'Strindbergs Svarta fanor', p.35.

67. See X:134 and *The Cloister*, pp.146-7, where the need for a confessionless 'monastery for intellectuals' is linked explicitly with 'an age when industry and

finance had pushed themselves so much to the fore'.
68. Suppressed foreword to *Black Banners*.

Conclusion

1. *The Art of the Novel* (New York, 1934), p.5.
2. *The Renaissance* (London, 1910), p.236.
3. 'The Storyteller', *Illuminations* (New York, 1968), p.94. Compare Tzvetan Todorov, *The Poetics of Prose* (Oxford, 1977): 'Narrative equals life: absence of narrative, death' (p.74).
4. *Anatomy of Criticism* (Princeton, 1957), p.41.
5. See e.g. Karl J. Weintraub, 'Autobiography and Historical Consciousness', *Critical Inquiry*, 1:4 (1975), 821-848, and the same author's *The Value of the Individual: Self and Circumstance* (Chicago, 1978).
6. *Breve fra J.P. Jacobsen* (Kjøbenhavn, 1899), p.95.
7. *The American Novel and Its Tradition* (London, 1958), p.199.
8. See e.g. the Flaubertian remarks of Maupassant in the preface to *Pierre et Jean*: 'Il y a, dans tout, de l'inexploré, parce que nous sommes habitués à ne nous servir de nos yeux qu'avec le souvenir de ce qu'on a pensé avant nous sur ce que nous contemplons. Le moindre chose contient un peu d'inconnu'. *Romans*, p.840.
9. *The Will to Power*, p.267.
10. *A la recherche du temps perdu* (Paris: Pléiade, 1954), III, 880.
11. *The Unnamable*, p.394.
12. The reviewer is in fact J.W. McFarlane, the review republished in *T.L.S. 1962* (Oxford, 1963), pp.27-35 (p.33). The quotation is here extended from the passage in McFarlane's review. It is taken from *Samlede Værker*, 5 vols (Kjøbenhavn, 1924-9), II, 93-4.

BIBLIOGRAPHY

A. August Strindberg

(i) Printed Sources

August Strindbergs brev, edited by Torsten Eklund, 15 vols to date (Stockholm, 1948-).

August Strindbergs dramer, edited with introductions by Carl Reinhold Smedmark, 4 vols to date (Stockholm, 1962-).

Brev till min dotter Kerstin, translated by Karin Boye and Åke Thulstrup (Stockholm, 1961).

En berättelse från Stockholms skärgård (Stockholm, 1949).

En dåres försvarstal, translation of Strindberg and Georges Loiseau's 1895 edition of *Le Plaidoyer d'un fou* by Tage Aurell (Stockholm, 1962).

En dåres försvarstal, translation of the Oslo manuscript of *Le Plaidoyer d'un fou* by Hans Levander (Stockholm, 1976).

'Efterslåtter bland Strindbergs brev', *Meddelanden från Strindbergssällskapet*, 59-60 (1978), pp.15-35; 61-62 (1979), pp.21-42; 63-64 (1980), pp.17-22.

Före Röda rummet: Strindbergs ungdoms journalistik, selected by Torsten Eklund (Stockholm, 1946).

Från Fjärdingen till Blå tornet. Ett brevurval 1870-1912, edited by Torsten Eklund (Stockholm, 1946).

Fröken Julie, edited by Göran Lindström (Lund, 1971).

Getting Married, translated and edited by Mary Sandbach (London, 1972).

Inferno, edited by C.G. Bjurström (Paris, 1966).

Inferno, Alone and Other Writings, edited and introduced by Evert Sprinchorn (New York, 1968).

Inferno and From an Occult Diary, translated with an introduction by Mary Sandbach (Harmondsworth, 1979).

Klostret, edited by C.G. Bjurström (Stockholm, 1966).

Lui et elle, translated and edited by C.G. Bjurström with Georges Perros (Paris, 1965).

'Nyfunna Strindbergsbrev', *Meddelanden från Strindbergssällskapet* 33 (1963), 1-10, 34 (1964), 7-18, 36 (1964), 7-14.

Ockulta dagboken, facsimile edition (Stockholm, 1977).

Samlade otryckta skrifter, edited by V. Carlheim-Gyllensköld, 2 vols (Stockholm, 1918-19).

Samlade skrifter, edited by John Landquist, 55 vols (Stockholm, 1912-20).

Spöksonaten, edited by Göran Lindström (Lund, 1963).

Strindbergs brev till Harriet Bosse (Stockholm, 1932).

Vivisektioner, edited by Torsten Eklund with parallel Swedish translations by Tage Aurell (Stockholm, 1958).

(ii) Manuscript Material

1. *Carlheim-Gyllenskölds samling Strindbergiana*, deposited in Kungliga Biblioteket, Stockholm.
2. 'En Tviflares anteckningar', in *Jöran Sahlgrens samling*, Universitetsbiblioteket, Uppsala.
3. *Nordiska Museets Strindbergsarkivalia*, deposited in Kungliga Biblioteket, Stockholm.
4. Strindberg's letters to Torsten Hedlund, Bonniers' Archive, Stockholm.
5. *Syndabocken* (Stockholm, 1907) with marginalia by Håkan Gillberg, Strindbergsmuseet, Blå tornet, Stockholm.

B. Secondary Sources

(i) Selected works either wholly or partly devoted to Strindberg.

Ahlberg, Alf, 'Det ondas problem i Strindbergs diktning', in *Filosofi och dikt* (Stockholm, 1924), 148-55.
Ahlström, Gunnar, *Det moderna genombrottet i Nordens litteratur* (Stockholm, 1947).
Ahlström, Stellan, 'Balzac och *Röda rummet*', *Svensk litteraturtidskrift*, 17:4 (1954), 175-9.
------'En dåres försvarstal', *Dagens Nyheter*, 15 September 1974.
------'Kommunarden Strindberg', *Ord och Bild*, 60:8 (1951), 453-8.
------*Strindbergs erövring av Paris* (Stockholm, 1956).
------'Zola och Strindberg', *Svenska Dagbladet*, 9 April 1954.
------ ed., *August Strindberg: Ungdom och mannaår* (Stockholm, 1959).
------ and Torsten Eklund, eds., *August Strindberg: Mannaår och ålderdom* (Stockholm, 1961).
Anderson, E.W. 'Strindberg's Illness', *Psychological Medicine*, 1:2 (1971), 104-17.
Axberger, Gunnar, *Diktarfantasi och eld* (Stockholm, 1967).
Bäfverstedt, Bo, and Erik Carlsson, 'Strindberg, alkohol och absint', *Recip Reflex*, 8:2, 3-4 (1975), 28-41, 24-36.
Bennich-Björkman, Bo, 'Fåglar och författarroller hos Strindberg', *Samlaren*, 83 (1962), 1-66.
------'Heidenstam, Strindberg och diktargagen', *Litteratur och samhälle*, 3:39 (1967), 1907-18.
Benston, Alice N., 'From Naturalism to the Dream Play: a Study in the Evolution of Strindberg's Dramatic Form', *Modern Drama*, 7:4 (1965), 382-98.

Berendsohn, Walter A., 'August Strindbergs Autobiographische Schriften', *Scandinavica*, 5:1 (1966), 41-9.

------'August Strindbergs *I havsbandet*', *Samlaren*, 26 (1946), 101-16.

------*August Strindbergs skärgårds- och Stockholmsskildringar: struktur- och stilstudier* (Stockholm, 1962).

------'Frida Uhls journalistik', *Dagens Nyheter*, 5 April 1950.

------'Strindberg's *Ensam*: a Study in Structure and Style', *Scandinavian Studies*, 31:4 (1959), 168-179.

------*Strindbergsproblem* (Stockholm, 1946).

------*Strindbergs sista levnadsår* (Stockholm, 1948).

------'Studier i manuskriptet till Strindbergs "Karantänmästarns andra berättelse"', *Samlaren*, 32 (1951), 16-28.

Bergom-Larsson, Maria, '*En dåres försvarstal* och mansmedvetandets kris', in *Författarnas litteraturhistoria*, 2, edited by Lars Ardelius and Gunnar Rydström (Stockholm, 1978), 84-97.

Bjarnason, Loftur L., *Categories of Søren Kierkegaard's Thought in the Life and Writings of August Strindberg* (unpublished doctoral dissertation, Stanford University, 1951).

Björck, Staffan, 'Strindbergs *Tjänstekvinnans son*', *Studiekamraten*, 41 (1959), 62-8.

Boëthius, Ulf, *Strindberg och kvinnofrågan till och med Giftas I* (Stockholm, 1969).

Bonnier, K.-O., *Bonniers: En bokhandlarefamilj*. 5 vols (Stockholm, 1930-56).

Böök, Fredrik, *Från åttiotalet* (Stockholm, 1926).

Borland, Harold, H., 'The Dramatic Quality of Strindberg's Novels', *Modern Drama*, 5:3 (1963), 299-305.

Brandell, Gunnar, *Strindbergs infernokris* (Stockholm, 1950). Revised edition translated by Barry Jacobs, *Strindberg in Inferno* (Cambridge, Mass., 1974).

Brandell, Gunnar, ed., *Synpunkter på Strindberg* (Stockholm, 1964).

Brunius, Teddy, 'Studier i August Strindbergs ungdomslyrik', *Samlaren*, 31 (1950), 102-9.

Burnham, Donald, L., 'August Strindberg's *Inferno* as a Case in Point of Sullivan's "Extravasation of Meaning"', *Contemporary Psychoanalysis*, 9 (1973), 190-208.

------'Restitutional Functions of Symbol and Myth in Strindberg's *Inferno*', *Psychiatry*, 36:3 (1973), 229-43.

------'Strindbergs kontaktdilemma studerat i hans förhållande till Harriet Bosse', *Meddelanden från Strindbergssällskapet*, 50 (1970), 8-26.

Carlson, Harry G., 'Ambiguity and Archetypes in Strindberg's *Romantic Organist*', *Scandinavian Studies*, 48:3 (1976), 256-71.

------*Strindberg and the Poetry of Myth* (Berkeley, 1982).

Dahlbäck, Lars, *Strindbergs Hemsöborna, en monografi* (Stockholm, 1974).

Dahlström, Carl E.W.L., *Strindberg's Dramatic Expressionism*, second edition (New York, 1968).

Delblanc, Sven 'Om Strindbergsstudier', *BLM*. 38:6 (1969), 406.

------*Stormhatten.* Tre Strindbergsstudier (Stockholm, 1979).

Edqvist, Sven-Gustaf, 'Elden och pånyttfödelsen: ett motiv hos Strindberg', *Ord och Bild*, 67:5 (1958), 333-44.

------*Samhällets fiende* (Stockholm, 1961).

Ekenvall, Asta, 'Strindberg, kvinnan och alstringen', *Meddelanden från Strindbergssällskapet*, 26 (1960), 11-16.

------'Strindberg och kvinnans fysiologi', *BLM*, 38:6 (1969), 457-64.

Eklund, Torsten, 'Strindberg under mask', *Dagens Nyheter*, 29 July 1928.

------'Strindbergs *I havsbandet*', *Edda*, 29 (1929), 113-44.

------*Tjänstekvinnans son. En psykologisk Strindbergsstudie* (Stockholm, 1948).

Falck, August, *Fem år med Strindberg* (Stockholm, 1935).

Falkner, Fanny, *August Strindberg i Blå tornet* (Stockholm, 1921).

Fehrman, Carl, 'Slutscenen i *Ett drömspel*', in *Poesi och parodi* (Stockholm, 1957), 84-95.

Flugrud, Sverre, '*En dåres försvarstal.* Ett Strindberg-manuskript på vandring', *Nordisk tidskrift*, 50:3 (1974), 125-37.

Forsell, Lars, 'Försvarstal för en dåre', *Dagens Nyheter*, 7 September 1955.

Frey, Torsten S:son, 'Medecinska synpunkter på August Strindberg', *Läkartidningen*, 77:4 (1980).

Fröding, Gustaf, ed., *En bok om Strindberg* (Karlstadt, 1894).

Gravier, Maurice, 'Strindberg écrivain français', *Revue d'histoire du theâtre*, 30:3 (1978), 243-65.

------*Strindberg et le theâtre moderne* (Lyon and Paris, 1949).

Hagemann, Sonja, 'Genienes inspiratrice: Dagny Juel Przybyszewska', *Samtiden*, 72:10 (1963), 655-88.

Häggqvist, Arne, 'Strindbergs *Samvetskval*', *Edda*, 39 (1939), 257-307.

Hagsten, Allan, *Den unge Strindberg*, 2 vols (Stockholm, 1951).

Hallberg, Peter, 'Strindbergs kammarspel', *Edda*, 58 (1958), 1-21.

Hallén, Sverker, 'Vem förföljde Strindberg? Kryptogram blev utmaning', *Ystads Allehanda*, 19 September 1970.

Harding, Gösta, 'Sin egen psykiater', *BLM*, 37:7 (1963), 556-8.

Hedenberg, Sven, *Strindberg i skärselden* (Göteborg, 1961).

Helmecke, Carl Albert, *Buckle's Influence on Strindberg* (unpublished doctoral dissertation, University of Pennsylvania, 1924).

Herrlin, Axel, 'Bengt Lidforss och August Strindberg. En studie över deras tankegemenskap och förhållande till samtida naturfilosofiska och metafysiska idéströmningar', in *Bengt Lidforss. En minnesskrift*, edited by Einar Sjövall (Malmö, 1923), 53-87.

Hildeman, Karl-Ivar, 'Strindberg, *The Dance of Death*, and Revenge', *Scandinavian Studies*, 35:4 (1963), 267-94.

Holmberg, Olle, 'Strindbergs skuld', in *Madonnan och järnjungfrun*, second edition (Stockholm, 1927), 203-20.

------'Tjänstekvinnans son - och husbonde', *Svensk litteraturtidskrift*, 37:3 (1973), 11-14.

Jacobs, Barry, 'Psychic Murder and Characterization in Strindberg's *The Father*', *Scandinavica*, 8:1 (1969), 19-34.

Jacobsen, Harry, *Strindberg og hans første hustru* (København, 1946).

Jensen, Thorkild Borup, 'Strindbergs forord til *Fröken Julie* som naturalistisk programskrift', in *Nordisk Litteraturhistoria - en bog til Brøndsted,* edited by Hans Bekker-Nielsen, H.A. Koefoed and Johan de Myliu (Odense, 1978), 233-47.

Johannesson, Eric O., *The Novels of August Strindberg* (Berkeley, 1968).

------'The Problem of Identity in Strindberg's Novels', *Scandinavian Studies*, 34:1 (1962), 1-35.

Jolivet, Alfred, 'Le Rousseauisme d'August Strindberg', *Revue de littérature comparée*, 24:2 (1950), 293-8.

------'Strindberg et Nietzsche', *Revue de littérature comparée*, 14:3 (1939), 390-406.

Josephson, Lennart, *Strindbergs drama Fröken Julie* (Uppsala, 1965).

Kärnell, K.-A., *Strindbergs bildspråk* (Stockholm, 1962).

Kulling, Jacob, *Att spjärna mot udden. En studie om Kristusgestaltens betydelse i Strindbergs religiösa utveckling* (Stockholm, 1950).

Lagercrantz, Olof, *August Strindberg* (Stockholm, 1979).

Lamm, Martin, *August Strindberg* (Stockholm: Aldus edition, 1961).

------'Quelques influences françaises sur l'autobiographie de Strindberg', in *Mélanges d'histoire littéraire générale et comparée offerts à F. Baldensperger*, 2 (Paris, 1930), 22-7.

------*Strindberg och makterna* (Uppsala, 1936).

------Strindbergs dramer, 2 vols (Stockholm, 1924-6).

Landquist, John, 'Diktaren och livssynen: Strindberg naturalisten' in *Humanism* (Stockholm, 1931), 176-91.

------'Strindbergs filosofi', in *Filosofiska essayer* (Stockholm, 1906), 263-301.

------'Litteraturen och psykologien', in *Dikten, diktaren och samhället,* edited by Alf Ahlberg (Stockholm, 1935).

Leifer, Leif, 'Den lutrende ild. En studie i symbolikken i Strindbergs kammerspil', *Samlaren*, 81 (1961), 168-94.

Levander, Hans, '*Svarta fanor*. Kring en nyckelroman', *Meddelanden från Strindbergssällskapet*, 17 (1955), 3-5.

Lie, Erik, *Minnen från ett diktarhem* (Stockholm, 1929).

Lindberger, Örjan, 'Heidenstams och Strindbergs brevväxling', *Svensk litteraturtidskrift*, 3:3 (1940), 124-141.

------'Hjalmar Bergman och Traditionen från *Tjänstekvinnans son*', *Hjalmar Bergman Samfundet Årsbok*, 1973, 12-23.

Lindblad, Göran, *August Strindberg som berättare* (Stockholm, 1924).
Linder, Sten, *Ibsen, Strindberg och andra* (Stockholm, 1936).
Lindström, Göran, 'Edvard Munch i Strindbergs *Inferno*', *Ord och Bild*, 64:3 (1955), 129-43.
------'Strindberg Studies 1915-1962', *Scandinavica*, 2:1 (1963), 27-50.
Lindström, Hans, *Hjärnornas kamp* (Uppsala, 1952).
------*Strindberg och böckerna* (Uppsala, 1977).
------'Strindberg, Per Staaff och *En dåres försvarstal*', *Ord och Bild*, 58:1 (1949), 13-18.
Lundegård, Axel, *Några Strindbergsminnen knutna till en handfull brev* (Stockholm, 1920).
McFarlane, James W., 'Letters from Strindberg', in *T.L.S. Essays and Reviews from the Times Literary Supplement* (London, 1963), 27-35.
Madsen, Børge Gedsø, *Strindberg's Naturalistic Theatre* (Copenhagen, 1962).
Meidal, Björn, ed., *Strindberg i offentligheten*, 3 vols (Uppsala, 1980).
Melberg, Arne, 'Sexualpolitiken, *Fru Marianne* och *En dåres försvarstal*', *Ord och bild*, 89:2-3 (1980), 50-65.
Milton, John, 'A Restless Pilgrim: Strindberg in the *Inferno*', *Modern Drama*, 5:3 (1963), 306-13.
Mörner, Birger, *Den Strindberg jag känt* (Stockholm, 1924).
Mortensen, Johan, *Strindberg som jag minnes honom* (Stockholm, 1931).
Norman, Nils, *Den unge Strindberg och väckelserörelsen* (Malmö, 1953).
------'Strindberg i Lund', *Svensk litteraturtidskrift*, supplement, 1943, 69-81.
------'Strindberg och Dante', *Svensk litteraturtidskrift*, 27:3 (1964), 103-15.
------'Strindberg och Napoleon', *Svensk litteraturtidskrift*, 22:4 (1959), 151-70.
Norrman, David, *Strindbergs skilsmässa från Siri von Essen* (Stockholm, 1953).
Ollén, Gunnar, *Strindbergs dramatik* (Stockholm, Prisma edition, 1966).
------*Strindbergs 1900-talslyrik* (Stockholm, 1941).
Östin, Ola, 'August Strindbergs *Ensam*', *Edda* 58 (1958), 81-99.
Philp, Anna von, and Nora Hartzell, *Strindbergs systrar berättar* (Stockholm, 1926).
Platen, Gustaf von, 'Strindberg, världsväverskan och tystnaden', *Expressen*, 29 January 1946.
Pohl, Margit, 'Några bärande motiv i *Svarta fanor*', *Meddelanden från Strindbergssällskapet*, 29 (1961), 12-19, 30-31 (1962), 20-29.
Poulenard, Elie, 'Les Influences françaises dans l'autobiographie d'August Strindberg', *Scandinavica*, 1:1 (1962), 29-50.
Printz-Påhlson, Göran, 'Allegories of Trivialization: Strindberg's View of

History', *Comparative Criticism*, 3 (1981), 221-36.

------'Strindbergs totemism', *Konstrevy*, 45:4 (1969), 154-60.

------'Tankens genvägar. Om Strindbergs antropologi', *BLM*, 38:6 (1969), 430-41; 38:8 (1969), 594-610.

Reinert, Otto, ed. *Strindberg: A Collection of Critical Essays* (NJ, 1971).

Rinman, Sven, 'En dåres försvarstal', *Svensk litteraturtidskrift*, 28:2 (1965), 63-75.

Robinson, Michael, 'P-aris:Notes for an Unwritten Volume of Strindberg's Autobiography', *Scandinavica*, 19:2 (1980), 63-7.

Romberg, Bertil, 'Strindbergs *Svarta fanor*', *Svensk litteraturtidskrift*, 32:3 (1969), 30-45.

Rothenberg, Albert, 'Autobiographical Drama: Strindberg and O'Neill', *Literature and Psychology*, 17 (1967), 95-114.

Schmidt, Torsten M., ed., *Strindbergs måleri* (Malmö, 1972).

Sjöstedt, N.A., *Søren Kierkegaard och svensk litteratur* (Göteborg, 1950).

Smedmark, Carl Reinhold, *Mäster Olof och Röda rummet* (Stockholm, 1952).

Smirnoff, Karin, *Strindbergs första hustru* (Stockholm, 1925).

Söderström, Göran, *Strindberg och bildkonsten* (Stockholm, 1972).

------'Tjänstekvinnans testamente', *Meddelanden från Strindbergssällskapet*, 51 (1971), 1-6.

Sprinchorn, Evert, *Strindberg as Dramatist* (New Haven, 1982).

Stenström, Thure, *Den ensamme* (Stockholm, 1961).

Stockenström, Göran, *Ismael i öknen. Strindberg som mystiker* (Uppsala, 1972).

------'The Journey from the Isle of Life to the Isle of Death: the Idea of Reconciliation in *The Ghost Sonata*', *Scandinavian Studies*, 50:2 (1978), 133-49.

Strindberg, Frida, *Strindberg och hans andra hustru*, 2 vols (Stockholm, 1933-4).

Strindbergssällskapet, *Essays on Strindberg* (Stockholm, 1966).

------*Strindberg and Modern Theatre* (Stockholm, 1975).

Svenaeus, Gösta, 'Strindberg och Munch i *Inferno*', *Kunst og Kultur*, 1 (1967), 1-30.

Tarschys, Karin, 'Några brev från Siri von Essen till August Strindberg som uteslutits i *Han och hon*', *Meddelanden från Strindbergssällskapet*, 45 (1970), 11-19.

Thorsell, Lennart, 'Den svenska parnassens "demokratisering" och de folkliga bildningsvägarna', *Samlaren*, 38 (1957), 53-135.

Tjäder, Per Arne, 'Strukturen i Strindbergs *Taklagsöl*', *Tidskrift för litteraturvetenskap* (Umeå), 7:1 (1978), 30-43.

Törnqvist, Egil, *Bergman och Strindberg* (Stockholm, 1973).

------*Strindbergian Drama: Themes and Structure* (Stockholm, 1982).

Uggla, Andrej, 'Przybyszewski och Strindberg: konflikter och utbyte', *Meddelanden från Strindbergssällskapet*, 53-4 (1974), 12-20.

Valbert, M.G., 'M. Auguste Strindberg et *Confession d'un fou*', *Revue des Deux Mondes*, 1 November 1893, 214-25.

Vogelweith, Guy, 'Attente et intuition de la psychanalyse dans le théâtre de Strindberg', *Scandinavica*, 12:1 (1973), 1-16.

------*Le Psychothéâtre de Strindberg: Un Auteur en quête de métamorphose* (Paris, 1972).

------'Strindberg et Freud', *Obliques. Littérature-Théâtre*, 1:1 (1972), 32-9.

Vowles, Richard B., 'Strindberg and the Symbolic Mill', *Scandinavian Studies*, 34:2 (1962), 111-9.

'Strindberg's *Isle of the Dead*', *Modern Drama*, 5:3 (1963), 366-78.

Ward, John, *The Social and Religious Plays of Strindberg* (London, 1980).

(ii) Autobiographies and Studies of Autobiography

Adams, Henry, *The Education of Henry Adams* (Boston, Sentry ed., 1961).

Augustine, Saint, *Confessions*, translated by Rex Warner (New York, 1963).

Barthes, Roland, *Roland Barthes by Roland Barthes*, translated by Richard Howard (London, 1977).

Beaujour, Michel, 'Autobiographie et autoportrait', *Poétique*, 32 (1977), 442-58.

Beyle, Marie Henri [Stendhal], *Vie de Henry Brulard*, edited by Henry Martineau (Paris: Classiques Garnier, 1953).

Blanchard, Jean Marc, 'Of Cannibalism and Autobiography', *Modern Language Notes*, 93:4 (1978), 654-76.

Blasing, Mutlu Konuk, *The Art of Life* (Texas, 1977).

Borel, Jacques, 'Problèmes de l'autobiographie', in *Positions et oppositions sur le roman contemporain*, edited by Michel Mansuy (Paris, 1971).

Bottrall, Margaret, *Every Man a Phoenix* (London, 1958).

Bourgeois, René, 'Signification du premier souvenir', in *Stendhal et les problèmes de l'autobiographie*, edited by Victor Del Litto (Grenoble, 1976), 87-91.

Braudy, Leo, 'Daniel Defoe and the Anxieties of Autobiography', *Genre*, 6:1 (1973), 76-95.

Bruss, Elisabeth, *Autobiographical Acts: The Changing Situation of a Literary Genre* (Baltimore, 1976).

Bryant, David, 'Fiction and Truth in Restif's *M. Nicolas*', *Trivium*, 14 (1979), 127-34.

Burr, Anna Robson, *The Autobiography: A Critical and Comparative Study* (London, 1909).

Cellini, Benvenuto, *The Autobiography*, translated by George Bull (Harmondsworth, 1956).

Coirault, Yves, 'Autobiographie et mémoires XVIIe-XVIIIe siècles, ou existence et naissance de l'autobiographie', *Revue d'histoire littéraire de la France*, 75:6 (1975), 737-53.

Conrad, Joseph, *A Personal Record* (London: Uniform Edition, 1923).

Delany, Paul, *British Autobiography in the Seventeenth Century* (London, 1969).

Didier, Béatrice, 'L'inscription musicale dans l'écriture autobiographique', *Poétique*, 37 (1979), 91-101.

------*Le journal intime* (Paris, 1976).

Dilthey, W., *Selected Writings* (Cambridge, 1976).

Downing, Christine, 'Re-Visioning Autobiography: The Bequest of Freud and Jung', *Soundings*, 60 (1977), 210-228.

Earle, William, *The Autobiographical Consciousness* (New York, 1972).

Eckermann, Johann Peter, *Conversations with Goethe*, translated by John Oxenford (London: Everyman's Library, 1930).

Ellis, David, 'Barthes and Autobiography', *The Cambridge Quarterly*, 7:3 (1978), 252-66.

Ellrich, Robert J., *Rousseau and his Reader* (Chapel Hill, 1969).

Fernandez, Ramon, 'Autobiography and the Novel', in *Messages*, translated by Montgomery Belgion (New York, 1927), 89-136.

Fleishman, Avrom, 'The Fictions of Autobiographical Fiction', *Genre* 9:1 (1976), 73-86.

Gelpi, Barbara Charlesworth, 'The Innocent I: Dicken's Influence on Victorian Autobiography', in *The Worlds of Victorian Fiction*, edited by Jerome H. Buckley (Cambridge, Mass., 1975), 57-74.

Gibbon, Edward, *Memoirs of My Life and Writings* (London, 1970).

Goethe, Johann Wolfgang von, *The Autobiography*, translated by John Oxenford, 2 vols (Chicago, 1974).

Goldberg, Jonathan, 'Cellini's *Vita* and the Conventions of Early Autobiography', *Modern Language Notes*, 89:1 (1974), 71-83.

Goodwin, James, 'Narcissus and Autobiography'. *Genre*, 12:1 (1979), 69-72.

Gunn, Janet Varner, 'Autobiography and the Narrative Experience of Temporality · as Depth', *Soundings*, 60 (1977), 194-209.

Gusdorf, Georges, 'Conditions et limites de l'autobiographie', *Formen der Selbstdarstellung: Analekten zu einer Geschichte des literarischen Selbstportraits*. edited by Günther Reichenkron and Erich Hasse (Berlin, 1956), 105-24.

------'De l'autobiographie initiatique à l'autobiographie genre littéraire', *Revue d'histoire littéraire de la France*, 75:6 (1975), 957-94.

Hart, Francis R., 'Notes for an Anatomy of Modern Autobiography', *New Literary History*, 1:3 (1970), 485-511.

Howarth, William L., 'Some Principles of Autobiography', *New Literary History*, 5:2 (1974), 363-81.

Jung, C., *Memories, Dreams, Reflections* (London, 1963).

Landow, George P., ed., *Approaches to Victorian Autobiography* (Athens, Ohio, 1979).

Leiris, Michel, *L'Age d'homme* (Paris, 1946).

Lejeune, Philippe, *L'Autobiographie en France* (Paris, 1971).

------'Autobiography in the Third Person', *New Literary History*, 9:1 (1977), 27-50.

------*Je est un autre* (Paris, 1980).

------'Le Pacte autobiographique', *Poétique*, 14 (1973), 137-62.

------*Le Pacte autobiographique* (Paris, 1975).

------'Stendhal et les problèmes de l'autobiographie' in *Stendhal et les problèmes de l'autobiographie*, edited by Victor dell Litto (Grenoble, 1976), 21-36.

------'Vallès et la voix narrative', *Littérature*, 23 (1976), 3-20.

Lifson, Martha Ronk, 'The Myth of the Fall: A Description of Autobiography', *Genre*, 12:1 (1979), 45-67.

Lo-Johansson, Ivar, *Pubertet* (Stockholm, 1978).

Mandel, Barret J., 'The Autobiographer's Art', *Journal of Aesthetics and Art Criticism*, 27:2 (1968), 215-226.

Marin, Louis, 'The Autobiographical Interruption: About Stendhal's *Life of Henry Brulard*', *Modern Language Notes*, 93:4 (1978), 597-617.

May, Georges, 'Autobiography and the Eighteenth-Century', in *The Author in His Work* (New Haven, 1978), 317-33.

------*L'Autobiographie* (Paris, 1979).

Mehlman, Jeffrey, *A Structural Study of Autobiography* (Ithaca, 1974).

Mill, John Stuart, *Autobiography* (Oxford, 1971).

Misch, Georg, *A History of Autobiography in Antiquity*, 2 vols (London, 1950).

Nabokov, Vladimir, *Speak Memory* (New York, 1966).

Nin, Anais, *Journals*, volume one (London, 1973).

Olney, James, ed., *Autobiography: Essays Theoretical and Critical* (Princeton, 1980).

------*Metaphors of Self: The Meaning of Autobiography* (Princeton, 1972).

Pascal, Roy, *Design and Truth in Autobiography* (London, 1960).

Pike, Burton, 'Time in Autobiography', *Comparative Literature*, 28:4 (1976), 326-42.

Pilling, John, *Autobiography and Imagination* (London, 1981).

Porter, C.A., *Restif's Novel, or an Autobiography in Search of an Author* (New Haven, 1967).

Porter, Roger, J., 'Gibbon's Autobiography: Filling Up the Silent Vacancy', *Eighteenth Century Studies*, 8:1 (1974), 1-26.

Raymond, Marcel, *Jean-Jacques Rousseau: La quête de soi et la rêverie* (Paris, 1962).

Renza, Louis A., 'The Veto of the Imagination: A Theory of Autobiography', *New Literary History*, 9:1 (1977), 1-26.

Restif de la Bretonne, *Monsieur Nicolas*, 6 vols (Paris, 1959).

Rousseau, Jean-Jacques, *Oeuvres complètes*, edited under the direction of
Bernard Gagnebin and Marcel Raymond, 4 vols (Paris, 1959-69).
Ryan, Michael, 'Narcissus Autobiographer: *Marius the Epicurean*',
ELH, 43:2 (1976), 184-208.
Sartre, Jean-Paul, *Les Mots* (Paris, 1964).
Sayre, Robert F., *The Examined Self: Franklin, Adams, James* (Princeton,
1964).
Shaftesbury, Anthony, Earl of, *Soliloquy: or, Advice to an Author*,
Standard Edition, Volume 1 (Stuttgart: fromman-holzboog, 1981).
Shapiro, Stephen A., 'The Dark Continent of Literature: Autobiography',
Comparative Literature Studies, 5:4 (1968), 421-54.
Shumaker, Wayne, *English Autobiography* (Berkeley, 1954).
Spacks, Patricia Meyer, *Imagining a Self: Autobiography and Novel in
Eighteenth-Century England* (Harvard, 1976).
Spengemann, William C., *The Forms of Autobiography* (New Haven, 1980).
Starobinski, Jean, *Jean-Jacques Rousseau: la transparence et l'obstacle*
(Paris, 1971).
------*L'Oeil vivant*, 2 vols (Paris, 1961-70).
------'The Style of Autobiography', in *Literary Style*, edited by Seymour
Chatman (Oxford, 1971), 257-65.
Sturrock, John, 'The New Model Autobiographer', *New Literary History*, 9:1
(1977), 51-64.
Szávai, János, 'La place et le role de l'autobiographie dans la littérature', *Acta
Litteraria Academiae Scientiarum Hungaricae*, 18 (1976), 398-414.
Thibaudeau, Jean, 'Le roman comme autobiographie', *Tel Quel*, 34 (1968),
67-74.
Tolstoy, Leo, *A Confession*, translated Aylmer Maude (Oxford, 1940).
Trollope, Anthony, *An Autobiography* (Oxford: World's Classics, 1950).
Vallès, Jules, *Jacques Vingtras*, edited by E. Casassus, 3 vols (Paris, 1968-70).
Vance, Christie, 'Rousseau's Autobiographical Venture', *Genre*, 6:1 (1973),
1-28.
Vance, Eugene, 'Augustine's *Confessions* and the Grammar of Selfhood',
Genre, 6:1 (1973), 1-28.
Voisine, Jacques, 'De la confession religieuse à l'autobiographie et au journal
intime: entre 1760 et 1820', *Neohelicon*, 2 (1974), 337-57.
------'Naissance et évolution du terme littéraire "autobiographie"',
La Littérature comparée en Europe orientale (Budapest, 1963), 278-86.
Webber, Joan, *The Eloquent 'I': Style and Self in Seventeenth Century Prose*
(Madison, 1968).
Weintraub, Karl J., 'Autobiography and Historical Consciousness', *Critical
Inquiry*, 1:4 (1975), 821-48.
------*The Value of the Individual: Self and Circumstance in Autobiography*
(Chicago, 1978).
Yeats, William Butler, *Autobiographies* (London, 1966).

(iii) Criticism - General

Abrams, M.H., *The Mirror and the Lamp* (Oxford, 1953).

Adams, Robert, *Surface and Symbol: The Consistency of James Joyce's Ulysses* (New York, 1962).

Bakhtin, Mikhail, 'The Forms of Time and the Chronotopas in the Novel. From the Greek Novel to Modern Fiction', *PTL*, 3:3 (1978), 493-528.

Barthes, Roland, *Le Dègre zéro de l'écriture* (Paris, 1953).

------*Image - Music - Text* (London, 1977).

------'Style and Its Image', in Seymour Chatman, ed., *Literary Style: A Symposium* (Oxford, 1971), 3-10.

Becker, George Joseph, ed., *Documents of Modern Literary Realism* (Princeton, 1963).

Booth, Wayne C., *The Rhetoric of Fiction* (Chicago, 1961).

Bradbury, Malcolm, and James McFarlane, eds., *Modernism 1890-1930* (Harmondsworth, 1976).

Clément, Catherine B., and Bernard Pingaud, 'Roman-Analyse', *Revue française du psychanalyse*, 38:1 (1974), 5-24.

Culler, Jonathan, *Structuralist Poetics* (London, 1975).

Eikhenbaum, Boris, 'On Tolstoy's Crises', in *Twentieth-Century Russian Literary Criticism*, edited by Victor Erlich (New Haven, 1975), 97-101.

Fath, Robert, *De l'influence de la science sur la littérature française dans la seconde moitié du XIXe siécle* (Lausanne, 1901).

Frye, Northrop, *Anatomy of Criticism* (Princeton, 1957).

Harari, Josué V., ed., *Textual Strategies. Perspectives in Post Structuralist Criticism* (London, 1979).

Hartman, Geoffrey H., ed., *Psychoanalysis and the Question of the Text* (Baltimore, 1978).

Kermode, Frank, *The Sense of an Ending* (Oxford, 1966).

Kierkegaard, Søren, *Samlede Værker*, edited by A.B. Drachmann, J.L. Heiberg, and H.O. Lange, second edition, 20 vols (København, 1962-4).

Lehmann, A.G., *The Symbolist Aesthetic in France 1885-1895*, second edition (Oxford, 1968).

Lukács, Georg, *Studies in European Realism* (New York, 1964).

------*Writer and Critic* (London, 1970).

Man, Paul de, *Blindness and Insight* (Oxford, 1971).

Melberg, Arne, ed., *Den litterära institutionen* (Stockholm, 1975).

Pingaud, Bernard, 'L'écriture et la cure', *Nouvelle Revue Française*, 18:10 (1970), 144-63.

Ricks, Christopher, *Keats and Embarrassment* (Oxford, 1974).

Roland, Alan, ed., *Psychoanalysis, Creativity, and Literature* (New York, 1980).

Said, Edward, *Beginnings* (New York, 1975).

Sollers, Philippe, *Loqiques* (Paris, 1968).

Todorov, Tzvetan, *The Poetics of Prose* (Oxford, 1978).
Trilling, Lionel, *Sincerity and Authenticity* (Oxford, 1972).

(iv) Other

a. Material pre-1900

Balzac, Honoré de, *Correspondance*, 5 vols (Paris, 1960-69).
------*Illusions perdues* (Paris: Classiques Garnier, 1956).
Baudelaire, Charles, *Oeuvres complètes* (Paris: Pléiade, 1951).
Benedictsson, Victoria, *Dagboksblad och brev*, 2 vols (Stockholm, 1918-20).
Bernard, Claude, *Introduction à l'étude de la médecine expérimentale* (Paris: Classiques Garnier, 1966).
Bernheim, Hippolyte, *De la suggestion et de ses applications à la thérapeutique*, second edition (Paris, 1888).
Brandes, Georg, 'Friedrich Nietzsche - En Afhandling om Aristokratisk Radikalisme', *Tilskueren* (1889), 565-613.
------*Hovedstrømninger i det 19 Aarhundredes Litteratur*, reprint of 6th edition, 6 vols (København, 1966-7).
------*Søren Kierkegaard* (København, 1877).
Brunetière, Ferdinand, *Le Roman naturaliste* (Paris, 1883).
Buckle, Thomas Henry, *History of Civilisation in England*, second edition, 2 vols (London, 1858).
Byron, Lord George Gordon, *Poetical Works* (Oxford, 1970).
Darwin, Charles, *The Expression of the Emotions in Man and Animals* (London, 1872).
------*The Origin of Species*, edited by J.W. Burrow (Harmondsworth, 1968).
Desprez, Louis, *L'Evolution naturaliste* (Paris, 1884).
Flaubert, Gustave, *Correspondance*, 9 vols (Paris, 1926-33).
Goncourt, Edmond and Jules de, *Journal*, 4 vols (Paris, 1956).
Hartmann, Edouard von, *Philosophy of the Unconscious* (London, 1931).
Ibsen, Henrik, *Samlede Verker i billigutgave*, 3 vols (Oslo, 1962).
Jacobsen, J.P., *Breve*, edited by Edvard Brandes (København, 1899).
------*Samlede Værker*, edited by M. Borup, 5 vols (København, 1924-5).
Keats, John, *The Letters of John Keats, 1814-1821*, edited by Hyder Edward Rollins, 2 vols (Cambridge, Mass., 1958).
Linné, Carl von, *Nemesis Divina*, edited Elis Malmeström (Stockholm, 1968).
Lytton, Bulwer, *Zanoni* (London, 1845).
Maeterlinck, Maurice, *Le Trésor des humbles*, fourth edition (Paris, 1916).
Marx, Karl, *Capital*, translation of 3rd German edition (London, 1970).

179

------*Early Writings*, translated by Rodney Livingstone and Gregor Benton (Harmondsworth, 1974).

Maudsley, Henry, *The Pathology of Mind* (London, 1879).

Maupassant, Guy de, *Romans*, edited by Albert-Marie Schmidt (Paris, 1959).

------*Sur l'eau* (Paris n.d.).

Michelet, Jules, *L'Amour* (Paris, 1859).

Nietzsche, Friedrich, *Beyond Good and Evil*, translated by R.J. Hollingdale (Harmondsworth, 1973).

------*The Portable Nietzsche*, edited and translated by Walter Kaufmann (New York, 1954).

------*The Will to Power*, translated by Walter Kaufmann and R.J. Hollingdale (London, 1968).

Nordau, Max, *Conventional Lies of our Civilization*, translated from the seventh German edition (London, 1895).

------*Paradoxes*, translated from the fifth edition (London, 1906).

Prel, Carl du, *The Philosophy of Mysticism*, 2 vols (London, 1889).

Ribot, Théodule, *Les Maladies de la personnalité*, 4th edition (Paris, 1891).

------*Les Maladies de la volonté* (Paris, 1883)

Sand, George, *Elle et lui*, edited with a preface by Henri Guillemin, (Neuchâtel, 1964).

Schopenhauer, Arthur, *The World as Will and Representation*, translated by E.F.J. Payne, 2 vols (New York, 1966).

Swedenborg, Emanuel, *Arcana Coelestia*, vols 1-4 (London: Swedenborg Society, 1939).

------*De Telluribus* (London: Swedenborg Society, 1894).

------*Heaven and its Wonders and Hell* (London: Swedenborg Society, 1958).

Zola, Emile, *Oeuvres complètes*, edited by Maurice Le Blond, 50 vols (Paris, 1927-29), *Madeleine Férat* and *L'Oeuvre*.

------*Le Roman expérimentale*, edited by Aimé Guedj (Paris, 1971).

b. Material post-1900

Adler, Alfred, *The Individual Psychology of Alfred Adler* (London, 1958).

Beckett, Samuel, *Molloy, Malone Dies, The Unnamable* (London, 1959).

Benveniste, Emile, *Problèmes de linguistique générale* (Paris, 1966).

Brandell, Gunnar, *Freud och hans tid* (Stockholm, 1970).

Burrow, John, *Evolution and Society* (Cambridge, 1966).

Carter, L.A., *Zola and the Theatre* (New Haven, 1963).

Derrida, Jacques, 'Freud and the Scene of Writing', *Yale French Studies*, 48 (1972), 73-117.

------*Of Grammatology* (Baltimore, 1976).

Ellenberger, Henri F., *The Discovery of the Unconscious* (London, 1970).

Forrester, John, *Language and the Origins of Psychoanalysis* (London, 1980).

Foucault, Michel, *Language, Counter-Memory, Practice* (Oxford, 1977).

Freud, Sigmund, *The Origins of Psychoanalysis* (London, 1954).

------*Standard Edition of the Complete Psychological Works*, 24 vols (London, 1953-74).

Gustafsson, Lars, *Språk och lögn* (Stockholm, 1978).

Hemmings, F.W.J., *Emile Zola*, second edition (Oxford, 1970).

Herman, M., *Un sataniste polonais: Stanislas Przybyszewski* (Paris, 1931).

Hillis-Miller, J., 'The Disarticulation of the Self in Nietzsche', *The Monist*, 64:2 (1981), 247-61.

Jakobson, Roman, *Essais de linguistique générale* (Paris, 1963).

Jameson, Fredric, 'Imaginary and Symbolic in Lacan: Marxism, Psychoanalytic Criticism, and the Problem of the Subject', *Yale French Studies,* 55-6 (1978), 338-95.

Jonsson, Inge, *Emanuel Swedenborg*, translated by C. Djurklou (New York, 1971).

Lacan, Jacques, *Ecrits: A Selection*, translated by Alan Sheridan (London, 1977).

------*The Language of Self*, translated with a commentary by Anthony Wilden (Baltimore, 1977).

Laing, Ronald D., *The Divided Self* (Harmondsworth, 1965).

------, H. Phillipson, and A.R. Lee, *Interpersonal Perception* (London, 1966).

Lemaire, Anika, *Jacques Lacan* (London, 1977).

Meisal, Perry, ed., *Freud: A Collection of Critical Essays* (New Jersey, 1981).

Reeves, Joan Wynn, *Thinking About Thinking* (London, 1965).

Ricoeur, Paul, *Freud and Philosophy* (New Haven, 1970).

------'What is a Text? Explanation and Interpretation', in David M. Rasmussen, *Mythic-Symbolic Language and Philosophical Anthropology*, (The Hague, 1971), 135-50.

Rieff, Philip, *Freud: The Mind of the Moralist* (London, 1960).

Saussure, Ferdinand de, *Course in General Linguistics* (London, 1974).

Steiner, George, *After Babel* (Oxford, 1975).

------*Extraterritorial* (Harmondsworth, 1975).

INDEX

Ån, 110.
Abraham, 99-100.
Abrams, M.H., 19,20.
Adams, Henry, 16.
Adams, Robert, 17.
Advice to an Author, 47.
'Affaire W-----l', 34, 98,150.
agoraphobia, 76.
Ahasverus, 110.
Ajax, 109.
alloted roles, 108.
Alone, 6, 12, 17, 20, 39, 43, 52, 63, 66, 135.
Amour, L', 74
Andersson, Nils, 107.
Anna O, 21.
Anno '48, 130.
Aragon, Louis, 27.
Arcana Coelestia, 13.
aristocratic radicalism, 88.
Armageddon, 53, 56-58, 71, 153-154.
Army Surgeon's Tales, The, 20.
Art of Becoming a Writer', 'The, 1, 24, 48, 95, 100-101, 143, 153, 158.
Artist, as protean, 77, his lack of identity, 78.
Asmodeus, 110.
'Aspasia', 71.
associational method, 25.
Atala, 115.
Atheism, 17, 88.
'At the Bier Side in Tistedalen', 76.
Autobiografia, 87.
autobiographical pact, 12, 132, 146.

autobiographical prerogative, the, 2.
Autobiographies, 108.
autobiography, as composition, 13; as event in the autobiographer's life, 13, 86; modernist, 27; narcissistic, 31; its scientific and documentary value, 5; as self-analysis, 22-23; singularity, 15; as supplement to the life, 13.

Bakhtin, Mikhail, 79,81.
Balzac, Honoré de, 9, 72, 74, 90, 108, 115-118, 162, 164.
Barthes, Roland, 10, 85, 118.
Battle of the Brains', 'The, 74-75.
Baudelaire, Charles Pierre, 118, 123, 164.
Beatrice, 108.
Beckett, Samuel, 79, 81, 141.
Beichte eines Thoren, Die, 127.
Benedictsson, Victoria, 11, 122, 133.
Benjamin, Walter, 138.
Bennich-Björkman, Bo, 130, 158.
Benveniste, Emile, 44, 49.
Berendsohn, Walter, 56, 123.
Berger, Alfred von, 148.
Berlin, 121, 123-124.
Bernard, Claude, 6.
Bernheim, Hippolyte, 22, 69, 74.
Betou, Sofia In de, 95.
Beyond the Pleasure Principle, 9, 44.
Bildungsroman, 12, 87.
Binet, Alfred, 22-23.
biographical criticism, 7, 9.

Lie, Jonas, 11, 29.
life, as a scientific project, 5, 15, 22, 95, 125; as staged, 3, 93; as writing, 1-2, 14, 76-77, 138.
Life in the Skerries, 114.
Like and Unlike, 51.
Lindberg, August, 130.
literary capital, 121-124.
literary housekeeping, 94, 122.
literary market, 114-121, 125-27.
Littmansson, Leopold, 16, 33, 39, 72-73, 107, 115, 117, 124, 137.
Locke, John, 76, 113.
L'Oeuvre, 118.
Loiseau, Georges, 23.
Lo-Johansson, Ivar, 66, 78, 80, 156.
Loke, 14, 110.
Longfellow, Henry Wadsworth, 99.
Louis Lambert, 91.
'Love-letter from Ingrid Persdotter', 102.
Lucas, Prosper, 75.
Lucidor, Lasse (Lars Johansson), 20.
Lui et elle, 96, 159.
Lukàcs, Georg, 115, 118, 132, 164.
Lund, 93, 117.
Lundegård, Axel, 37, 91, 122.
lying, 49-52, 55-56, 58, 133.

Madame Bovary, 102, 159.
Madeleine Férat, 75.
Madman's Defence, A, 6-8, 11, 17, 23, 29, 34-35, 42-43, 47, 70, 74, 77, 91-92, 95, 97-98, 100-101, 104, 124-128, 135, 137, 143, 146, 150, 155, 158-159, 164.
Maeterlinck, Maurice, 57.
Magie der Zahlen als Grundlage aller Mannigfaltigkeit und das Scheinbare, Die, 151.
makterna, 116.
Maladies de la Mémoire, Les, 149.
Mallarmé, Stéphane, 11, 118, 164.
¹mö, 99.

Mame, Louis, 115.
Manfred, 3.
Manilius, 109.
Manon Lescaut, 115.
Man, Paul de, 10.
Marx, Karl, 87, 118, 127, 132.
Mäster Ensam, 107.
Master Olof, 8, 33, 88, 96, 120, 131, 149, 160.
Maudsley, Henry, 22, 72, 87, 148.
Maupassant, Guy de, 6, 10-11, 166.
Maurois, André, 9.
Mauthner, Fritz, 50.
Médecin de campagne, Le, 116-117.
Medeltidens magi, 108.
'Med flaska och det ärliga ögat', 70.
Melberg, Arne, 118.
Memoirs of My Life, 143.
memory, 1, 7, 34, 36, 39-40, 60, 76, 80-81, 97, 116, 146, 151, 156.
Merlin, 106-107, 110.
Mesmer, Franz Anton, 74.
'Metamorphosis', 164.
Michelet, Jules, 74.
Mirror and the Lamp, The, 19.
Miss Julie, 11, 17, 68-69, 72, 74, 86, 102, 104, 114, 125, 130, 139, 165.
modernism, 17.
modernist, 129.
modernist aesthetic, 7, 26, 124.
Monsieur Nicolas, 5.
Mörner, Birger, 2, 73.
Munch, Edvard, 70-71, 93, 107, 124.
Musil, Robert, 139.
Musset, Alfred de, 96, 102-03, 159.
Musset, Paul de, 96, 159.
Mysticism of World History', 'The, 122, 139.

Nadja, 27.
Napoleon, 110.
narrative, 31, 40, 44, 80, 87, 89, 108.

Naturalism, 4-6, 14-15, 22-23, 54, 75, 86-87, 126, 129, 136, 139-140, 143, 160.
Naturalist aesthetic, 125.
Naturalist discourse, 55.
Naturalist model, 139.
Naturalist period, 129.
Nausée, La, 89.
nekrobios, 43.
Nemesis, 33, 42, 87-88, 90, 106.
Neue Freie Presse, 22.
New Introductory Lectures on Psychoanalysis, 41.
New Kingdom, The, 51, 77.
Niels Lyhne, 119, 141.
Nietzsche, Friedrich, 3, 9, 22, 47, 50, 73-74, 88, 132, 139-140, 148, 151-152, 164.
Nietzschean, 152.
Nightingale of Wittenberg, The, 150, 153.
Nin, Anais, 13.
Nordau, Max, 25, 51.
Norman, Nils, 3, 106, 109.
Norrtullsgatan, 8, 14, 34, 94.
Novels of August Strindberg, The, 8.

Occult Diary, 6, 12, 26, 28, 32, 35, 71, 75, 86, 90, 93, 109-110, 131, 135-136, 140, 143, 145, 149-150, 153.
Oedipal scenario, 34.
Oedipus, 139.
Omphale, 108, 136.
'On the General Discontent', 11, 53.
ontological security, 66.
order, 14, 31, 40-41, 58.
Orfila, Mathieu Joseph Bonaventura, 117.
Orpheus, 141.
Österling, Hans, 127-28.
own progenitor, 76.

Paris, 99, 115, 117, 124.

Pascal, Roy, 146.
Passant, Le, 101.
Pater, Walter, 138.
Pathology of Mind, The, 22.
patriarchal family, 87.
Paul, Adolf, 70, 93.
Paul et Virginie, 115.
Paysan de Paris, Le, 27.
Peer Gynt, 134.
Péladan, Joséphin, 108.
Pelican, The, 21, 55, 59-60, 151-153.
Pendennis, 165.
People of Hemsö, The, 2, 7.
Perrault, Charles, 115.
personal myth, 14.
Petit Chose, Le, 23.
Phaedrus, 62.
Philosophie der Mystik, 136, 149.
Philp, Hugo von, 96.
Pierre et Jean, 166.
pietism, 3, 86-87.
pietist, 4-5, 87, 144.
Pietists, 51.
Pingaud, Bernard, 30-31.
Plaidoyer d'un Fou, Le, 146.
Plato, 62.
Playing With Fire, 17, 48, 144.
Poe, Edgar Allan, 9.
Popper, Karl, 49.
Portrait of Dorian Gray, The, 132.
posthumous perspective, 15-16, 23, 43.
Potiphar, 111.
Prel, Carl du, 136, 149.
Pretenders, The, 105.
Printz-Påhlson, Göran, 26, 37, 151.
Protestantism, 122.
Proust, Marcel, 139-140.
Przybyszewski, Stanislaw, 70-71, 124.
psychological naturalism, 22.
Psychopathology of Everyday Life, The, 26.
Public Lie, The, 50-51, 152.